BEYOND A LITTLE LEARNING

BEYOND A LITTLE LEARNING

Portraits of 25 Distinguished
Old Boys of Leeds Grammar School

Neill Hargreaves

With a contribution from John Davies, Archivist at GSAL
Line drawings courtesy of Doreen Greenshields

Scratching Shed Publishing Ltd

Copyright © Neill Hargreaves 2022
All rights reserved
The moral right of the author has been asserted.
First published by Scratching Shed Publishing Ltd in 2022
Registered in England & Wales No. 6588772.
Registered office:
47 Street Lane, Leeds, West Yorkshire. LS8 1AP
www.scratchingshedpublishing.co.uk
ISBN: 978-1838489939

No part of this book may be reproduced or transmitted in any form or by any other means without the written permission of the publisher, except by a reviewer who wishes to quote brief passages in connection with a review written for insertion in a magazine, newspaper or broadcast.

A catalogue record for this book is available
from the British Library.

Typeset in Oriya MN Bold and Palatino
Printed and bound in the United Kingdom by

Short Run Press Ltd
Bittern Road, Sowton Industrial Estate, Exeter. EX2 7LW
Tel: 01392 211909   Fax: 01392 444134

Contents

Foreword by Sue Woodroofe,
Principal of The Grammar School at Leeds.................vii
Introduction and Acknowledgements..................ix

The book offers biographies of 25 of the most distinguished Old Boys of LGS. There is an emphasis, where possible, on their school career before leading on to the impact they have made nationally and internationally. They are:

John Harrison	1579-1656	St John's Church; the new School (1624)	1
John Smeaton	1724-1792	Eminent Civil Engineer; the Eddystone Lighthouse	13
Sir Charles West Cope	1811-1890	Artist and Engraver	25
Sir John Hawkshaw	1811-1891	Eminent Civil Engineer; the Severn Railway Tunnel	35
George Dixon MP	1820-1898	Educational Reformer	45
Col. Edmund Wilson	1838-1914	Co-founder of the Thoresby Society	59
William G Nicholson	1845-1918	Field Marshal; 1st Chief of the Imperial General Staff	71
		[*above entry contributed by John G Davies*]	
Col. G F R Henderson	1854-1903	Military Strategist and Historian	81
John Nicholson Ireland	1879-1962	Composer	93
Ernest Bristow Farrar	1885-1918	Organist and Composer	101
William Potts & Sons		Clock Makers	109
		[*Five Potts family members attended LGS*]	
Geoffrey A S Kennedy	1883-1929	Army Chaplain better known as Woodbine Willie	119
Arthur Michael Hollis	1899-1986	Anglican Bishop and Ecumenical Leader	131
Christopher Hollis MP	1902-1977	Author and Publisher	139
Sir Roger Henry Hollis	1905-1973	Intelligence Officer; Head of MI5	151
Geoffrey Crowther	1907-1972	Journalist, Educator, Co-founder of the Open University	159
Godfrey Talbot	1908-2000	Journalist and Royal Correspondent	167
Geoffrey Wooler	1911-2010	Pioneer Heart Surgeon	177
John Connell Freeborn	1919-2010	Battle of Britain Fighter Ace	187
Rodney Hill	1921-2011	Professor of Applied Mathematics	201
John Rowe Townsend	1922-2014	Children's Author and Literary Critic	209
Sir Gerald Kaufman MP	1930-2017	Politician and Member of the Shadow Cabinet	217
Barry Cryer	1935-2022	Comedy Script Writer & Entertainer	229
Lord John Dyson	1943-	Eminent Legal Figure and Retired Master of the Rolls	241
Ricky Wilson	1978-	Lead Singer with the Kaiser Chiefs and Media Celebrity	259

Afterword – by Professor Tristram Hope MEng, CEng, FIStructE, MICE.................273

Foreword

THE CURRENT MOTTO of The Grammar School at Leeds is 'Be Inspired'. We continue to espouse the importance of academic standards alongside the development of the whole person, aiming to enthuse and prepare every student to achieve their personal best, in school and beyond, in every walk of life – Renaissance men and women are alive and well in Leeds in 2022!

However, the new school is rooted in the alumni successes of its two founding schools. Woven through every page of Neill's text, humbling and inspiring in equal measure, you will read of centuries of LGS men who have excelled in their chosen fields, including; medicine and engineering, science, politics and law, the military and religion, art and music, literature and journalism.

It is wonderful to read how LGS inspired such vision, such entrepreneurial spirit, such deep-rooted commitment to others, from men who travelled the world and those who stayed closer to home. It is our privilege to maintain this tradition and to inspire the next generations of global citizens and leaders to similar success and an impact far beyond Yorkshire's boundaries.

Sue Woodroofe, BA (Hons.), Med, NPQH
Principal
The Grammar School at Leeds

Introduction and Acknowledgements

THE IDEA OF writing a book outlining the lives of famous Old Boys of Leeds Grammar School first came to me as I set about the task of compiling a database of every OL at the School during the course of the nineteenth century, using the Admission Registers from 1820 to 1901. In this I was helped greatly by an unlikely hero of mine, Edmund Wilson (1838-1914), himself an OL, who went to great lengths to identify and contact as many ex-pupils of the School as was possible and then published his research in 1906 under the title of *Leeds Grammar School Admission Books from 1820 to 1900*. Wilson lived in one half of Denison Hall, a grand edifice that may be found today overlooking Hanover Square in Woodhouse. He kept up a correspondence (always hand-written letters) with as many OLs as he could contact until his death in 1914.

It was while I was entering scholars' names onto the database that I became very much aware of the many OLs who could justifiably be called distinguished (there is a separate listing of boys who left the School prior to 1820) and I thought it a good idea to record their achievements for posterity. Bearing in mind that this process started in 2011, I did not then see any relevance to the centenary of the OLA in 2019, but various people, including Professor Tristram Hope and John Davies, pointed out to me the obvious connection.

If I were not to produce a volume or volumes of the length of *War and Peace*, I had to start making choices – it is a measure of the School's success in educating great achievers that this was a difficult task. I have had to leave out a great many famous people for no other reasons than the practicalities of publishing and not

Introduction and Acknowledgements

putting at risk my happily married relationship with my long-suffering wife. Having made my selection, I find that most of my subjects are dead, and I suppose that this affords the opportunity for a more complete assessment of their lives and careers.

There is no attempt at precedence or ranking. All my subjects are of equal value to me and I believe that each in his own way has made a significant contribution to the city of Leeds and far beyond. So the order of presentation is simply chronological.

Anyone seeking ground-breaking revelations or exciting new observations regarding the lives of my subjects will be disappointed. I have used for the most part published sources that any curious reader may consult by judicious use of my bibliographies. Any factual errors are mine alone. I have in many cases imposed what some might see as an undue emphasis on their years at school, but my reasoning is that their experiences there largely influenced their later careers.

Many people have helped me in the production of this book. First, I must thank the Principal of GSAL, Mrs Sue Woodroofe, who provided encouragement and financial assistance. Professor Tristram Hope, President of the OLA, has been wholly supportive of the idea of marking the centenary of the Association with a celebration of the School's influence in the city and the achievements of its scholars and has also given financial assistance. Others have offered advice and proof-reading services, including John Davies, my fellow archivist and friend at GSAL, who has generously contributed the entry on Field Marshal William Gustavus Nicholson, and Robert Dyson OL, whose knowledge of local history is all-embracing and who has provided much help in my chapter on his brother. Andrew Smith OL helped me with some details regarding Bands Night and Nevile House Plays. Dr Kevin Grady kindly put me right regarding aspects of John Harrison's life. Phil Caplan OL at Scratching Shed Publishing has gone to great pains to guide me through the process of transforming Word documents into a book and has never once pointed out my ignorance of the procedures involved. My thanks to Geoffrey Wooler's nephew, Peter, who provided photographs from the family albums and who allowed me to view a DVD featuring Geoffrey's career. Anne Wickes at The Second World War Experience Centre (then at Walton but now on Boroughgate in Otley) kindly allowed me to browse the archival material relating to Geoffrey as well as Godfrey Talbot, and gave permission to quote material from the Centre's website. Barry Cryer OL granted permission to quote extracts from his books *Butterfly Brain* and *The Chronicles of Hernia*, as well as his poem "Ode to Leeds Grammar School", presented to LGS on 25 February 1999. Michael S Potts was kind enough to point out some errors and omissions from my chapters on the Potts family and William Potts as well as giving permission to use photographs and extracts from his book. Chris Hindle, editor at the Thoresby Society, gave me permission to include many quotations and images from its excellent series of publications. Doreen Greenshields has contributed a number of splendid line drawings to enhance the text relating to several OLs. Professor Michael J Sewell kindly gave permission for me to make extensive use of his Biographical Memoir on Rodney Hill. Hodder & Stoughton allowed extracts from Geoffrey Studdert Kennedy's *Rough Rhymes of a Padre*. My wife, Pam, has patiently endured my fascination with Potts clocks, among other things, and the long hours I have spent secluded in my study while wrestling with the complexities of English syntax and style.

Finally, I hope this book goes some way to demonstrating the incontrovertible fact that the School has in many ways contributed to the cultural life of the city of Leeds and this in turn has spread outwards to embrace Yorkshire, Great Britain as a whole and beyond. It is not the only Leeds institution to do so but it is an important one.

Neill Hargreaves
February 2022

John Harrison's portrait hangs at St John's Church, New Briggate

1

John Harrison 1579-1656
Merchant and Benefactor
At LGS dates unknown [C.1589-1595]

THERE IS AN assumption by many local historians, including David Thornton, Steven Burt and Dr Kevin Grady, that John Harrison the Younger attended Leeds Grammar School. This may in part explain why later, in 1624, he provided the land and funds to move the School to a spot close to where the Grand Theatre is to be found today. The previous location was almost certainly the New Chapel or Chantry of our Lady in Lady Lane, just off the Headrow. According to Burt and Grady, 'it [the School] became the owner of an old Chantry chapel on the Headrow and thereafter used the building as its school house'. [B&G, *WP&T*, p.16] According to A C Price in his *History of the Leeds Grammar School*, the School was here in 1620. [Price, p.86] In fact, it may well have moved on a number of occasions although the exact sequence of those moves is not known. The most popular theory is that it was originally located at a Chapel close to Bridge End. Be that as it may, Ralph Thoresby, himself possibly a former Leeds Grammar School scholar, wrote in his *Ducatus Leodiensis* (1715) that 'the famous Mr. Harrison removed it to a pleasant Field of his own which he surrounded with a substantial Wall and then in the midst of the Quadrangle built the present Fabrick of the School'. [ACP, p.86] His will, written in 1653, elaborates upon this:

> Whereas I have of my own charge and upon my own land erected and built one new house now used and employed [as] a grammar school and walled the yard thereunto belonging with a stone wall as the same

abutteth upon the land of Henry Rhodes upon the north and upon my own land upon south east and west my mind and will is that the same shall be for a Master and an Usher to teach Scholars in for ever. [ACP, pp.86-87]

This school, with some modest additions and improvements, including Godfrey Lawson's library extension (1692), remained in use until Dr Barry removed it to Woodhouse Moor in 1858; it was officially opened on 27 June 1859.

John Harrison the Younger was born in 1579, the son of John Harrison the Elder (died 1601), a cloth merchant of Leeds, and Elizabeth Marton, daughter of a Holbeck clothier (died 1602). The family lived in Pawdmyre, a district of the town now known as Upper Briggate. He was baptised in the Parish Church of St Peter on 16 August. Exactly when young John attended the school is not yet known but he must have had some affection for the place in view of his later generosity, added to which his father was a Trustee. Little is known of his early life but it is possible he spent much of his childhood in the house of his uncle, John Kitchingman, who lived at Chapel Allerton. There is an appealing though possibly apocryphal story that, at quite an early age, he gave his coat to a beggar but sadly this cannot be verified.

In 1601 Harrison inherited the greater part of his father's estate and business interests, including a large tract of land lying at the top of Briggate, and this made him a very wealthy man indeed. He purchased the North Hall estate, at the junction of Vicar Lane and Lady Lane, and Rockley Hall, which he later used as a storehouse for food and clothing for the poor, and, in the following year, he married Elizabeth, the daughter of Thomas Foxcroft who lived at Barr Grange. He then built himself a substantial house on Briggate, described by Thoresby as 'a good old-fashioned House, with a quadrangular court in the midst' [Thoresby, *Ducatus*] Being fond of felines, Harrison 'had Holes or Passages cut in the Doors and Ceilings, for the free passage of Cats'. [*DL*]

He was not content, however, to live off his father's munificence, but was sufficiently industrious to add considerably to his personal finances. Moreover, he was quite happy to put a good part of his fortune to philanthropic purposes and in this he was carrying on the good work of his father before him. He may well have been deeply affected by the death of his mother in 1602, and this was quite possibly a stimulus to his charitable benefactions. He caused a rather stylish Market Cross to be erected at the north end of the Middle Row, a mean street which split Briggate into two halves and ran from present-day Commercial Street to the Queen's Arcade. According to Thoresby, it 'was a stately Cross for Conveniency and Ornament of the Market [RT, *DL*; Hornsey, p.116].It was rebuilt in 1776, but sadly demolished in 1825, though in 1933 its remains formed part of a gateway near the top of Lady

Harrison's school, 1624

Lane. He then built New Kirkgate (now New Briggate) which ran from the junction of Lowerhead Row to immediately opposite the steps at the south east corner of St John's churchyard. The rents from New Street were dedicated to charitable purposes, especially caring for the poor, the improvement of the local highways and the Grammar School. Later, sometime between 1632 and 1640, he founded Harrison's Hospital, two groups of twenty almshouses, built in such a way as to form a quadrangle adjacent to the Church. In all there was sufficient accommodation for forty poor women who each received a handsome pension from an annual endowment of £80. [MAH, *TS*, pp.123-4] According to the inscription on his monument in St John's, written by Dr Lake, the Vicar of Leeds, these almshouses were for 'the Relief of Indigent Persons of good Conversation, and formerly industrious'. [Stocks, *TS*, Vol. xxiv (1919), p.190] By an indenture of enfeoffment dated 21 April 1653, he dedicated the income from several properties to his hospital, the trust fund to be administered by four worthies of his acquaintance. In 1791, Arthur Ikin gave money to allow the building of 12 extra units across the centre of the quadrangle (see 1906 OS Map). Later, in 1849-50, the almshouses were completely rebuilt around a double courtyard which faced into Wade Lane. Harrison's legacy continues with the building of additional almshouses in 1876-77 at Raglan Road, now run by the Harrison and Potter Trust. The Wade Lane buildings were demolished in 1960.

Following his father's example, Harrison had, by 1624, become a Trustee of the Grammar School and, as described above, he arranged for it to move to what were then considered superior surroundings, half an acre of grounds with a building offering commodious accommodation. Following the move, he decided that the school should be governed by Trustees like himself rather than the Committee of Pious Uses, set up in 1620 to administer charitable funds, some members of which Harrison was known to dislike. A good number of benefactions had been made to the School and the portfolio of properties whose income was dedicated to it had grown substantially and he believed the Committee was incapable of acting with due probity. It was in part this increase in income and funding that led him to provide a building that served not only a function but also possessed some elaborate features, especially the roof. Sadly, no heating system was provided and all classes, no matter of what age, were taught together in the large single schoolroom. As a concession to comfort, seating was installed for the pupils in 1708 and heating by means of a single fireplace was provided in 1751.

As well as the Grammar School, Harrison looked to the spiritual needs of the growing population of Leeds. There simply was not sufficient seating capacity in St Peter's, described in the 1628 Survey of Leeds as a 'verie faire church built after a Cathedrall structure', to accommodate would-be worshippers. [*The Survey of Leeds* (1612), quoted from DT, *Story of Leeds*, p.57] In 1631, his wife, Elizabeth, died (they had no children) and in her memory he started work on St John's Church, now the inner city's oldest surviving place of worship and with a seating capacity then of 1200. At the Service of Consecration, Harrison spoke of his joy at seeing the building completed and ready for its first services:

> Whereupon I the said John Harrison, duely Considering how great necessity there was of making further Provision to Suply the defect of that place [St Peter's] of my owne free Will and accord, in Zeale and pious disposition to the honour of God and benefit of the People have built and Erected this Chappell att my onely proper costs and charges with intent and Purpose that it might be dedicated to the Worship of God, And that his holy and blessed Name might there be reverenced and called upon by me the said John Harrison and Such and So many of the Inhabitants as shall repair thither for divine Service… [Stocks, *Consecration*, p.429]

It was to be a further 40 years before another place of worship, Mill Hill Chapel, was built in Leeds. Between 1837 and 1841, St John's functioned temporarily as the Parish Church when St Peter's was being rebuilt after the foundations of the mediaeval church were found to be rotten. [HWD, p.54] [SB & KG, p.182] It remains a magnificent monument to his generosity and is undoubtedly one of the finest seventeenth-century churches in the country, and one that unusually, within its internal structural details, catered for different and competing elements within the church at that time.

High Anglicans and Presbyterians alike could worship there, but unfortunately they were disinclined to tolerate each other and the place became a source of distress for its founder. The Archbishop of York, Richard Neile, objected to the new church on several grounds as he thought it too close to St Peter's and too likely to fall under the sway of the Puritans, in particular the newly appointed Puritan Vicar of Leeds, Henry Robinson. In what might be regarded as a confrontational move, Harrison, who leaned towards middle-of-the-road Anglican Church sentiments, appointed the moderate Puritan Vicar of Ledsham, Robert Todd, as Curate of St John's, in one way a fortuitous appointment because, when plague struck the town in 1645 he remained in post when many lesser clergymen might have fled to the relative safety of the countryside. J E Stocks, in his *St John's Church, Leeds*, suggests that Todd's Puritanical leanings may well have saved the beautiful internal woodwork from destruction by the more zealous soldiery of the New Model Army. This is particularly important bearing in mind the detailed study that Stocks made in 1934 of the carvings in which he praises the craftsmanship of the woodwork, evident for all to see.

When the church was consecrated in September 1634, the inaugural sermon was preached by the Archbishop of York's chaplain in the High Anglican style. However, on that very same day, in the afternoon, Robert Todd preached a stirring puritanical sermon denouncing everything the chaplain had espoused and this so angered the archbishop that he immediately suspended Todd. It took the joint persuasive efforts of Harrison and Sir Arthur Ingram of Temple Newsam to persuade Neile to reverse his decision the following year.

There is no question that ecclesiastical wrangling caused Harrison a great deal of grief. From our perspective, it seems tragic that his greatest gift to the town should be the cause of so much controversy, especially considering the fact that, on his death, his funeral service took place not in St John's but in St Peter's. Equally disconcerting, Whitaker, in his *Loidis and Elmete*, brutally condemned the church in uncompromising terms; St John's had, 'all the gloom and all the obstructions of an ancient church without one vestige of dignity and grace'. [W, p.62] He felt obliged to add:

John Harrison – Merchant and Benefactor

Harrison's Blue Plaque at St John's

At this period architecture, especially church architecture, was at its lowest ebb. The highest effort of church builders was to produce a clumsy imitation of our ancient churches, no whit better than the works of their tasteless successors of the present day. This church in particular is a most unhappy specimen of this taste. [Whitaker, p.61]

In 1865, when the fabric of the building required some restoration, other detractors, including the Leeds architect John Dobson (who hoped to design the projected replacement church), took Whitaker at his word and advocated total demolition. Such a drastic step was fiercely opposed by Richard Norman Shaw, a London architect who reported in 1865, expressing disbelief at the prospect of destruction and concluding his report with the words:

> …one cannot escape the conviction that it is simply a matter of duty never to destroy good old work if it can possibly be retained, and were the dilapidations of the church three times greater than they are, I would still say restore it, and restore it only where absolutely necessary – touch nothing you can avoid touching. [Stocks, *TS*, p.220]

Thankfully, Shaw's advice, backed up by the famous Sir George Gilbert Scott, was accepted by the Trustees of the church, albeit reluctantly, and some modest restoration took place.

Interestingly, by the time of Walter Farquhar Hook, Vicar of Leeds from 1837 to 1859, St John's was very High Church indeed, the *Leeds Mercury* describing worship there as 'Cathedral Service' and praising in particular the quality of the music, prayer and impressive Holy Communion. [HWD, p.54]

In 1885, the Harrison Memorial Window was installed in the church, the work of John Burlison and Thomas Grylls, whose firm of stained glass makers was founded in 1868. It depicts some of the more memorable aspects of his life such as the gift of gold coins to Charles I, the construction of the Market Cross, the great man at prayer, and a touching scene in which he helps an elderly lady into one of his almshouses.

He, like Leeds, prospered to such an extent that he was able to purchase a large house, built of brick, opposite the east end of Boar Lane. The town was on the up: the population of 3,000 in 1600 was to rise to 6,000 by 1700. Its wealth was derived chiefly from the woollen cloth trade, sharing with the West Country and East Anglia the lion's share of the country's output. Naturally, the local Leeds merchants wanted more control over how that wealth was distributed, so in 1626 they successfully petitioned the Crown for a charter and 'this was the most important landmark in the history of Leeds, for the charter gave the town important powers of self-government'. (SB & KG, *IHoL*, p. 33] These movers and shakers comprised about thirty dynamic merchants, 'young adventurers lately sprung up who at little or no charge buy and engross as they please'. [B&G, *WP&T*, p. 13] One of those merchants was John Harrison. The government of Leeds was now in the hands of one alderman (later called the mayor), nine principal burgesses, of whom Harrison was one, and twenty assistants, all of whom were given the role of Justice of the Peace. He deputized for Sir John Savile, the alderman, before taking the position himself. In 1629 he was one of the nine townsmen who purchased the manor of Leeds (excluding the rights over the manorial corn mills) for the princely sum of £2,710 from the Corporation of London who had bought it from an impecunious Charles I. For the London Corporation this represented a quick profit of 80% in one year.

He was now truly the driving force in the development of Leeds into a thriving commercial centre. He and his coterie of dynamic merchants most likely met in the new Moot Hall, built for the transaction of public business in 1618, and were able to ensure that the cloth they produced was of good and consistent quality. This Moot Hall was in all probability the centre of a kind of unofficial civic life. [Hornsey, p.115] Moreover, they could exclude any potential rivals from threatening their near-monopoly control over the market. Just to cement their hegemony, they obtained an Act of Parliament that created a corporation in order to control cloth making throughout West Yorkshire, although this occurred five years after Harrison's death. In all this, they had the support of Sir John Savile of Howley, a neighbouring landowner and courtier.

With the advent of the Civil Wars (1642-49), Harrison was placed in a very difficult position. He naturally tended towards moderate Anglicanism and loyalty to the Crown, despite his dislike of Archbishop Laud's High Anglicanism, and the vicissitudes of war caused him great consternation and certainly affected his health. When Charles I was taken prisoner and held at Red Hall in Leeds, he visited the monarch and begged to be allowed to proffer a silver, lidded tankard of ale. It was indeed a heady brew because the tankard was full of gold coins 'which his Majesty did, with much celerity, hasten to secrete about his royal person'. [quoted from the Wikipedia entry on John Harrison].True or not, this magnanimous gesture, almost certainly a simple act of kindness to someone in impoverished circumstances, cost him dear because he was later tried at York by the Parliamentarians and fined £464, a huge sum in those days. The actual charge against him was that he had supplied two horses to the Royalist army, though he claimed he had done this under duress and threat of punishment. [Hornsea, p.144] And this was despite evidence known to his persecutors that Harrison had shown even greater generosity towards them, as a Memorandum from W Harrison, Treasurer to Parliament, shows:

> Whereas by Ordinance of Parliament bearing date the 24th day of November, 1642, the right honble. Ferdinando Ld. Fairfax (or whom he should appoint Treasurer for that purpose) was enabled to engage the public faith of the Kingdom for all such Plate, Money, Armes and Horse as should be voluntarily lent or raysed for the service of the State in the Northern Counties. In pursuance of the said ordinance John Harrison of Leeds Esq., did in the yeare of our Lord 1642 furnish and lende the Sume of fower score and Ten poundes in money and also [an] Horse and Armes, being valued at Twenty Poundes, in all amounting to the sum of One Hundred and Ten poundes, the Publique Faith of the Nation is to bee engaged unto the said John Harrison. In Testimony whereof I have hereunto put my hand and seale.
>
> *W. Harrison, Treasurer*

He was tried in absentia because his health was so poor and eventually he became bedridden. Some indication of his state of mind may be deduced from a letter he wrote to his judge, Francis, Baron Thorpe, in 1652:

I am on the point of seventy-two years of age and therewith weakened with so many infirmities, as I am indeed bed-ridden, and have been little better this twelve years. I therefore humbly crave pardon for this boldness that instead of speaking I am forced to present my thoughts in writing… And it may be thought fitting by my adversaries, that I should (whether right or wrong) suffer for both, which if so, I must beg to conclude with the saying of a royal queen - If I perish, I perish, so if I must sell my father's inheritance, I must sell it. Fiat voluntas Dei [may God's will be done], My lord, I am, your lordship's servant, J Harrison. [quoted from JGD, p.22]

Thorpe treated Harrison in a most unfair manner, sometimes appearing conciliatory but on other occasions acting with vindictive cruelty. Worst of all, he allowed his detractors to humiliate Harrison, knowing that the man was virtually on his death bed. He alone must bear responsibility for the draconian fine imposed upon the ailing benefactor. His hostile attitude was noted by some of those present at the hearing, including one Thomas Dixon, who wrote in a letter to an unknown recipient, 'Here, they [those speaking against Harrison] stuck a great while, and baron Thorpe did so squeeze it and grind it, that a counsellor sitting by (I know him not) whispered me in the ear, and said I perceive much malice'. [Hornsea, p. 145]

By any standards, this was shoddy treatment of a man who had, throughout his adult life, shown nothing but the utmost compassion in his support of charitable deeds towards those less fortunate than him. His most outstanding characteristics were his piety and his benevolence and we must judge his reputation on those qualities. He was known to hate hypocrisy, at the same time loving truth and justice. Even in his business affairs, he was shrewd but fair, and was genuinely surprised at the malevolence shown towards him by some of the younger, competing merchants of the town during the trying period of his sequestration.

Harrison died on 29 October 1656, aged 77, in unhappy circumstances, bed-ridden and possibly lonely. His memorial service took place in St Peter's and, on 8 November, according to some authorities, he was interred in his orchard close to where Kirkgate Market now exists, though Hornsea casts doubt on this assertion. Later, his remains were fittingly removed to St John's and buried beneath a monument of black marble, over which was placed, until recently, his portrait in full length municipal robes.

It has now [2020] been moved to the rear of the Church and can be found in the far corner on the left hand side as you enter the Church. Boys eating their lunch in the refectory at Moorland Road will surely remember a large copy of this portrait hanging on the wall at the far end where the staff table was situated. In 1904, when the House system was set up under the headmastership of the Rev. Canon J R

John Harrison – Merchant and Benefactor

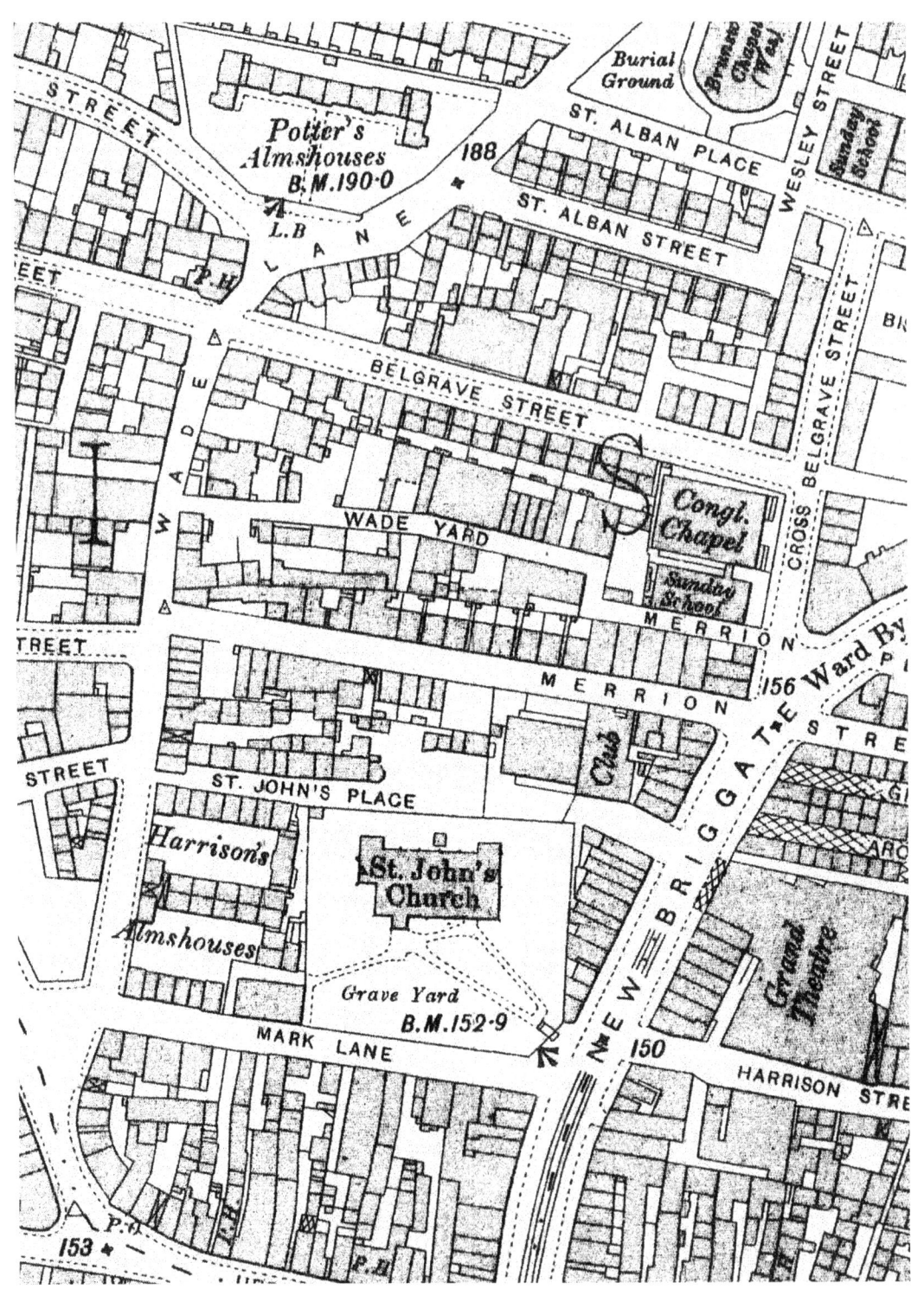

*Harrison and Potter's Almshouses on a 1906 OS Plan,
Reproduced by permission of the Ordnance Survey*

Wynne-Edwards, Harrison House was named in honour of the great benefactor. The other Houses were Sheafield, Lawson and Barry.

Leeds has treated him more kindly than those ardent Parliamentarians. There is a statue of him in City Square, the work of Henry Charles Fehr, that depicts him in a long robe, book in hand, looking kindly upon his fellow Loiners. As Margaret Hornsey writes, 'John Harrison, perhaps, did more for Leeds than any of his contemporaries'. [MAH, p.104]

Bibliography

Beresford, M W & Jones, G R J (eds.), *Leeds and its Region*, Leeds Local Executive Committee of the British Association for the Advancement of Science (Leeds: 1967)

Burt, Steven and Grady, Kevin, *The Illustrated History of Leeds*, Breedon Books (Derby: 1994)

Burt, Steven and Grady, Kevin, *War, Plague & Trade. Leeds in the Seventeenth-Century*, Burt and Grady (Leeds: 1985)

Dalton, Harry W, *Anglican Resurgence under W. F. Hook in Early Victorian Leeds*, The Thoresby Society (Leeds: 2002)

Davies, John G, *From Bridge to Moor*, Leeds Grammar School (Leeds: 2002)

Hornsey, Margaret A, '*John Harrison, the Leeds Benefactor, and his Times*', in *Miscellanea*, Volume XXXIII, Thoresby Society Publications (Leeds: 1935)

Linstrum, Derek, *Architects and Architecture*, Lund Humphries (London: 1978)

Marshall, James W D, *Floreat Per Saecula. From Age to Age Excel*, Smith Settle (Otley: 1997)

Price, Aubrey Charles, *A History of the Leeds Grammar School*, Richard Jackson (Leeds: 1919)

Sprittles, Joseph, *Links with Bygone Leeds*, The Thoresby Society, Volume LII, No. 15 (Leeds: 1969)

Stocks, J E, "The Consecration Service of St. John's Church, Leeds", in The Thoresby Society Publications, *Miscellanea*, Volume XXIV, pp. 421-434 (Leeds: 1919)

Stocks, John Ellis, with Thompson, Herbert, *St John's Church, Leeds 1634-1934*, Whitehead & Miller Ltd (Leeds: 1934); also in Thoresby Society, *Miscellanea*, Volume XXIV, pp. 190-226 (Leeds: 1919]

Thoresby, Ralph, *Ducatus Leodiensis*, First Edition, Maurice Atkins (London: 1715)

Thornton, David, *The Story of Leeds*, The History Press (Stroud: 2013)

Whitaker, Thomas Dunham, *Loidis and Elmete*, Robinson, Son, and Holdsworth (Leeds: 1816)

John Smeaton's marble memorial (detail) at Whitkirk Church, courtesy of the Faith Team at St Mary's Church, Whitkirk

2

John Smeaton FRS 1724-1792
The First British Civil Engineer
At LGS 1734-1740

JOHN SMEATON was the great grandson of John, a watchmaker at York who moved his family to Whitkirk. His grandfather, also John, built Austhorpe Lodge which stood in about six acres of grounds. John's father, William, was an attorney who married Mary Stones of Beal. He prospered and the couple had three children, of whom only John, born on 8 June 1724, and his sister, Hannah, born 10 April 1732, outlived their father. William, the other sibling, died in October 1732, aged only five.

He was first educated, at home, by his mother, Mary, but in 1734 he started at Leeds Grammar School under the headmastership of the Rev. Thomas Barnard. Samuel Smiles, in his *Lives of the Engineers*, observed that

> At a proper age the boy was sent to school at Leeds. The town then possessed, as it still does, the great advantage of an excellent Free Grammar School, founded by the benefactions of Catholics in the early times, afterwards greatly augmented by the endowment of one John Harrison, a native of the town, about the period of the Reformation. At the school, Smeaton is supposed to have received the best part of his school instruction, and it is said that his progress in geometry and arithmetic was very decided; but, as before, the chief part of his education was conducted at home, amongst his tools and his model machines. There he was incessantly busy whenever he had a spare moment. [SS, Vol.2, p.106]

John Smeaton – First British Civil Engineer

C A Lupton paints a rather gloomier picture of the grammar school in his Presidential Address given at the annual meeting of the Thoresby Society in 1969. The School was

> a somewhat austere seminary with a hard earth floor and no heating, where education was concerned on religion, logic and the classics with the stimulating influence of the rod, 'God's instrument to cure the evils of their conditions, to drive out that folly which is bound up in their hearts'. [CAL, *TS*, Vol. 15, Part 3, p.217]

A C Price, in his *A History of the Leeds Grammar School*, when writing of eminent Old Boys who did not go up to Cambridge, describes Smeaton as 'the famous engineer, of whom tradition says that even as a child he had a taste for mechanics and distinguished himself at school in geometry and arithmetic'. [ACP, pp.120-121]

During his six years at the school he 'proved to be an enthusiastic and attentive scholar, but not so inclined towards sports and other activities'. [RFL, *Smeaton of Austhorpe*, p.4] He received a good grounding in mathematics, geometry and Latin – very much the staple diet, along with Greek and Divinity, of the curriculum at that time. He was, apparently, a shy boy who shunned the company of his fellow pupils, who rather unkindly dubbed him 'Fooley Smeaton' because he preferred the company of artisans and workmen, particularly those who were adept at using their tools and machinery. He delighted in making models and soon began to explore the potential of simple machines. One of these was a water pumping engine, which he built after watching workmen set up some pumps at Garforth Colliery, and which he applied to his father's fish pond so successfully that he managed to kill off most of the fish. Despite this, John prevailed upon his father to allow him the use of one of the outhouses adjacent to the house as a workshop. This is surprising because William was aghast that his son consorted with artisans and workers who were deemed to be of a lower class and he was determined that John should follow him into the Law.

A letter written after 1742 by John Holmes, John Smeaton's cousin, gives a vivid impression of a young man totally consumed by the delights of engineering and experimentation:

> In the year 1742 (when Smeaton was 18), I spent a month at his father's house, and being intended myself for a mechanical employment, and a few years younger than he was, I could not but view his works with astonishment; he forged his iron and steel, and melted his metal; he had tools of every sort… He had made a Lathe, by which he cut a perpetual

screw in brass, a thing little known at that day, and which I believe was the invention of Mr Henry Hindley, of York… Mr Hindley was a man of the most communicative disposition, a great lover of Mechanics, and of the most fertile genius. Mr Smeaton [John] soon became acquainted with him, and they spent many a night at Mr Hindley's house till day light, conversing on those subjects. [quoted from the Dedication Service at Westminster Abbey, p.9]

To bring his father's plan regarding his son's career into fruition, on leaving LGS John was put to work copying legal documents as part of his training to become an attorney. He was then sent to London in 1742 to work in the Courts of Westminster but this did not suit him at all and after two years he told his father he wished to take up mechanical engineering instead. Again, William was displeased, seeing his son's inclination to be a perverse loss of status and certainly poorer prospects, viewing engineering as a vocation for menials. It is true that, at that time, almost all mechanical work was performed by millwrights and others at labourers' wages.

John must have been a persuasive negotiator because his father did agree that he might return to Austhorpe and he would support John financially.

John lived through a period prior to the Industrial Revolution. The eighteenth century was a time of small, localised industry but there were signs of a growth in major capital investments such as canals and ports, a reflection of Britain's emerging empire and trade. This period of change is exemplified by the fact that when John was born, the only real industry in his locality was coal mining and small scale broad cloth manufacture, yet by 1792 Leeds was fast developing into a major centre of the woollen industry. It was the impetus given by the need to improve communications to facilitate this growth that provided John with many of his projects, particularly after 1760.

Whilst in London, around 1748, John had befriended Benjamin Wilson (who, like Smeaton, was expected to train as a lawyer but instead became a successful portrait painter) and through his auspices he met members of the Royal Society, some of whom encouraged him to consider becoming a professional instrument maker. It was around this time that he began attending French lessons (LGS did not offer modern languages) and he met and fell in love with a young lady, much to the alarm of his parents as she was deemed an unsuitable match. In the event, the romance fell through, though at some cost to John, chiefly because some of his friends believed he had behaved dishonourably.

Another friend, Dr Gowan Knight FRS (himself an Old Boy of the Grammar School), persuaded John to set up in business as an instrument maker. This he did in 1748 and he began to make a name for himself. Sadly, on 17 April 1749 his father

John Smeaton – First British Civil Engineer

Austhorpe Lodge

died so John brought his mother and his sister, Hannah, to stay with him in the capital.

John worked on improving the vacuum pump as well as developing, in conjunction with Knight, a mariners' compass which in time became standard issue in the Royal Navy. Success followed and business was so brisk that he had to move to larger premises at Furnival Inn Court, near Holborn. His reputation as an instrument maker grew and he began to divert a portion of his energy into studying the effects of the motive power of wind and water, something crucial when he came to tackle his most famous project, the Eddystone Lighthouse. Such was his growing reputation that he was invited to become a Fellow of the Royal Society in March 1753. The happiness this afforded him was tempered by the death of his sister Hannah some weeks later on 8 June.

He quickly became aware that he could not earn a successful living from making mathematical instruments alone so he made the decision to concentrate on his engineering studies and in this he was demonstrating an awareness that the country was in need of developing a commercial infrastructure that relied on invention and innovation. John became renowned for his determination to approach every project with the same meticulous attention to detail, creating superb drawings and making scale models for every scheme under consideration. The commissions which followed gave rise to his reputation as a civil engineer. He designed a windmill, then a water mill; and after studying the works of engineers in France and Holland, he undertook the design and construction of stone bridges and land drainage. It was soon after a trip to the Continent to see for himself what was being achieved there that he heard of the destruction by fire of Rudyerd's wooden lighthouse at Eddystone, thirteen miles south-west of Plymouth. He quickly completed all other tasks in hand and found the time to fall in love with and then marry, in June 1756, Ann Jenkinson, whose father was a merchant tailor and Freeman of the city of York. It is possible that, having secured the contract for re-building the Eddystone lighthouse and the financial security that entailed, he felt he was in a good position to take on the obligations and responsibilities of marriage. The couple were to go on and have three daughters.

Smeaton was invited to re-build the Rudyerd lighthouse on the recommendation of the then President of the Royal Society, Lord Macclesfield, and at the behest of Trinity House, the organization set up in 1514 and responsible for purchasing privately owned lighthouses and improving them. In some ways he was an unusual choice in that his fame at that time was based solely as a mathematical instrument maker, albeit an able mechanic with a reputation for painstaking thoroughness. He surveyed the incredibly challenging site of the ruined structure and came to the conclusion that his lighthouse would be constructed in stone, a ground-breaking and deeply contentious decision. Trinity House was adamant that 'nothing but wood could possibly stand on the Eddystone' [RFL p.20; SS, p. 28] but Smeaton persevered and started by adapting Rudyerd's design on paper by enlarging the foundations and tapering the circular walls in order to minimise resistance to wind and waves. He then decided to add strength by forming dovetail joints in the stonework.

In April 1756 he managed to land on the reef and set about the task, taking measurements and testing the hardness of the base rock. He paid careful attention to the logistics of the exercise: a work-yard was set up close to Mill Bay between Plymouth and Devonport; a comprehensive set of regulations governing working practices was produced – an early forerunner of today's Health and Safety legislation; and he chose Cornish granite for the exterior and Portland stone for the interior. Despite all their earlier misgivings, Trinity House gave him a carte blanche to proceed as he thought fit

On 3 August 1756 work commenced and Smeaton himself oversaw the preparation of the base on which to build the first course of stone. He shared the hardships and terrors that afflicted the workmen, never shirking from arduous and dangerous situations.

The winter of 1756-57 was spent cutting and dressing the stone ready to place onto the base rock. Knowing the strength of the elements, he developed a waterproof cement to fix the stones in place. As a further precaution, he learned from the example of Lostwithiel Church, whose spire had been destroyed by an electric storm, as well as that of Benjamin Franklin, who in 1747 had written a paper on the nature of electrical energy generated during a thunderstorm, that a lightning conductor would be essential. On visiting the site after a particularly strong series of autumn gales, Smeaton was delighted to note that, 'Not a block had been moved. The cement was found to have set as hard as the rock itself'. [RFL p.27] Despite this comforting news, he insisted on double-checking all his calculations. Moreover, whilst living at Plymouth, each morning he would stand on the Hoe and peer through his telescope to seek reassurance that the structure was still standing. He need not have concerned himself. Slowly the column rose up from the base, each layer of stone carefully dovetailed into its neighbours and at last

> The column was now erected to its specified height of seventy feet. The last mason's work done was the cutting out of the words "Laus Deo" ["Praise God"] upon the last stone set over the door of the lantern. Round the upper storeroom, upon the course [of stones] under the ceiling, had been cut at an earlier period, "Except the Lord build the house, they labour in vain that build it" [Psalm 127] (words the observant visitor may descry written on the walls of the Victoria Hall at Leeds Town Hall as part of a series of stirring sentiments). [SS, p.152]

He designed the ironwork that would sit atop the lighthouse and the cupola placed as a decorative feature on top of the lantern room. He even chose personally to screw down the gilt ball above the cupola with the help of his assistant, Roger Cornthwaite. This must have been a daunting task, given that they were working 120 feet above a seething sea, perilously balanced on a wooden board. Every last detail was checked and double-checked and Smeaton personally attended to the window fittings, the glazing of the lantern and the installation of the lightning conductor.

Three years after its completion, one of the most ferocious storms ever known at that time raged for days along the south-west coast, causing terrible damage to harbours and shipping in the area, but the lighthouse stood firm, 'all the damage done to [it] was repaired by a little gallipot of putty'. [SS, p. 45]

The construction of a stone lighthouse caught the public imagination at the time and it became an attraction in its own right. 120 years later, when the lighthouse was deemed to be in need of replacement, the residents of Plymouth and the surrounding area were horrified to hear that the authorities planned to blow it up, so they raised funds by public subscription and had the structure dismantled stone by stone and re-erected on Plymouth Hoe thirteen miles away as a monument to Smeaton and there its stands today, splendidly restored. It is a testimony to him that lighthouses built around the world after Eddystone were designed on the same engineering principles employed by him.

Smeaton was never one to waste his time and during those spells of inclement weather when work on Eddystone was impossible, he tackled a range of other, more land-based, projects. He surveyed the upper River Calder with a view to making it navigable; he worked on Dysart Harbour at Kirkaldy; and he prepared a Paper on the power of water and wind to turn mills, a treatise so highly regarded he was presented with the prestigious Copley Medal, awarded annually by the Royal Society, in 1759. The citation for the award read as follows:

> On account of his curious experiments concerning Water-wheels and Wind-mill Sails, communicated to the Society. For his experimental enquiry concerning the powers of water and wind in the moving of Mills.

Following the death of his mother on 18 October 1759, Smeaton returned to Austhorpe and in one sense returned to his Yorkshire roots, focusing his energies on more local assignments, starting with extensive renovations and additions to Austhorpe Lodge, where he built a tower that housed his office and workshops. 'When he entered his sanctum [in the tower], strict orders were given that he was not to be disturbed on any account. No one was permitted to ascend the circular staircase that led to his study. When he heard a footstep below, he would call out and enquire what was wanted.' [SS, p. 75] All this building work caused him some financial problems despite the fact that he was able to increase his daily rate of remuneration to one guinea as a consulting engineer. This situation was eased somewhat when he was appointed Receiver of the Derwent Water Estates of Greenwich Hospital with a handsome annual salary of around £450. At the same time he took on more consultancy work which proved to be financially beneficial. There followed major projects on the River Calder, and the River Aire at its confluence with the Ouse at Airmyn. He produced his usual detailed reports on the proposed Louth Canal and the Trent and Mersey Canal.

Whilst maintaining a demanding workload he still found time to do good work in his local community. Smeaton remained a devout Christian all his life. He supported St Mary's Church at Whitkirk and became a 'Governor' of the local Charity school. Civil engineering projects included building a water-ram system to provide water for Temple Newsam House as well as hanging the gates there (the Sphinx gates are the only survivors, built in association with Capability Brown); a steam engine for pumping water out of Middleton Colliery; and a five-sail windmill used for crushing flint at the Leeds Pottery at Burmantofts.

The Seacroft area was well suited to the development of small-scale industry, having coal, wood, iron ore and lime in the immediate vicinity. Smeaton's improvements to the old ironworks there overcame the problem of an inconsistent water supply that reduced power to the furnace. He advised the use of an overshot wheel, by which water enters the wheel from the top, to provide power to the bellows, and a steam engine to return surplus water back to the reservoir in the wetter seasons. Further work on improving Newcomen's steam engine led to greater efficiency and reliability. The *Yorkshire Evening Post* waxed eloquent over the wheel, built around 1780, now providing power to a flour mill:

> But the feature that stamps the mill with the impression of John Smeaton is the great water wheel that supplied it with power. This wheel is still housed in a narrow brick building attached to the back of the mill itself and is still almost as perfect as it was made by Smeaton. The claim is made for it that it is the largest wooden water wheel in the country, and certainly its proportions are quite awe-inspiring when viewed from near at hand. [*Yorkshire Evening Post*, 11 October 1934, p.14]

Further investigation at the time led to the conclusion that the wheel in its then present condition had been renovated and restored, using Smeaton's original engineering design and dimensions. It was still working well until around 1912. When the wheel was threated with destruction in order to make way for the new Seacroft housing estate, there was much debate concerning its preservation. Once again, the *Yorkshire Evening Post* was moved to make a strong case in favour of retaining the wheel in one form or another:

> The huge water wheel designed by Smeaton, the famous Leeds engineer of over a hundred years ago, and still standing on what is now the Seacroft housing estate, is to be dismantled and destroyed….One prominent citizen was greatly interested in the possibility of preserving the relic. He was most anxious that it should be kept for posterity, and he was even prepared to spend as much as £1,000 for that purpose. [*YEP*, 30 May 1938, p.12]

The 'prominent citizen' referred to was a Mr Roland Winn but sadly this laudable attempt at conservation proved futile. The City Council, determined to develop the 800 acres bought from the Wilson family, approved a resolution 'that the wheel be dismantled and broken up, so that the Housing Director could get on with the development of the Seacroft estate'. [ibid]

Another area of civil engineering was bridge building. He was consulted over

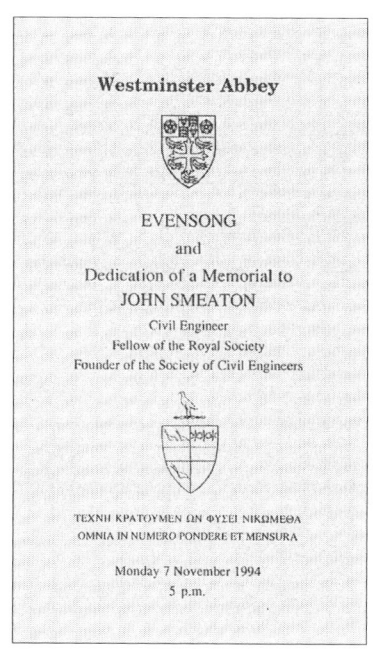

Memorial dedication order of service

the parlous condition of the Old London Bridge, which had had some of its piers removed and was in danger of collapse. Smeaton recommended that the stones taken from the city gates be positioned in the water adjacent to the bridge to reduce the water surge. This was done and the "temporary" solution lasted over 60 years. He designed bridges at Coldstream (1766), Perth (1772) and Banff (completed after 1772) but was less successful when he designed and built the bridge at Hexham (1777-1780) spanning the River Tyne. He took into account the Tyne's reputation for severe flooding and overwhelming water surge (an earlier bridge by Jonathan Pickernell had been destroyed within one year of construction) and factored in the unstable river bed, but even so his bridge collapsed after only two years. He was disconsolate: 'All our honours are now in the dust...the news came to me like a thunderbolt'. [SS, p.63]

Smeaton undertook work at several harbours including St Ives, Eyemouth, Rye, Peterhead and Aberdeen. In all, he either supervised the work or drew up reports on 30 different harbours, and this represents the greater part of his civil engineering projects. At Ramsgate there was a problem due to silting on such a great scale that it threatened to choke the harbour. Smeaton proposed a basin within the harbour that would fill with water at high tide and this water would be released back into the outer harbour through sluices, taking the sand with it. With a few modifications, this solved the problem.

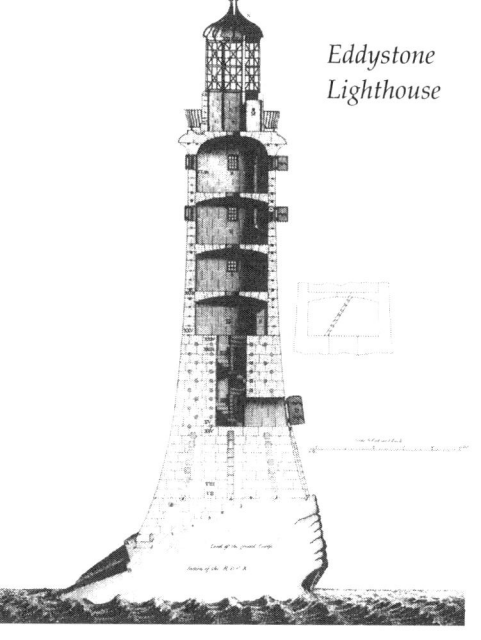

Eddystone Lighthouse

Smeaton's influence on the future development of civil engineering may be gauged by those who followed him in the profession. His pupil, the great canal engineer William Jessop, worked with Thomas Telford on the Ellesmere and Caledonian canals. Telford in turn worked closely with Sir William Cubitt on the Birmingham and Liverpool Junction Canal. Cubitt worked with Edward Leader Williams who undertook the improvement of the River Severn; and it was his son, Edward, who became Chief Engineer on the Manchester Ship Canal project. This close liaison between the early civil engineers, spanning many years, suggests close collaboration and this led to the founding of the profession's first association, indeed the first engineering society in the world, the Society of Civil Engineers (known after his death as the Smeatonian Society), and Smeaton was one of the seven founding members. The idea was that, as professional engineers, they would occasionally dine together with a view to exchanging ideas and avoiding any potential clashes of interest. In time, these informal gatherings led, in 1818, to the formation of the Institution of Civil Engineers, the body that today governs the profession in the United Kingdom. [P&A, Chapter 3, *TGJC*]

Following the death of his wife on 17 January 1784, Smeaton to a large extent withdrew from public life for three years, a move made easier for him by the failure of his bridge at Hexham. However, by 1787 he was once again able to respond to requests for his advice. He increased his fee to ten guineas a day but even this failed to diminish his work load. Sadly, his health was failing and a difficult session before a Parliamentary Committee giving evidence concerning the proposed Birmingham and Worcester Canal led to his retirement.

In the year before his death, he decided to concentrate on writing up detailed accounts of his achievements in the field of civil engineering. He wrote from his lodgings in Gray's Inn on 6 October 1791:

> Mr Smeaton begs leave to inform his Friends and the Public in general, that having applied himself for a great number of Years to the business of a Civil Engineer, his wishes are now to dedicate the chief part of his remaining Time to the Description of the several Works performed under his Direction. The Account he lately published of the Building of the Eddystone Lighthouse of Stone has been so favourably received, that he is persuaded he cannot be of more service to the Public, or show a greater Sense of his Gratitude, than to continue to employ himself in the way now specified. He therefore flatters himself, that in not yielding to the many applications made to him lately for further Undertakings, but confining himself in future to the Objects above mentioned, and to such occasional Consultations as will not take up much Time, he shall not incur the Disapprobation of his Friends. [SS, pp.81-82]

In September 1792, while walking in the grounds of Austhorpe Lodge, he suffered a stroke, from which he partially recovered, but he was now very frail and he died at Austhorpe on 28 October 1792. He is buried in the chancel of Whitkirk Church and on the north wall there is a marble tablet that records his fame:

Sacred to the memory of John Smeaton FRS
A man whom God had endowed with the most extraordinary abilities, which he indefatigably exerted for the benefit of mankind in works of science and philosophical research: more especially as an engineer and mechanic. His principal work, the Eddystone Lighthouse, erected on a rock in the open sea, (where one had been washed away by the violence of a storm, and the other having been consumed by the rage of fire) secure in its own stability and the wise precautions for its safety, seems not unlikely to convey to different ages, as it does to every nation of the globe, the name of its constructor.

The School afforded him the honour of having one of the Junior School Houses, created by the Headmaster, Terry Thomas in 1923, named after him. (The other House was named after Field Marshal Lord Nicholson.) Sadly, after his death, his workshop was cleared of much of its contents and 'a fire was kindled in the yard, and a vast quantity of papers, letters, books, plans, tools, and scraps of paper of all kinds, were remorselessly burnt'. [SS, p.77]

Bibliography
Lawrence, R F, *Smeaton of Austhorpe: the Father of English Civil Engineering*, Leeds History and Archaeology Society (Leeds: 2007)
Holland, David [Past President of the Smeatonian Society], Readings given at the Dedication of the Memorial to John Smeaton at Westminster Abbey on Monday 7 November 1994, p. 9
Lupton, C A, 'John Smeaton', in *Thoresby Society Publications*, New Series, Volume 15, Part 3, *Miscellany* (Leeds: 1973)
Petticrew, Ian and Austin, Wendy, *The Grand Junction Canal. A Highway Laid with Water*, published online (2013)
Platt, George Moreton & Morkill, John William, *Records of the Parish of Whitkirk*, M.T.D. Rigg Publications, Guiseley; facsimile edition printed by Smith Settle (Otley: 1990)
Price, Aubrey Charles, *A History of the Leeds Grammar School*, Richard Jackson (Leeds: 1919)
Skempton, A W, *John Smeaton FRS*, Thomas Telford Ltd (London: 1981)
Smiles, Samuel, *Lives of the Engineers, Volume 2, Smeaton and Rennie*, John Murray (London: 1862)
Yorkshire Evening Post dated 11 October 1934 and 30 May 1938

Sir Charles West Cope, Self Portrait, National Portrait Gallery

3

Sir Charles West Cope Kt 1811-1890
Water Colour Landscape Painter, Muralist, Etcher and Engraver
At LGS 1821-1827

ANYONE WISHING to research the life and times of Charles West Cope has the undoubted advantage of being able to refer to his fascinating and informative autobiography, *Reminiscences*, completed in 1889 less than a year before his death in 1890. Cope may not have been in the first rank of painters but his work is accomplished, technically proficient and aesthetically pleasing. He earned a degree of prominence and prestige from his decorative panels in the Houses of Parliament.

He was born on 28 July 1811 at Park Square, Leeds, the son of an accomplished historical painter, Charles Cope. Charles was named "West" in honour of the artist Charles West; his sister, Ellen Turner, was similarly named in honour of J M W Turner. Both of those renowned artists were friends of the Cope parents. Sadly, the mother died shortly following the birth of Charles and he was sent to foster parents, Mr and Mrs William Sharp, at Woodhouse Moor for two or three years, followed by a spell in London. He attended Mrs Johnson's boarding school in Camberwell and from there he was sent to Terry's School at Great Marlow, where he was bullied and his elbow was broken, an injury that left him with a crooked arm for life. This incident is described in *Reminiscences*:

> One day two big boys each held an end of a hedge-stake on their shoulders; another placed me astride it, and if I attempted to hold on with my hands I received a rap on the knuckles, so that I was obliged to try and balance myself. The boys occasionally gave a jerk, and the

> amusement consisted in seeing the awkward contortions of the victim. Of course, I was upset, and falling across my left arm, it was dislocated, and also broken at the elbow-joint. [R, p.4]

Life did not get a great deal better for him because he was then entered into Leeds Grammar School in 1821, under the watchful eye of the headmaster, the Revd G Walker. The under master, the Revd W C Wollaston, was no better than he should be, was excessively harsh in his punishments and treated all pupils in his charge as dunces and acted accordingly. In *Reminiscences*, Charles describes at length his treatment at the hands of his tormentor:

> He was a very severe master, and for his extreme cruelty he had been deprived of the power of flogging, and sent all his delinquents to be flogged by the head-master…a very humane man (*after* he'd had breakfast). To make up for this deprivation, W[ollaston] invented other punishments, such as pulling boys' ears, sometimes till they bled, knocking knuckles with his ruler, pulling hair out, causing boys to stand or kneel on forms holding up a heavy leaden inkstand, etc., until some imposition, such as a hundred lines of Virgil, was executed, to be doubled each day if they were not finished. [R, p.6]

This dreadful situation obtained for quite a period of time until Charles senior intervened by sending a letter to Wollaston and thereafter the relationship improved and Charles was able to concentrate on his studies. Again, Charles recollected:

> I believe this to have been the turning point in my life, as I was led for the first time to *reflect* on conduct and the consequences of idleness. After this I got on pretty well at school, but I found it hard work trying to make up for lost time, often sitting up late at night doing with difficulty what ought to have been easy. However, I got a remove into the fourth form, and next term gained a prize and removal into the fifth, under the head-master, to my great content, though I found myself sadly handicapped by my previous idleness. [R, p.8]

Charles enjoyed a close relationship with his father, who on numerous occasions took him off on holiday, during one of which, in Teesdale, he was introduced to the sport of fishing, a pastime he was to embrace with great enthusiasm for the rest of his life.

We went to Greta Woods, Rokeby, Barnard Castle, up to Middleham and over the Winch Bridge (then made of planks, and supported on chains), and so up to the High Force waterfall and the Cauldron Snout, a long cascade down the hill-side coming out of a moorland pool called the Wheel, which may be considered the source of the river Tees. [R, pp.13-14]

Clearly, Charles was impressed with the landscape in which he found such joy fishing. 'This tour in Teesdale made a great impression on me, and its consequences tinctured my whole future life, and also created in me a passionate love for romantic scenery.' [R, p.15]

In contrast, an engraving by J Cousen of a drawing by Charles' father depicting the scene downstream of Leeds Bridge, shows that by 1830 the area was already afflicted by the blight of numerous mills with their chimneys churning out smoke. His drawing clearly shows the increased industrial activity above and below the dam or spillway in the centre of the picture. The mill on the island at this time was the Bank flax mill of Hives and Atkinson. Behind the mill Leeds Parish Church is clearly visible, while to the right in the background is John Harrison's St John's Church. The spire of Holy Trinity Church, Boar Lane has been afforded a loftier status by the artist.The construction of the Leeds to Selby railway line was in part responsible for this escalation of commercial activity and its attendant pollution. As some anonymous wit wrote around this time:

> *The Aire below is doubly dyed and damned;*
> *The air above, with lurid smoke is crammed;*
> *The one flows steaming foul as Charon's Styx,*
> *Its poisonous vapours in the other mix.*
> *These sable twins the murky town invest,*
> *By them the skin's begrimed, the lungs oppressed.*

The loving bond with his father was tragically ended when Charles senior was killed in a coaching accident on 24 November 1827, shortly after Charles had been entered for Sass's academy of art in Bloomsbury. At Sass's, he met and befriended Francis Cary as well as Charles Stonhouse, a pupil of Wilkie, the latter famous for his *Siege of Saragossa* paintings. A year later he enrolled as a student at the Royal Academy [RA] and obtained a silver medal from the Society of Arts in 1829, awarded for his first still life painted in the manner of Wilkie, and a second medal from the Royal Academy Life School, a feat that earned him a life studentship. At this time he was living in lodgings in Great Russell Street, Bloomsbury.

While a student at the RA, Cope and his friends, Price and Cary, took up sailing as a hobby, and had a fine boat built, called the *Siren*. In this they happily sailed along the Thames and the south coast, around Hale, Greenwich and Herne Bay. On one occasion, they rounded the Foreland between Margate and Broadstairs, barely escaping with their lives in the choppy waters. The following day, they entered Sandwich Harbour and were promptly arrested by a revenue cutter on suspicion of smuggling. On being released they manoeuvred their craft as far as Sheerness, only to be challenged again by the customs people. A quick round of drinks ameliorated the anger of the excise men.

In 1832 he travelled to Paris with his friend, Cornelius Harrison, staying at the Hotel Wagram, and copied some 'old masters', particularly Titian and Rembrandt, in the Louvre. Whilst at Paris, he met a close friend of Charles Lamb, Edward White, whom he later encountered in Italy. In 1833, he exhibited a painting called *The Golden Age* at the Royal Academy. A short while later he visited Italy at the invitation of Cornelius White, and travelled around that country for two years, stopping at Florence, Rome, Orvieta, Assisi, Perugia and other places in Umbria. He was particularly taken with Florence and its wealth of art treasures:

> This morning I visited the Pitti Palace, and was as much delighted as the day before at the Gallery. Really, one fine thing after another started up in such quick succession, that they were almost too much for me. Two Titians, to begin with – one a most lovely female portrait…"Titian's favourite", and a "Holy Family." No wonder the former *was* a favourite; she is bewitching enough on canvas. The dress of the lady is most beautiful; blue silk embroidered with blue – and such blue! And the neck is so delicate; the eyes, too, looking at you – such sweet eyes they are, too! I was desperately smitten myself. [R, p.49]

Having appreciated the art on offer, he was careful to note the techniques used by the masters and was determined to emulate them in his own paintings.

During his visit to Rome, he visited the Sistine Chapel and St Peter's. Through the auspices of Cromek, the son of the engraver of Turner's works, he met Arthur Glennie who was to become another life-long friend. 'I used to go out sketching from nature with Cromeck or Glennie in water-colours, which I had not before practised, and soon began to be at home in it under their advice.' [R, p.53] He also made many drawings in pen-and-ink of the antique Greek marbles in the Vatican and the Capitol.

When he travelled on to Naples, arriving there on 6 May 1834, he was astonished to see Mount Vesuvius erupt. At first, 'The eruption was slight, but very beautiful; and from a large hole in the cone flowed a stream of red-hot lava, which extended for about a quarter of a mile before getting stiff and black'. [R, p.82] Later,

Works of Charles West Cope (clockwise): Florence Cope Saying Grace at Dinnertime (Fine Art America);

The Council of the Royal Academy Selecting Pictures for Exhibition (RA);

The First Trial by Jury (source unknown)

while staying at Sorrento, where he spent the summer, the volcano erupted in earnest:

> The lava was streaming down and covering the vineyards and trees, while the natives of a village being submerged lay about in picturesque confusion on the ground, having barely escaped with what household goods they could save from the burning lava, which gave out a lurid red light, except where the hot cinders were stopped by a tree and were heaped up against it. [R, pp.85-86]

He was disappointed with Herculaneum but most impressed by Pompeii. Florence was the city that most attracted him and he returned to stay there from late 1834 to early 1835. Whilst there, he painted a number of pictures, including an initial version of *The Firstborn*, later exhibited at the British Institution and bought by William Beckford of Fonthill. Another commissioned painting, *The Convent Door*, was for William Hey of Roundhay. It was during his stay at Florence that he experienced a strong earthquake that damaged many of the old houses. At Mantua, he studied the frescoes of Giulio Romano: 'The Palazzo del Te was both built and adorned by him, and truly he has indulged in the wildest freaks of an unrestrained imagination'. [R, p. 101]

He travelled on to Venice where he enjoyed gondolier rides along the canals to the accompaniment of music. He studied paintings in the galleries and practised techniques in the same style. 'I made studies in oil in the galleries of the 'Assumption of the Madonna', and part of the [Santa Maria Gloriosa dei] Frari Titian, one of his finest works; also the 'Peter Martyr' in watercolour, and a few sketches from nature.' [R, p.106] After an enjoyable and rewarding three months in the city he moved north along the Rhine.

Eventually, he returned to England and met up with his friend, Stonhouse, at Newman Street. He took lodgings with the Kiallmark family at 1 Russell Place, using members of the Kiallmark family as models, particularly the daughter, who was 'tall, rave and grand in form'. [R, p.111] He painted *Paolo and Francesca* and *Osteria di Campagna*, both of which were exhibited at the RA. Both paintings sold for very respectable prices and Cope's reputation began to grow.

In 1839-40, he painted a large altar-piece for St George's Church, Leeds and exhibited it at the RA in 1840. Cope eventually donated it to the church. In *Reminiscences*, he makes reference to this important work:

> About the end of my sojourn in Russell Place, my friend John Atkinson [possibly the John Atkinson, artist, listed in Wilson's *Admission Books* under the entry for his son John Beaumont, at LGS from 1830] was interested in building a new church at Little Woodhouse, near Leeds; and it was determined that instead of a large east window, the space should be filled by an altar-piece; and I offered to paint it and present it to the church, on condition that my expenses (only) were paid... I took as my theme the text: 'He ever liveth to make intercession for us.' ... The picture was about sixteen feet high by about twelve, I think. [R, p.119]

In order to paint such a large picture, it was necessary for Cope to move from Russell Place to Lisson Grove.

Whilst living at Russell Place, Cope, along with his friend Richard Redgrave, helped to found the Etching Club whose members experimented with the medium, discussed their plates, sold a few, and enjoyed simple suppers together.

With Redgrave, Cope went on a sketching and fishing holiday in Teesdale, during the course of which he met Charlotte Benning, a surgeon's daughter, whose mother was not particularly keen on Cope as a potential son-in-law and was never slow to show it. This did not deter him; from the outset he was struck by her beauty:

> There were other young ladies [present at Stubb House] whom I thought rather too forward; and they kept Miss Charlotte Benning constantly at the piano, although they talked loudly all the time she played. I thought, 'How amiable that girl is!' This was my first impression of her: modest, retiring, quite contented to be overlooked, and to make herself useful. [R, p.125]

Somehow he, to some extent, overcame this prejudice and the couple were married on 1 September 1840. The day was not without incident. Cope left the wedding ring in his room and had to send his friend Redgrave to fetch it. Then, with immaculate timing, as the happy couple stepped into their post-chaise to commence their honeymoon, Mrs Benning rushed forward and, in a voice loud enough for the whole assembly to hear, cried out, 'Oh, you poor victim!' It was with relief that they travelled on to Helmsley to spend a blissful fortnight, after which they took up residence in Hyde Park Gate, Kensington Gore, in 1841.

While staying with his friends the Sullivans at Ashford, Middlesex, he had been visibly affected by a scene at a meeting of a board of guardians at Staines and he made this the subject of a picture called *Poor Law Guardians: Board-day application for bread* which he exhibited at the RA in 1841. Although it remained unsold there, the painting was eventually purchased for £105.

The old Palace of Westminster burned down on 16 October 1834 and the new building was designed by the architect Charles Barry. One of his sons, Edward Middleton Barry, was later responsible for the design of the Moorland Road School; and another son, Alfred Barry, was the Headmaster who moved the School from the old Harrison building close to what is now the Grand Theatre. With regard to the new Palace, a Fine Arts Commission was appointed, headed by Prince Albert, and it decided that a series of historical pictures, wood carvings and sculptures would reflect the glory of English history and serve to educate the populace. It was at this point that Cope was appointed as one of the artists to execute this work.

As a result, he now concentrated on a series of competitions for the decoration of the Houses of Parliament and in 1843 he won a prize of £300 for his cartoon (a full-size drawing made as a preliminary design for a painting) of *The First Trial by Jury*. Buoyed up by this success, he was keen to learn the art of fresco painting and for the 1844 competition he proffered a beautiful design of the *Meeting of Jacob and Rachel*. On the strength of this, he was commissioned in July 1844 to prepare cartoons, coloured sketches and specimens of fresco painting for the decoration of the Peers' Corridor in the House of Lords. He won a further prize of £400 for his design of *Prince Henry, afterwards Henry V, acknowledging the authority of Chief-justice Gascoigne*. He was commissioned to produce this in fresco, along with another depicting Edward the Black Prince, a task he completed quickly, but due to damp and dust these works were soon in ruins. Notwithstanding, he was now so heavily engaged in work for the House of Lords that he had very little time for other work apart from a few small-scale studies in oils.

In 1845, Cope, concerned by the rapid deterioration of his early fresco work due to damp and atmospheric pollution, accompanied Mr Horsley to Italy to examine the technical methods of fresco painting, and from there he visited Professor Hess in Munich. He learned that Hess was using a process known as 'Waterglass' (a solution of potassium silicate or sodium silicate), whereby the art work was painted directly onto the wall surface and then glazed. He exhibited *Cardinal Wolsey's Reception at Leicester Abbey*, a work he had produced for Prince Albert, in 1848, and followed this with a fresco of *Griselda* on the wall of the upper waiting hall of the House of Lords. In all, he produced eight paintings to adorn the Peers' Corridor and there can be no doubt that his work attracted a great deal of praise:

> Inaccurate and anachronistic in much of their detail (none more so than the *Mayflower* scene), Cope's Stuart frescoes are nevertheless a peculiar triumph. They not only celebrate the intensity of Victorian interest in the Stuart period, and represent vividly the 19th century idea of the artist as antiquarian; they also confirm the conviction of the Victorian Englishman that his political good-fortune was unrivalled. The struggles shown in Cope's Peers' Corridor frescoes had established the basic principles of the constitution – the prevention of arbitrary rule by the monarch; the rights of both Houses of Parliament to freedom of speech; and the determination of minorities of the population to establish their right to freedom of religious worship. [Bond, p.93]

The following year (1849) he exhibited *The First-born*, a life-size painting commissioned by a Mr Dewhurst of Manchester, and probably his best known work. This was followed by *King Lear and Cordelia*, painted for the 'Shakespeare room' at Isambard Kingdom Brunel's home, who was at that time renowned as an accomplished engineer. There followed a series of fine paintings for a number of different clients, including *Othello relating his Adventures to Dessdemona* [sic] which was sold to a Mr Leather of Leeds [probably John Wignall Leather, an artist and father of two OLs].

At this time, Cope fell seriously ill from an internal tumour but he recovered and produced further works, one of which meant a great deal to him personally, *The Friends*, which depicted two of his own children, Charles and Charlotte. In 1857, he exhibited *Affronted*, a portrait of Charlotte and followed this with a fresco of *The Burial of Charles I* in the Peers' Corridor.

Cope was fortunate to attract the friendship and support of Prince Albert and in 1865 his posthumous portrait of the Prince was hung in the large room of the Society of Arts. Perhaps this homage in art was a reflection of the gratitude Cope felt towards Albert, whose consistent kindness meant so much to him.

Apart from his painting and fresco work, Cope was heavily involved in other spheres. He was appointed Professor of Painting to the RA, delivering six lectures a year until 1875; and he became secretary of the building committee tasked with making the arrangements to remove the RA from Trafalgar Square. He was one of the artists selected to report on the paintings in oil at the great exhibition in Paris.

In 1868, Cope was devastated by the death of his wife but after a brief period of mourning, he once again produced paintings to be exhibited at the RA. He joined a group of fellow artists to report on fresco painting in the House of Commons. He painted *The Council of the Royal Academy – Selection of Pictures*, exhibited in 1876, which he presented to the RA and it hangs today in the council room. In the same year he accompanied Peter Graham to represent the RA at the centennial exhibition in Philadelphia.

In 1879, Cope married his second wife, Miss Eleanor Smart, and settled at Maidenhead in a house overlooking the Thames. In 1883, he retired onto the list of honorary members of the RA and ceased painting as a profession, though he did continue to paint for his own pleasure and act as an examiner in painting for the South Kensington Schools of Art. He spent much of his time writing his memoirs, *Reminiscences*, at the instigation of his eldest son, the Rev. Charles Henry Cope, completed in 1889. He died at Bournemouth on 21 August 1890 after a brief illness.

Cope may not be included amongst the very best artists, but he exhibited 'considerable accomplishment, [was] versed in technical methods, a capable draughtsman and designer, and a good etcher. Engaged mainly on large historical compositions, and obtaining a ready sale for the smaller domestic pictures which occupied his lighter hours, he lived an industrious and honoured life.' [WCM, *DoNB*, 1901 Supplement]

Bibliography
Bond, Maurice (editor), *Works of Art in the House of Lords*, HMSO (London: 1980)
Cope, Charles West, *Reminiscences*, Richard Bentley & Son (London: 1891)
Monkhouse, William Cosmo, "Charles West Cope", in *Dictionary of National Biography, 1901 supplement* [Internet]
Wilson, Edmund, *Leeds Grammar School Admission Books*, Thoresby Society (Leeds: 1906)

Sir John Hawkshaw FRS – (GJ Stodart, 1888)

4

Sir John Hawkshaw Kt, FRGS, FRS, 1811-1891
Eminent Civil Engineer
At LGS 1823-1824

IT IS a remarkable fact that Leeds Grammar School can count among its Old Boys several of the most eminent Civil Engineers this country has ever produced. John Smeaton may properly be regarded as the father of British civil engineers and Sir John Hawkshaw is in no way inferior to him in output and genius. If Smeaton is forever associated with the Eddystone Lighthouse, then Hawkshaw's name is synonymous with the Severn Tunnel. Another distinguished engineer was William Gustavus Nicholson, Field Marshal of the British Army.

John Hawkshaw was born on 9 April 1811, the son of Henry, the licensee of the Golden Cock Inn at 13-14 Kirkgate (now re-developed and a branch of Superdrug), and his wife Sarah. John was the fifth of their six children. One of his earliest memories was being taken to see the Middleton Railway, the world's first commercially successful steam railway operating from 1812. This almost certainly sparked John's life-long interest in steam engines and the burgeoning rail network.

Henry died in 1820 when John was nine years old, and two years later Sarah married Ralph Coulson, a tenant farmer from Rothwell. Immediately following their marriage, Ralph took over the running of the White Cross Inn on Briggate, assisted by his new, rather older – and more experienced – wife.

John was sent to school at Jonathan Lockwood's Academy in Brunswick Terrace where he met James (later Sir James) Falshaw, who was himself to become an eminent civil engineer and Lord Provost of Edinburgh. John's step-father decided to send him to Leeds Grammar School and the boy was admitted on 4

August 1823. The Headmaster, the Revd G Walker, had done little to widen the curriculum away from the precepts laid down at the school's foundation, despite the recommendations of the Eldon Judgement of July 1805; that is, a grinding insistence on the pre-eminence of Divinity, Greek and Latin (with a little Hebrew thrown in for light relief) rather than more "modern" subjects like foreign languages, history and geography. As a sop to modernity and the recommendations of Eldon, the school did include some teaching of Classics, English and Mathematics and this may well have engaged the young Hawkshaw as he sat at his unheated long bench with his fellow pupils (the single fireplace was for the convenience of the masters). Be that as it may, despite major extensions and improvements to the school in 1823, he was taken away on 29 November 1824, aged thirteen, to commence work with the famous Leeds engineer, Charles Fowler.

Fowler was building turnpike roads at this time and he put the young Hawkshaw to work as an apprentice surveyor. Whilst engaged in this, he developed an interest in geology, in particular the comparative hardness of different rocks and the natural qualities of shales, soils and clays. All this was to have an important bearing on his later professional career.

In 1829 he left Leeds and joined Alexander Nimmo, who was busy developing railways in North West England. Hawkshaw assisted Nimmo with the survey work associated with a proposed Liverpool to Leeds route, itself part of an intended coast-to-coast line. He was associated with the railway company that emerged from these early proposals, the Lancashire and Yorkshire Railway, for most of his working life.

In 1832, he was sent by Nimmo's associates or clients (Nimmo had died) to take charge of the British-owned Bolivar Mining Association's copper mine in Aroa, Venezuela. Using his keen eye for geological formations, he made notes on the different rocks of the area and found the presence of potential copper-bearing veins of steatite. After a journey full of incident and adventure, he finally arrived at Aroa and took charge of a workforce of over 1200 personnel, including many Cornish miners. In his book *Reminiscences of South America* (1838) he wrote on a wide variety of topics relating to, among others, the geology and natural history of Venezuela, and commenting on the decline of the Catholic Church there, hoping that Christian (Protestant) missionaries from England might be induced to proselytise the locals. Regarding his journey from the port of Tucacas to Aroa, he wrote:

> Our way lay along the sea shore until we arrived at the mouth of the river [Aroa], where there were several workshops and a considerable number of English workmen employed. We then passed up the banks of the river for nearly thirty miles, and stayed for the night at one of the company's farms. [*RoSA*, p.83]

The mines had first been worked using slave labour and were left in a parlous condition. He immediately set about dealing with the transport logistics which, until his arrival, had been entirely unsatisfactory. He built a sound new cart road on which to carry the ore to the Aroa river, improving that river's navigability and building a loading pier fit for purpose. Again, he wrote in his *Reminiscences*: 'Altogether about two hundred English workmen were employed, and upwards of a thousand Creoles. About forty of the English workmen were miners, chiefly from Cornwall; the remainder were carpenters, smiths, boat-builders etc.' [*RoSA*, p.106] One problem was the shortage of trained horses, the local breed being wild and unpredictable in temperament and quite unsuited to hauling the carts filled with ore. Moreover, the locals lived in fear of them but the English navigators (navvies) were up to the task:

> One poor Irishman was killed, and one or two horses were knocked down by the flying carts; and, in one instance, a horse with a cart behind him ran off the road, and dashed right through the gable end of a house, and out the other side, completely gutting it in his course; but, with these exceptions, the horses were all got ready in about three months. [*RoSA*, p.108]

As a result of these and other endeavours, the movement of ore from the mine to the smelting works at St Helens was expedited. Ideally, he would have liked to build a light railway along the valley of the Aroa from La Hacha down to the river mouth at Boca de Aroa, but this was not to be. Sadly, in 1834, ill health forced him to return to England, but not before he had established a close friendship with Venezuela's ruler, General Paez.

Reminiscences of South America, published in 1838, was the first example of a literary work of this type written by a civil engineer.

On his return to England, he worked for a short time with Jesse Hartley on the Liverpool Dockyard project before moving to the office of James Walker, the newly elected President of the Institution of Civil Engineers (ICE). Under Walker's supervision, Hawkshaw surveyed the Leipzig to Dresden Railway.

In 1835 he married Ann Jackson, daughter of the Methodist minister at Green Hammerton, near Harrogate, and they subsequently moved to Manchester. She was a lively woman, well educated and full of ideas and with a vivid imagination, publishing volumes of poetry that received some critical acclaim. The couple had six children, two of whom sadly died in childhood and they suffered the further loss of their grown-up daughter who died in childbirth.

In 1836, Hawkshaw was accepted as an Associate of the ICE and was

Sir John Hawkshaw - Eminent Civil Engineer

Middleton Railway

contracted by the directors of the Manchester, Bury and Bolton Canal Navigation and Railway to complete that enterprise which had for various reasons stalled. This he did in good time (1838) and was rewarded with full membership of the ICE.

In the same year he was asked to draw up a report on whether or not it was desirable to maintain and extend the broad gauge system of the Great Western Railway. Rather boldly, he argued strongly against the GWR broad gauge, chiefly because it created a huge problem with the ideal of a future integrated railway network. The GWR and I K Brunel chose to ignore his advice, but later events proved him to be the wiser counsel.

In 1844, he was appointed Consulting Engineer to the Manchester, Bury and Rossendale Company which later developed into the East Lancashire Railway Company. The following year he became the Chief Engineer of the Manchester and Leeds Railway Company which itself eventually became known as the Lancashire and Yorkshire Railway Company in 1847. For 41 years, in fact for the remainder of his professional career, he held this post, serving the company with both loyalty and distinction, developing the system until it covered 428 miles. It was while he was working on this railway project that he investigated the feasibility of steeper gradients of up to 1 in 44 (made necessary by the difficult terrain through which the routes passed) and came to the conclusion that, despite being opposed by no less an authority than Robert Stephenson, steeper gradients were quite possible.

The advantages attached to this finding were obvious: a more direct line could be surveyed as opposed to a more circuitous one that would be less cost effective.

He was responsible for the construction of several viaducts, including the Lockwood Viaduct and those at Denby Dale and Holmfirth, the latter built of wood when the stone masons went on strike.

In 1850, Hawkshaw moved from Manchester to 33 Great George Street, Westminster where, from 1870, he was joined by his son, John Clarke Hawkshaw, and Harrison Hayter. From this new address, he was responsible for drawing up reports and offering advice on a huge number of projects world-wide. He continued to construct railways and deliver reports to Parliamentary Committees, always presented in meticulous detail and assertive in the interests of his employers. When dealing with foreign contracts, he would visit the sites to monitor progress and the quality of the workmanship. This meant travelling to, or writing reports on, projects for, among other places, Russia, India, Mauritius, Bengal, Brazil and Portugal.

He was responsible for building many tunnels necessitated by the hilly terrain through which some proposed routes lay. His most famous achievement in this field is surely the Severn Tunnel, built for the GWR between 1873 and 1887. At over four miles long the tunnel had to cross under the estuary of the Severn where there is a tidal rise of almost 50 feet. For a century it was the longest submarine tunnel in the world. There were immense problems. Initial drillings encountered a succession of fresh water springs which flooded the workings. Hawkshaw, as Consulting Engineer, clashed with the Chief Site Engineer, Charles Richardson, who was eventually dismissed. Further flooding occurred when water from the Severn entered the tunnel and there were problems with the pumps that had been installed to drain the workings. Then, to cap it all, an unusually high tidal wave caused a new flood which trapped 83 men, though fortunately they were all rescued. By the time the Sudbury pumping house had been built to cope with the worst excesses of flooding spring water, and other unavoidable expenses had been incurred, the total cost to the GWR of the Severn Tunnel was estimated to be just short of £2,000,000. Even so, the Great Spring broke through into the workings once more and Hawkshaw finally decided on an even greater pumping capacity and this allowed a trial coal train to pass through the tunnel on 9 January 1886. He had overcome a series of dreadful obstacles, mostly to do with drainage, and the Board of Trade inspection noted that the pumping capacity insisted upon by Hawkshaw was 66,000,000 gallons per day, twice that of the worst case scenario envisaged by the engineers. The report concluded:

> The difficulties of dealing with the large quantity of water, and particularly of dealing with the underground stream, which runs at a great velocity, have been considerable, but have now been successfully

overcome, and the result is a tunnel of unusually large dimensions, which is particularly dry. [quoted from MB, p.123]

In July 1863, the Viceroy of Egypt, Said Pasha, asked Hawkshaw to visit his country in order to inspect the site of the proposed Suez Canal and to report to the Egyptian government. He spent just under a month examining the area to be traversed by the canal and reported in very favourable terms that he could see no serious impediment to the proposal, a conclusion that was anathema to Lord Palmeston, who favoured a railway linking the Red Sea to the Mediterranean. Such was Hawkshaw's reputation that the French engineer, de Lesseps, freely admitted that it was the Englishman's affirmation of the feasibility of the project that ultimately convinced the Egyptians that the canal should go ahead. De Lesseps is reported to have introduced Hawkshaw to the site engineers with the words, 'This is the gentleman to whom I owe the canal'. [quoted from the 1891 obituary, words of Lord Houghton; the original in Reid's *Life of Richard Monckton Milnes, First Lord Houghton*, p.217]

The following year, Hawkshaw was asked by the Viceroy to report on the possibility of canalising the first cataract of the Nile with a view to making it navigable. He sent his son, along with his partner, Hayter, and the surveyor, Graham, to survey the whole area and on their return to England, he not only affirmed that canalization was possible but he drew up detailed engineering plans to back up his favourable opinion.

Another major project was the possibility of constructing a Channel Tunnel connecting Britain to mainland Europe. Between 1872 and 1886, he worked alongside Sir James Brunless as engineer to the Channel Tunnel Company, although he had spent a considerable amount of time and energy prior to this working on preliminary investigations that led him to believe that such an astonishing engineering feat could be realised with the intention of integrating the railway systems of Britain and France and, further afield, the entire Continent. Hawkshaw employed an eminent geologist, Hartzinck Day, to examine the Cretaceous strata on both coasts and trace their course beneath the Channel as far as was practicable. At the same time he employed Henry Marc Brunel, second son of the illustrious Isambard Kingdom Brunel, to make a marine survey of the Channel and ascertain

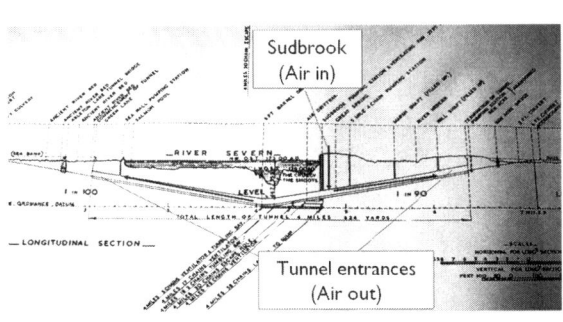

A diagram of the Severn Tunnel (Network Rail)

the nature of the strata forming its bed. Brunel reported favourably and this induced Hawkshaw to cause deep borings to be made at Dover and Calais. Later, engineers from the French railway companies and from the South Eastern Railway Company confirmed that the project was feasible. However, having investigated the possibilities of such a tunnel from a purely engineering point of view, Hawkshaw then gave much thought to the strategic, military and security concerns, and concluded that, though the Channel Tunnel *could* be built, it was inadvisable to open up Britain to the threat of political and military intervention from the Continent.

Hawkshaw was responsible for the building of a great many bridges and viaducts, including the South Bridge at Hull, the Londonderry Bridge and the Nerbudda Bridge in India. Alongside W H Barlow, he completed the Clifton Suspension Bridge, begun by Isambard Kingdom Brunel but never completed. He finished the work on the harbour at Holyhead, Anglesey, and was praised by the Prince of Wales at the opening ceremony in 1873. Indeed, he fully

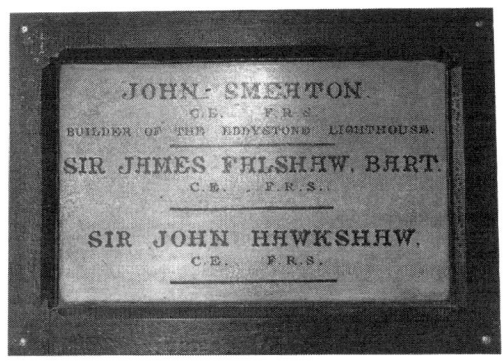

The honours board in the reception corridor

deserved this approbation because Hawkshaw had overcome a succession of seemingly insoluble problems starting with the major damage to the site caused by the great storm of 24-25 October 1859 when 200 ships were wrecked in British waters, including the single greatest loss of life aboard the *Royal Charter* which foundered off the north coast of Anglesey. He created a superstructure from huge blocks of stone that rose almost 40 feet above low water, on top of which he built a massive parapet. He then designed and built a breakwater which terminated in a head 150 feet long and 50 feet wide, surmounted by a square lighthouse rising 70 feet to provide maximum light. In June 1873, after 25 years working relentlessly on the project, Hawkshaw was able to pronounce the job completed. After the official opening ceremony, he was invited to Balmoral Castle to be knighted by Queen Victoria on 30 August 1873. Rather unusually, this investiture took the form of a private audience with Her Majesty in the presence of the Prime Minister of the day, W E Gladstone. It must have been of great comfort to those present that the Holywell harbour provided a safe refuge from the violent storms to which the west coast of Anglesey was, and still is, prone.

Among his many other assignments, mention must be made of his work on flood control and sewage installations. He may be said to have strongly influenced the government of the day to accept Joseph Bazalgette's scheme for creating a series of underground sewers to take away the effluent of an increasing London population rather than simply discharging it into the Thames. In this, both men were assisted by Dr John Snow, who had promoted his own theory that cholera was caused by drinking contaminated water rather than being spread by a miasma of odorous air caused by the stench of human waste. As for his own schemes to reduce pollution, Hawkshaw designed and installed the intercepting and outfall sewers at Brighton, carefully following Bazalgette's example of installing seven foot diameter sewers that allowed for a projected increase in population. Indeed, the demographic figures for Brighton speak for themselves: 110,000 in 1874; 160,000 in 1961 and 273,000 by 2011. Brighton's sewers have become an unlikely tourist attraction catering for the enthusiasm of aficionados of Victorian engineering, something that would have amused and pleased Hawkshaw. Lastly, he undertook a number of flood control and drainage schemes, including widening and deepening the River Witham, the drainage of the Middle Level District in Norfolk, and work on the Humber Estuary. He drew up plans to help alleviate the problem of flooding in and around Lincoln, around Norwich and then at Burton-on-Trent.

Hawkshaw had the reputation of being a forceful man when it came to dealing with the promoters of the various schemes in which he was chief engineer. It was quite common for promoters, those who paid for the work and who took ownership of the finished product, and the chief engineer, whose role was to translate the promoters' concept into a viable design, to come into conflict, particularly over costings. One such confrontation is described in *The Grand Junction Canal. A Highway Laid with Water*:

> A story is told about Sir John Hawkshaw who, attending a promoters' meeting, was faced with a refusal to pass for payment a certificate issued by him as chief engineer on the basis it exceeded estimate. When silence eventually fell on the meeting he said, quietly, "*Excuse me! What John Hawkshaw signs, you pay*" – and that was the end of the matter. [IP & WA, Chapter 3]

As befits a man of his genius and standing, Hawkshaw received many honours in addition to his knighthood. He became a Fellow of the Royal Geological Society of London in 1838 and was elected a Fellow of the Royal Society in 1855. He was President of the ICE in 1862-63 and President of the British Association in 1875. In 1880 he was made an Honorary Member of the American Society of Civil Engineers. For many years he was associated with the Volunteer Movement, a forerunner of the Territorial Army, in particular the Engineer and Railway Transport Volunteers and gained the rank of Lieutenant-Colonel Commandant in 1878.

He eschewed politics but was a keen field sportsman, owning estates in Scotland and Sussex. In 1865, he bought a 4,000 acre estate at Hollycombe in

Hampshire, as a country retreat for his family. Above all, he was meticulous in all his professional duties, never supporting any proposed scheme until he had given it careful consideration, but when he was convinced of the practicability of a project he would give it his full support and was capable of presenting lucidly the facts before Parliamentary Committees. His obituary in *Engineering News* (1891) sums up these qualities:

> Mr Hawkshaw early established a high reputation as a Parliamentary witness. The care and precision with which his evidence was always given, and the fact that both from high conscientiousness of character and great powers of memory he was never found to contradict himself, no matter after what interval of time, gave to his testimony great weight and value. [*Engineering News*, Vol.25, Issue 595, 1891]

Sir John Hawkshaw died at his town residence, Belgrave Mansions, Grosvenor Gardens, on 2 June 1891 with his reputation at its zenith. He was buried at Bramshott, Hampshire, next to his beloved wife, Ann, who had died on 29 April 1885. His tombstone bears the inscription, 'In memory of Sir John Hawkshaw, Knt. Of Hollycombe, Sussex, Born April 11, 1811, Died June 2, 1891.', a succinct rendition of the facts. For a more fulsome summary of his career, the ICE offered this appraisal:

> Sir John Hawkshaw was undoubtedly one of the greatest engineers of the century...This distinguished engineer [left] a reputation such as few have achieved for variety of good and honest work. Certainly no man has done more to enhance the honour and reputation of the profession. [From *Minutes of Proceedings of the Institution of Civil Engineers* Volume 106, Issue 1891, Part 4, p.335]

Bibliography

Beaumont, Martin, *Sir John Hawkshaw 1811-1891: The Life and Work of an Eminent Victorian Engineer*, The Lancashire & Yorkshire Railway Society, (Arnold, Nottingham: 2015)
Chrimes, Mike, *Oxford Dictionary of National Biography*, OUP, 2004, Online edition 2016
Dictionary of National Biography 1901, John Hawkshaw
Engineering News, 1891 (*Obituary*)
Grace's Guide, John Hawkshaw and *Obituary* 1891
Hawkshaw, John, *Reminiscences of South America from two and a half years' residence in Venezuela*, Jackson and Walford (London: 1838)
Minutes of the Proceedings of the Institution of Civil Engineers, Volume 106, Issue 1891, Part 4, published on-line (2015)
Petticrew, Ian and Austin, Wendy, *The Grand Junction Canal. A Highway Laid with Water*, published online, 2013

A portrait of George Dixon (Wilson)

5

George Dixon MP 1820-1898
MP for Birmingham and Birmingham Edgbaston
and Educational Reformer
At LGS 1829-1837 [with a break of around 12 months]

GEORGE DIXON was born at Gomersal, West Yorkshire, on 21 July 1820, the son of Abraham Senior (this to distinguish him from his eldest son, Abraham), a Commission Agent, whose role was a middleman between sellers and buyers, and his wife Laetitia (née Taylor). George was baptised into the Anglican Church at Kirkheaton on 15 October 1821. He was the seventh of the couple's eight children. Quite a lot is known of their family circumstances, in part due to the fact that Laetitia's family, who lived at Red House, Gomersal, were close friends of Charlotte Brontë. Abraham Senior hailed from Cumberland and was an inventor connected with the woollen industry.

George was educated at Leeds Grammar School at a time when the fall-out from the Eldon judgement of 1805 caused the curriculum at the School to be widened to include the teaching of science and, a little later, mathematics and English. Price in his *History of the Leeds Grammar School* offers the intriguing suggestion that the pupils themselves petitioned the Headmaster for a more 'modern' education that embraced some ancient history and even geography. Price quotes from the memoirs of a Dr Heaton, who was at the School more or less at the time Dixon was there:

> The scholars of each form sit round their proper table, having their slates placed before them, and being under the direction of the monitor and sub-monitor, who sit at the top and bottom of the table and are

those two boys in each form who had the highest amount of marks of merit for their labours of the preceding week. [Price, p.162]

It is a beguiling picture of the conditions in which pupils like Dixon and Heaton knuckled down to their studies, remembering that at this time the benches were made of unyielding wood and there was inadequate heating in the colder months. Price goes on to describe a more traditional lesson:

> In a grammar lesson each boy in his turn reads one word of a sentence, and all of them copy upon their slates what is read, until the period is finished; this period is then continued to be read from the slates in like manner until every boy is able to repeat it; the subsequent periods are so learnt until the whole lesson is finished. In a construing lesson the words of each period are read, parsed, and construed according to the same plan, the lexicon also is consulted, notes are read, maps are inspected, and other explanatory books referred to, at the discretion of the monitor, and the English of each period is thus written down on every boy's slate. [P, p.162]

If war is hell, then education in the early nineteenth century would appear to be no less so. A number of pupils were sufficiently disenchanted with the tedium of lessons such as these to demonstrate a rebellious streak. When not subjecting new boys to the traditional initiation rites – some of which, according to Price, were positively lethal - the more bumptious pupils would crouch behind the railings and ambush innocent passes-by with well-directed peashooters. As if this were not bad enough, during snowy periods, they would take on soldiers going about their lawful business:

> When snow lay on the ground we pelted the regiments marching down North Street…and the soldiers when off duty would retaliate and a fierce engagement followed. The steps of the School were lost and won amidst the cheers of the victors as the fortune of war varied, and the soldiers would roll their unfortunate prisoners in the dirty snow in the middle of North Street to the great derangement of vehicular traffic. [quoted from Price, p.191]

The boys themselves became victims of malicious prejudice when confronted by the townie lads for whom the School was a bastion of privilege. Disguise might afford some escape, but the introduction of the LGS cap with tassels made life much more difficult. Again, Price gives some indication of the age-old problem of town and gown:

> ...a constant feud or vendetta had been waged between the Grammar School boys and the town boys. The town boys were in the habit of waylaying us in gangs as we went to and from school, and many bloody encounters ensued. We of course imitated their tactics and marched in well-ordered battalions from the school gates, dispersing our several ways when safely through the enemy's country. [However] the mortar-boards revealed us wherever we went, and solitary individuals were often chivvied to the very door by the enemy; it became a serious matter for us to reach the School without molestation, and many ruses and disguises had to be resorted to in order to foil the vigilance of our foes. [quoted from Price, p.191]

There is some confusion over the year in which Dixon left the Grammar School. James Dixon in *Out of Birmingham* gives 1837 [JD, p.20] while Wilson in his *Admission Books* claims he was withdrawn in June 1832. [W, p.31] There is a possible explanation for this discrepancy. James Dixon writes that George suffered from eyesight problems when he was about 12 years old and as a consequence his elder sister taught him Spanish at home. For over a year he was forced to wear a bandage or sit in a darkened room and it is likely he had some private tuition at the same time. It is probable that he returned to the School in 1833.

Two other Dixon siblings were at Leeds Grammar School. William (1818-1884) attended between 1829 and 1832, though it is possible he was there for a little longer as Wilson states he, too, was 'removed' in June 1832 and this is no guarantee that he did not return as a senior pupil. He eventually became Vicar of Chilthorne Domer in Somerset and officiated at the christening of all of George's six children. William's own son, Frederick, led the choir at George's funeral in Birmingham in 1898. Thomas (1821-1865) would appear to have had a short stay at LGS, from January to August 1829, though sadly the reason for his removal is not known.

On leaving school, George spent a year in France learning the language. In 1838 he moved to Birmingham with his brother, Abraham Junior, and joined the firm of Rabone Brothers, exporters of, among other merchandise, jewellery made in Birmingham. He proved himself so capable that he was first made a partner and then took over as head of the firm when Abraham, who had done much to build up the business, retired in 1866. The site occupied by Rabone Brothers was very extensive and a part of it was taken over by Cadbury Bros., the chocolate manufacturers. When they moved to Bournville, George Dixon used the premises to set up a pioneering Technical School.

Around this time, he bought a 99-year lease on a large house called 'The Dales' at 42 Augustus Road and here he lived for the rest of his life. There followed

W E Gladstone

a period in which little is known of his movements or career, but it is very probable that he was living in Canada for some time.

By 1853 he had joined the Committee of the Birmingham and Midland Institute, an organization providing cultural activities for the wealthier men of the town.

On 11 September 1855 he married Mary, the daughter of James Stansfield, a judge of the County-Court of Halifax. She was some thirteen years his junior and a lady of great charm as well as being an accomplished musician with a beautiful voice. There was the problem of their belonging to different denominations of the church, George being an Anglican and Mary came from a Unitarian background.

With commendable common sense they respected each other's beliefs and this sense of compromise was to be a feature of George's political career. They had six children, all but one of who lived to a ripe old age. Their eldest son was the architect Arthur Stansfield Dixon (1856-1929).

George and Mary spent three years in Australia and New Zealand, serving the interests of the firm and whilst there he took a keen interest in the educational system which appeared to him to be more liberal and inclusive than that found in England. He was also impressed by the standard of living enjoyed by the people there, comparing it favourably with that back in the UK. Two children, Arthur and Helen, were born over there.

George and Mary returned to Britain in 1858 and he was pleased to find that John Bright had been elected Liberal MP for Birmingham and that the tax on newspapers had been abolished. This led to an enormous increase in public interest in current affairs and social reform. The *Birmingham Daily Post* had a particularly strong influence over public opinion in the town.

Wherever he was, his main concern was for the promotion of the family business. 'Keen, broadminded, well informed, scrupulously honourable, he was well fitted to raise the tone and enlarge the sphere of commercial dealing, and he speedily put his firm in the front rank of Birmingham merchants.' [JHM p.52] He remained in this capacity for the rest of his life. Between 1840 and 1870, the value of exports from Britain quadrupled and Rabone Brothers shared in this bonanza. The range of goods exported by the firm grew significantly to include railway rolling stock, bridges and track, cutlery, garden tools, anchors and chain cables. The American Civil War created a massive demand for guns made in Birmingham.

He was a great philanthropist. In 1864, mainly due to his efforts, Aston Hall and Park were purchased for the town after a rather tragic accident in which the 'Female Blondin', a tight-rope walker, fell and was killed at a fair in the Park. Queen Victoria, who had visited Aston Hall in 1858, wrote protesting against 'the demoralising taste' displayed in the Park which she herself had opened a few years earlier. As a consequence, Dixon and his brother, Abraham, contributed generously to the funds needed to effect the purchase of the Hall and Park, and Birmingham gained a valuable public amenity that exists to this day. The parallel here with the purchase of Kirkstall Abbey by Colonel North is quite clear as the move was prompted by the fear that a tawdry commercial firm had put in a bid to turn the grounds of Aston Hall into an amusement park.

His political life began when he entered Birmingham town council as member for the Edgbaston Ward. Three years later he was elected Mayor of the town in November 1866. He had promoted the Rifle Volunteer Movement in Birmingham in 1859 and in June 1867 he displayed commendable bravery by personally intervening in the anti-Popery riots led by William Murphy and George Hammond

Whalley against an angry crowd of Irish immigrant labourers. An estimated 50,000 to 100,000 antagonists clashed, causing serious damage to buildings. James Dixon, quoting in part from Dent's *Old and New*, paints a vivid picture of the scene:

> Murphy was a fanatical Protestant Electoral Association rabble-rouser who exhorted the crown to attack ritualism of any kind. The chief magistrate had declined the use of the Town Hall for the purpose of these lectures [given by an itinerant demagogue fulminating against perceived 'Popery'], and this tacitly gave the rough element in the town to understand that he was not to be afforded any protection. 'A number of the lowest roughs, delighted at the prospect of a "row" and probably not caring two straws for either cause, took possession of Park Street, stripped many of the houses of their contents, tore off the tiles from the roofs of most of the buildings in the street, and there ensued such a scene of destruction as had not been equalled since the Chartist riots of 1839.' [JD, p.68]

A squadron of hussars was called in to quell the mob but Dixon 'rode boldly among the enraged crowd at the Bull Ring and read the Riot Act'. The crowds dispersed and the hussars returned to barracks without drawing their swords.

As Mayor, he convened a private conference at his house at which many of the leading Birmingham figures were present 'to remedy the want of education' in the town. [JHM p.53] They also deprecated the employment of young children unless due provision was made for their education up to the age of eleven. As it happened, the Factory Extension Act of 1867 and the Hours of Labour Regulation Act (Workshops Act) between them had cast many children out of employment and onto the streets, where they accounted for a mini crime wave. Unusually for the time, the coming together of so many men of discordant opinions at this conference led to a consensus of opinion that reform of the provision of education was vital if the town was to prosper. In March 1867 a public meeting was held in the Town Hall at which an Education Aid Society was formed, following the earlier example of Manchester. The Society raised sufficient funds to pay the school fees of the children of the more indigent parents.

The aim of the Society was, in Dixon's own words, to work towards 'a gradation of schools – schools that is, not uniform, not of the same character, but so diverse that they should be adapted to the wants of every class of the community'. [JHM p.55]

In July 1867, on the death of William Scholefield, the sitting MP, he resigned his office of Mayor to stand as parliamentary candidate for Birmingham, and was elected with a good majority.

In February 1869 the National Education League was set up with Dixon as chairman, assisted by other luminaries including Joseph Chamberlain. Its avowed aim was 'the establishment of a system which should secure the education of every child in England and Wales' and to this end carried on an active propaganda campaign throughout the country. With a fund of £14,000, the League's somewhat over-ambitious objectives were that all local authorities be compelled by law to provide school accommodation for every child in their district; that the cost of funding and maintaining such accommodation be provided out of local rates, supplemented by Government grants; that all such schools be managed by the local authority and subject to Government inspection; that all schools thus funded be non-sectarian; that all places at such schools be free of fees; and that, with school accommodation being provided, the local authority to have the power to compel the attendance of eligible children. Had these principles been put into effect, they would have far exceeded the provisions enshrined in the Forster Education Act of 1870.

The League was so popular it attracted 2,500 paying members before any public meetings were held. Local committees were formed in all the major towns and it attracted an annual subscription of over £6,000. The first general meeting was held in October 1869, with Dixon presiding. Those present feared a great deal of opposition to their aspirations, but nevertheless a resolution was carried that a bill be prepared for presentation to Parliament. Over the following months, Dixon worked hard to promote their cause, employing his Commons experience to guide and encourage his fellow reformers.

Their fears regarding intransigent opposition to their proposals were well founded. Gladstone's Whig government was by no means driven by reforming zeal but the Vice-President of the Council and spokesman for educational matters, William Edward Forster, was acutely aware of the growing agitation for reform, not least from Dixon himself. For his part, Forster argued that over £800,000 annually was allocated by Parliament as funding for existing schools, but acknowledged that in many parts of the country there were no schools at all. Like Dixon, he knew that a part of the problem lay in the vested interests of religious societies who were loath to lose their grip on whatever primary education was available.

Forster announced that he was proposing to introduce a bill dealing with the whole subject and Dixon, knowing that intransigent opposition could scupper the bill, wisely agreed to suspend further action. As it turned out the Government Bill was only a half-measure and fell far short of the League's aspirations. Compulsion was left to the local authorities; School Boards were only to be created where there was a desperate dearth of schools; religious denominations were given time to improve their provision of schools; and fees were permitted, though School Boards *could* grant remission. Dixon moved an amendment arguing that 'provided' schools should be forbidden to teach a specific religious catechism but this was rejected. On 9 August the Act was passed and over the succeeding months School Boards were elected.

Digressing from our main theme for a moment, what was the effect of the Forster Act on educational provision in Leeds generally and at Leeds Grammar School in particular? Prior to 1784, there was little on offer for the children of the working classes, but in that year the Sunday School movement began in earnest and over the course of the following thirty years, up to 5,000 Leeds children were receiving a day's teaching, concentrating on the essentials of reading, writing and arithmetic. There followed the Royal Lancastrian School (1811) catering for up to 500 boys, and the National School in 1813, at which 320 poor boys and 180 girls were taught. There was fierce rivalry between the different religious denominations in the town, each seeing the value of capturing the hearts and minds of the children and their parents. More schools were founded, mainly due to the philanthropic generosity of the middle classes who could see the advantage of an educated and engaged proletariat. The main point to bear in mind here is that most of these schools offered free tuition as opposed to the Grammar School. By 1837 it was estimated that up to 1,400 Leeds youngsters were receiving some sort of education, but even so there were many more children who did not attend any school. Moreover, the quality of instruction varied enormously, so there was no room for complacency on the part of the providers.

By the middle of the nineteenth century, the situation improved markedly. Denominational schools in the borough offered good quality teaching, catering for the needs of over 20,000 pupils. With assistance from government grants, this laudable situation was further improved. However, children were still leaving school far too early, chiefly because poor parents valued the extra income their offspring could contribute to the family finances. Furthermore, attendance was far too irregular to allow for any real and sustained improvement in academic performance. As the provision of day schools improved, so the Sunday Schools lost ground.

The Forster Act to some extent responded to the increasing demands for a more coherent educational strategy. The Industrial Revolution created the urgent need for a more educated workforce and this, combined with the widening franchise brought about by the 1832 and 1867 Reform Acts (that implied that votes should be subject to *informed* opinion), simply reinforced the notion that the existing situation could not prevail. Leeds, as a dynamic and progressive industrial and commercial town, needed reform as much as, if not more than, most other conurbations in the country, and the borough's administrators responded with alacrity to the provisions in the Act. They set up the first School Board and its primary duty was to rectify the appalling situation whereby only 27,000 school

William Edward Forster

places were available for a potential school population of nearly 50,000. The progress made in improving this parlous situation was quite remarkable. By 1878, 31 large schools had been built to host around 19,000 pupils. Much of the cost of this expansion was borne by the ratepayers, some of whom thought the cost to be exorbitant, but their objections were to no avail. The Board Schools increasingly offered some form of *secondary* education, with a proper emphasis on the three Rs and technical and commercial subjects. Higher Grade Schools began to appear in

Leeds, the first being opened in 1889, the imposing Central Higher Grade School, later known as the City of Leeds School. Such was the scope and quality of its curriculum that the Grammar School began to feel the adverse effects of competition. The Central School offered subjects that provided a much better foundation for a modern education: these included French, German, Science and Drawing without any undue emphasis on Classical languages and literature. This was in contrast to the stultified curriculum of the Grammar School which, even as late as 1900, still insisted on a quite unnecessary emphasis on Greek and Latin. The consequence was that the School roll declined to 161 in 1895 and the Headmaster, J H D Matthews, attributed this decline directly to the competing attraction of the Central High School for lower middle class parents.

 Other alternatives to the Grammar School were on offer; middle class parents could consider sending their boys to the Mechanics' Institute's Mathematics and Commercial School, opened in 1845. Indeed, by 1852, this *fee-paying* day school had 211 pupils, more than North Street or, subsequently, Moorland Road could boast. The pupil roll rose to around 300 in 1869 and was described in one Schools Report as the best provider of secondary education in Leeds. Two years later, a similar education was offered to girls when the Leeds Educational Institute for the Education of Girls (later known as Leeds Girls' Modern School) was established, thus pre-empting the foundation of Leeds Girls' High School in 1876. Parents of children attending these two schools were likely to be shopkeepers, clerks, travellers and other lower middle class occupations, who almost certainly considered the Grammar School to be of little relevance to their aspirations.

 The response from the Grammar School was hesitant and piecemeal. Matthews upgraded the teaching of French and German. The science syllabus was extended and this attracted many of the pupils away from the Classics. Pupils lower down the School were allowed to choose between Greek and German. Music became a subject in its own right. Workshops were set up. Oddly enough, the Headmaster wanted to construct a swimming pool but the Charity Commissioners refused their permission, though gymnastics did find a place on the curriculum. However, there were still serious deficiencies in the facilities. The building as a whole, despite or perhaps because of its attractive Gothic appearance, was deemed to 'fall very far short of the modern standard of requirements'. [Assistant Commissioner's Report, 1895, quoted from Marshall, p. 36]. The heating system was wholly inadequate (no change there) while in summer the rooms were stifling and 'the interior was dingy and unattractive, and it is little wonder that parents preferred to send their sons to schools where healthier and more comfortable conditions prevailed'. [Marshall, p. 37] Even the quality of the teaching came in for serious criticism. Just to add salt to the wounds, the recently founded Yorkshire College offered 'preparatory classes for students who in age and attainments differed little from schoolboys' and taught more effectively those subjects for which potential Sixth Formers might have opted. [Price, p. 247] As the Report tersely put it, the School had been 'allowed to drift into a backwater apart from the main current of educational progress'. [Assistant Commissioner's Report, quoted in Price, p. 260]

Real and effective change occurred only after this damning report and the Board of Trustees (early Governors) pushed through reforms of the Governing Body, the criteria for selecting the Headmaster, and, most importantly, a wider curriculum to attract more parents who wished to see the School compete favourably with other schools in the city. Henceforth, the School was to be non-denominational. As a result of these much-needed improvements, the School roll rose to 600 by 1923 and continued to increase until by 1939 numbers stood at around 1,000.

Forster's Act, despite its inadequacies, did give rise to a groundswell of public interest in education and a very substantial increase in state funding. Given the strength of the opposition from conservative and religious interests, it was a good stepping stone towards later educational legislation.

It is worth remembering that the Education Bills of 1896 and 1906 were both withdrawn due to the strength of the opposition to further reform. The Balfour Education Act of 1902 led to further discontent despite the fact that it abolished all School Boards in England and Wales, placed all elementary education in the hands of local education authorities, made provision for secondary and technical education and encouraged the provision of free places to grammar schools for the children of impoverished parents.

Dixon could be seen to be ahead of his times in relation to secondary and technical education. In 1870 he was elected onto the Birmingham School Board and became its chairman in 1876, but in the same year felt obliged to retire from Parliament because of Mrs Dixon's poor health. (However, in 1885, he was elected MP for Birmingham Edgbaston, and he continued as MP for that constituency until his death in 1898.) Free from his parliamentary duties, he was able to concentrate on his role as chairman of the School Board. He constantly advocated that Board schools should offer the very best education possible and to back up his views he subscribed generously to the scholarship funds and even set up at his own expense a 'technical school' at Bridge Street in 1884. He allowed the Birmingham Board to rent the premises at Bridge Street which were to serve as a central seventh grade school accommodating 400 boys. Manual instruction formed a large part of the syllabus, which also included geometry, chemistry and freehand drawing. Dixon wrote:

> I would invite the manufacturers of the town and neighbourhood to inspect this school, and having done so to consider whether it will not

be to their interest to reserve their best places for those who have passed successfully through it. All are now agreed that if this country is to retain its commercial supremacy it is essential that our artisans should have that training and education which will best fit them for the workshop. We are seeking to carry this out in the Bridge Street School. [W B Stephens (Ed.), *A History of the County of Warwick: Volume 7*, the City of Birmingham, Victoria County History, London 1964]

The Bridge Street School served as a model for other schools of similar character throughout the country.

In yet another way Birmingham led the field in educational reform when, in 1891, following the Education Act of 1890, all fees in all of the city's [Birmingham received its city charter in 1889] local education authority schools were abolished.

On 25 March 1885, Mrs Mary Dixon died, having suffered ill health for a number of years. A growth debilitated her, and she was prescribed homeopathic medicines which had little effect so an operation to remove the growth was carried out by Lawson Tait, an eminent Birmingham surgeon. Sadly, she passed away three days later.

Unquestionably, the people of Birmingham had the highest regard for George Dixon. He was made an honorary freeman of the city at the very end of his distinguished life, the ceremony taking place at his home on 4 January 1898. As the *Birmingham Post* reported:

> It will be a satisfaction to Mr Dixon's friends to know that the freedom of the city has been formally presented to him. On Saturday evening he received the Lord Mayor (Councillor Beale), who presented to him the copy of the council resolution conferring the freedom. Though he was extremely feeble, Mr Dixon was able to sign the roll of honorary freedom, and to express his gratification at this mark of respect from the Council on behalf of the town. [*BP* 17 January 1898]

Dixon's health continued to decline. His elder sister, Mary, had died in August 1897 and this affected him deeply. He died at his home on 24 January 1898, a week after receiving his honour from the city. 'The funeral of the late Mr George Dixon MP at Witton Cemetery, near Birmingham, yesterday [28 January], was marked by evidence of public sympathy and affectionate interest unsurpassed…by any similar event in the previous history of the city.' [*London Evening Standard* 29 January 1898] He was buried in the same grave as his wife alongside his sister Mary's grave. Today, it is not a peaceful location – the M6 motorway is close by.

What is striking about George Dixon's reforming zeal is that he continued to strive for social improvement, and particularly the provision of education, when, like Abraham Junior in 1866, he could so easily have retired in comfort and luxury and enjoyed good health surrounded by a loving family. The inference here is clear; Abraham, who had moved to a grand house, Cherkley Court in Surrey, lived until 1907. George, whose health declined over the last years of his life, refused to leave his Birmingham base and perhaps paid the ultimate price.

Bibliography
Birmingham Post, 17 January 1898
Dixon, James, *Out of Birmingham. George Dixon (1820-98), 'Father of free education'*, Brewin Books (Studley: 2013)
Jones, John Morris, *George Dixon, the Man and the Schools* (1969)
Kenrick, George H, "George Dixon" in *Nine Famous Birmingham Men*, edited by J H Muirhead, Cornish Brothers Ltd (1909)
London Evening Standard, 29 January 1898
Marshall, James W D, *Floreat Per Saecula. From Age to Age Excel. A History of Leeds Grammar School*, Smith Settle (Otley: 1997)
Price, A C, *A History of the Leeds Grammar School*, Richard Jackson (Leeds: 1919)
Wilson, Edmund, *Leeds Grammar School Admission Books from 1820 to 1900*, Thoresby Society (Leeds: 1906)

Colonel Edmund Wilson, courtesy of the Thoresby Society

6

Colonel Edmund Wilson VD FSA 1838-1914
Solicitor, Volunteer and Social Reformer
At LGS 1853-1856

INCLUDING EDMUND WILSON amongst the other distinguished Old Boys of Leeds Grammar School contained in this book may seem at first an anomaly, but there are at least three very good reasons for doing so.

First, he was instrumental in acquiring Kirkstall Abbey and its grounds for the people of Leeds; second, he was a founder member of the Thoresby Society; and, third, he was the author of the *Leeds Grammar School Admission Books, from 1820 to 1900*, published by the Thoresby Society, as well as privately, in 1906.

In his book, Wilson lists all the pupils of the School to be found in the hand-written registers and this was certainly a herculean task because, in preparation before publishing, he chose to write hundreds of letters to those worthies whose addresses he could discover in order to determine their post-LGS careers. Thereafter, he continued to glean information from as many OLs as he could contact right up to his death, incorporating hand-written emendations into a special 1906 printed edition containing interleaved blank pages for that purpose. He was the first to admit that he had not written a history of the School; or a mere list of pupils who gained university distinctions. He wrote in the 'Introduction' to his book, 'I do not think that the School should be judged by the number of high dignitaries to be found amongst its former pupils'. [W, p.vi] Wilson was at pains to distance himself from an earlier publication listing OLs, compiled and written by J H D Matthews, Headmaster from 1884-1902, and Vincent Thompson, published in 1897, which he found to contain errors and omissions, the most serious of which was the absence of any leaving dates of former pupils of the School. In justification of his own compilation, Wilson wrote:

> Let me now say that my object has been simply the good of the School. It is a Leeds School; and it is right that every inhabitant of Leeds should have the means of ascertaining, as far as possible, how it has been managed, and whether what has been done in recent years has been what would have had the approval of the grand old founder of the institution. [W, p.viii]

He goes on to write, 'If it be true that the object of education is to fit the pupil for a career in life, one should be able to judge the merits of a school by the success in life of its pupils; therefore I have tried to record what became of every pupil after he left the School.' [W, p.xx] He does attempt a rough analysis of these careers and found that certain professions were popular with former pupils: out of 4,300 entries, he discovered that the church attracted 251, the law 173, medicine 208, other professions 451, the Army and Navy 88 and business 661 (with 2,468 unknowns). It is interesting to note that a major criticism of the School during this period, 1820-1900, was that its curriculum simply did not prepare boys for a life in commerce, but Wilson's analysis would appear to confound this notion.

James Singleton, in his review of the life of Wilson, wrote of the effort involved in producing the *Admission Books*. They

> entailed much labour and expense, and occupied much of his time for many years. After its appearance in 1908 [actually 1906], he continued to gather information regarding the old pupils of the school, and a considerable amount of interesting matter has been accumulated which can be incorporated in a future edition brought down to a later date, if such a publication should be thought advisable.

Edmund Wilson was born in September 1838, the fourth son of Thomas Wilson, MA, of Banks Hall, Barnsley, whose antecedents were of yeoman stock living in the Featherstone area. A few years later, the family moved to Crimble's House in Leeds and Thomas became the auditor and comptroller of the Aire and Calder Navigation.

Edmund joined Leeds Grammar School on 1 August 1853 and his entry in the *Admission Books* reads:

> *Wilson, Edmund – Thomas, Gentleman, Leeds – 14.*
> *Admitted a solicitor T. 1863. Red Hall, Leeds. Aire Street, Goole.*
> *Registrar of the Goole County Court. A volunteer from 1863 to 1900.*

Lieut.-colonel commanding (hon. Colonel) 3rd Volunteer Battalion West Yorkshire Regiment. V.D. Nine years in the Leeds Town Council. F.S.A. Denison Hall, Leeds, 1905 (See also pp. 125 and 126.)

On page 125 he is listed under the Upper Department of 1856 and he is an exact contemporary of Robert Jarratt Crosthwaite, later Bishop of Beverley. Of the other boys in the Upper Department of 1856, 21 went on to Oxford or Cambridge. The list for 1857 includes William Gustavus Nicholson, later Field Marshal.

Edmund had followed his elder brothers to LGS: Herbert who was there from 1849-1852; and Arthur, there from 1851-1853. Herbert went up to Magdalene College, Cambridge on a Milner scholarship, gained first class honours in Classics (1856) and joined the Indian Civil Service. He died at Futtehghur, India, in June 1866. Arthur has the enigmatic entry in Edmund's book: 'died 8 Feb., 1857, from injuries received whilst at school'. [W, p.112]

Another brother, Kenneth, was at LGS (Upper Department) from c. 1856 to c.1861. He went up to St John's College, Cambridge and ended up as Principal of Wellington College, New Zealand and was still living in that country in 1905. The *Leeds Intelligencer* dated 22 December 1861 contained an article on the LGS Amateur Theatricals in which both Edmund and Kenneth are congratulated for their performances in John Tobin's comedy *The Hangman*, Edmund taking the part of Count Montalban and Kenneth that of Rolando, a Captain. [LI, 22 December 1861]

On leaving the School, Edmund was articled to John Hope Shaw, a prominent Leeds lawyer who was also a Trustee of the Grammar School.

In 1863 he was admitted a solicitor and joined the firm of Shaw, Tennant, Newstead & Wilson. The practice moved from Albion Street to Red Hall, the old house where John Harrison presented Charles I with a tankard filled with gold coins. Wilson continued to practise with James Shaw Newstead and in time set up on his own at Red Hall then later moved house to one wing of Denison Hall in Woodhouse. For a time he was President of the Leeds Law Society and in 1867 was appointed Registrar of the County Court at Goole, a position he kept until ill health forced him to resign in 1912.

Wilson possessed a deep social conscience. As part of his duties as Registrar at Goole, he witnessed the proceedings against debtors and the sequestration of property from defaulters, in particular poor people with no means of repaying their debts. He opposed imprisonment for those unfortunates who could not comply with the requirements of the Court and was particularly offended by the seizure of their property, usually furniture, which was then sold on. He worked hard to circumvent the procedure by advising and encouraging the debtors to pay off their creditors and in this he was remarkably successful.

His career with the Volunteers spanned the years 1863 to 1900 and he served

Colonel Edmund Wilson – Solicitor, Volunteer and Social Reformer

the organization with distinction. He joined the Leeds Rifles as a Private and stayed with them until, in 1867, he was commissioned as Lieutenant and was promoted to Captain in 1869. This was followed by further advancement, to Major, in 1878. The pinnacle of his career came when, in 1885, he was given the rank of Honorary Colonel and appointed Commanding Officer. Apart from his duties as a solicitor, the Volunteers took up much of his time and energy, so much so that, in 1892, he was one of the first officers to receive the Volunteer Decoration, 'given by Her Majesty Queen Victoria for conspicuous service with the Volunteer force'. [James Singleton, in TS, *Miscellanea*, Vol. xxiv, 1919, p.26]

During his time as CO, he worked hard to move the old headquarters of the battalion from Oxford Place to much larger premises in Carlton Hill, where they still exist today. He was the first Volunteer officer to carry out an experimental mobilisation, and he commanded the first battalion of Yorkshire Volunteers that visited Aldershot where 'he had the honour of being personally complimented by His Royal Highness the Duke of Connaught'. [JS, p.27]

In politics, he was a Liberal, being elected the first Honorary Secretary of the old Leeds Liberal Association and then President of the North Leeds Liberal Association. In 1880, he acted as the Election Agent to Gladstone. For nine years he represented the Headingley Ward in the Leeds Town Council.

In keeping with his liberal tendencies, he was keen to ameliorate the dreadful housing conditions of the destitute in Leeds. He founded the Leeds Industrial Dwellings Company and sought to remove the worst of the slum areas and create more fitting housing in more salubrious areas. He gave lectures on the subject in his home town and also at the Royal Society of Arts in London who thought fit to award him their medal.

An article in the *Leeds Mercury* dated 25 June 1900 reported on this occasion: 'Mr. Edmund Wilson, of Leeds, is among the recipients of the silver medal of the [Royal] Society of Arts, for his paper, read during the last session, on the "Housing of the Working Classes".' [*LM*, 25 June 1900]

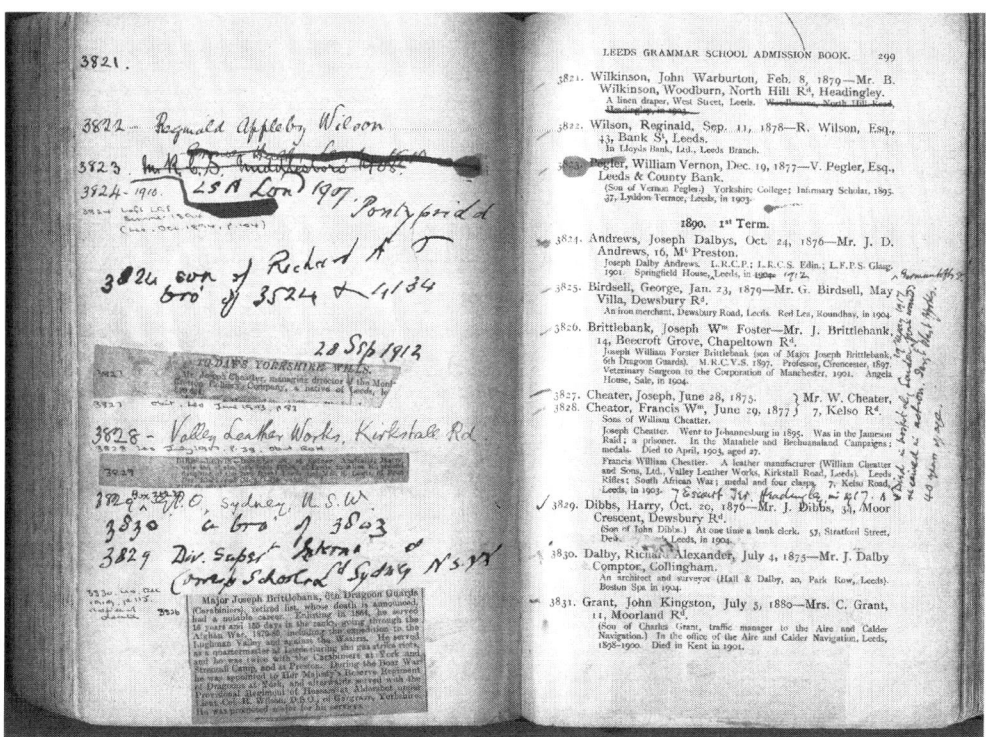

A typical page in Wilson's amended register

He joined the Leeds Philosophical and Literary Society in 1876 and eleven years later was elected a member of the Council. In the Council Minutes of the Society for April 1889, the following entry appears: 'Mr. Edmund Wilson was granted use of the Library without charge for a meeting to promote the formation of a Leeds Historical Society. At this meeting the Thoresby Society was instituted.' [KC, *History of the Leeds Philosophical and Literary Society*, p. 103] [See below]

From 1896 to 1898 he was President of the Philosophical and Literary Society. He read two papers before the members, one on "Slums" in 1894 and another on "Jersey" in 1896. The paper on "Slums" was instrumental in forging public opinion in favour of clearing out the worst areas in Leeds and undertaking a programme of re-housing. In May 1897, an entry under Council Minutes states that, 'The Council resolved to support a representation about to be made to the City Council against the proposed demolition of the old Grammar School'. [KC, p.112] Almost certainly, Wilson was a prime mover of this initiative.

He was an ardent campaigner for educational reform and improvement. He was highly effective in raising funds and acting as Treasurer to two organizations: the Leeds Educational Council and the Yorkshire Board of Legal Studies. The Leeds

Colonel Edmund Wilson – Solicitor, Volunteer and Social Reformer

Educational Council had, among its many objectives, the provision of scholarships for boys of straightened means from the Leeds Elementary Schools in Leeds, Holbeck and Bramley to attend Leeds Grammar School:

> In the first term of 1878 this Council sent its first batch of scholars… They were five in number; of these one gained an Exhibition at Queen's College, Oxford, took his B.A. in 1887 and M.A. in 1890; and three entered Government offices. [JS, p.28]

The first-mentioned boy was Edwin Lincoln Fearnside who had attended Carlton Hill Board School. He rose to become a woollen manufacturer, Fearnside Brothers of Ossett, and was able to move to 8 Sholebroke View in Chapeltown, then a highly-desirable residential area for the aspiring middle classes.

However, he was not averse to criticising Leeds Grammar School if he felt some injustice was being done.

One example of this was the misuse of income from the Poor's Fund, a levy on the middle classes for the relief of poverty, which should have been allocated to the education of boys and girls from poorer backgrounds. He found that LGS was not complying with this and a letter to the *Leeds Mercury* states his objections. A part of that letter is as follows:

> Five years ago [1877] there was an estate in Leeds called the Poor's Estate, to the income of which the poor of Leeds were solely entitled.
>
> The trustees of the Leeds Grammar School framed and obtained the sanction of Parliament to a scheme for appropriating to educational purposes the surplus income of this estate – about £700 a year.
>
> Under this scheme a large portion of this surplus income is enjoyed by the children of parents who do not belong to the poor of Leeds [*LM*, 21 November 1882]]

The Yorkshire Board of Legal Studies aimed to improve the education of articled clerks in solicitors' offices and gave a large grant to the Yorkshire College, later Leeds University, towards the expenses of a lecturer in law. Ultimately, this led to the creation of a Chair for the Faculty of Law at the university. Wilson served as a member of the Court of Governors at the Yorkshire College, and subsequently at the university, from 1885 to 1911.

In 1904, he was one of the founders of the Girls' High School at Chapel Allerton. He formed the company and raised the capital to set up the school and

Kirkstall Abbey - as illustrated by another old boy, Rodney Hill, see page 201

he became its first Honorary Secretary. The Leeds Education Authority took over the school in 1914.

He was a keen amateur antiquarian with a life-long interest in archaeology and was for many years on the Council of the Yorkshire Archaeological Society. But perhaps his greatest achievement in the pursuit of the arts was his association with the Thoresby Society, founded in 1889.

As previously mentioned, he was one of the founder members and was a key figure at its inception. He was both President and Treasurer of the Society for many years. He contributed articles to Volumes IX and XI of the *Miscellanea* series. He also produced his annotated *Leeds Grammar School Admission Books* for Volume XIV. One of the articles in Volume IX concerns "A Law-Suit in the 16th Century" and it makes reference to the fact that John Harrison purchased the North Hall estate and he quotes from Thoresby's *Ducatus Leodiensis*:

> On the West-side of the said Rivulet [the stream that rises in Adel and flows into the Aire] was the seat of the Falkinghams, called the North-hall, Part of which was standing in the reign of King Charles I, when the last of the Family sold the Estate to Mr. John Harrison, the Benefactor. [W, in TS, Volume IX, *Miscellanea*, p. 2; Thoresby, DL, 1st edition, 1715, p.111]

The other article describes in detail two old maps of Leeds, the Cossins Map of 1725 and the Jeffreys Map of 1771. The article in Volume XI describes the so-called Waterloo Map of Leeds, published in 1815, and Wilson uses the accompanying

Colonel Edmund Wilson – Solicitor, Volunteer and Social Reformer

An illustration of Red Hall, built in 1628

commentary to vent his anger on the re-naming of some of the Leeds streets, a process that had been encouraged by local architects who visited the Great Exhibition of 1851 in London:

> May I say a word about the naming of streets? I would express a devout hope that the good old names may not give place to new names copied from London thoroughfares.
>
> Leeds has already suffered in this respect. Butts Lane is now called Basinghall Street, probably because the Bankruptcy Court, which is there no longer, was once at its south end.

> The street south of St. John's Church is still called Mark Lane, though the Corn Exchange is no longer there. Merry Boys Hill – Butts Hill on our map – is now known as Guildford Street, and only a few months ago it was actually proposed to call Vicar Lane "the Strand" – a monstrous piece of vandalism. The Strand in London is so called because it runs along the north bank of the Thames. I know of no reason for giving that title to Vicar Lane. [EW, TS Volume XI, *Miscellanea*, pp.284-5]

He would have been equally offended by the development of Hyde Park Corner, Hyde Park Road and the surrounding streets of Kensington Terrace, Regent Park Terrace, Midland Road, Grosvenor Road and Grosvenor Terrace by those same architects, who commissioned a builder to erect substantial – and admittedly beautiful – houses. His sole objection would have been the choice of London street names. [Robert Dyson by email communication]

Wilson is possibly best known for his endeavours to save the historic ruins of Kirkstall Abbey and grounds from being converted into a tawdry pleasure resort by a group of Manchester businessmen. The problem was that the Abbey had been allowed to deteriorate in such a way that, despite its romantic appearance, it was in danger of falling down. The ironmasters of Kirkstall Forge, the Beecrofts and the Butlers, leased Abbey House from the owner of the Kirkstall estate, Lord Cardigan – he of the Charge of the Light Brigade – and they enjoyed the spectacular views of the ruins and their surrounds.

On his death in 1868, his widow took the difficult decision to sell the Abbey and its grounds at public auction in 1888. When the "For Sale" notices went up, Wilson and others negotiated with the owners with the intention of buying the estate for the benefit of the people of the town. Those negotiations came to naught and the real danger was that Lady Cardigan would sell at auction to the highest bidder whose plans for the area were inconsistent with the grandeur of the setting. Wilson, driven by urgency, was bold enough to sign a contract for the purchase *on his own responsibility* for the sum of £13,500 and paid the deposit but had not the means to pay the balance.

Colonel John Thomas North (the title "Colonel" came from his appointment as honorary Colonel of the Tower Hamlets Volunteer Engineers), the Nitrate King, whose fortune was based in part from the extraction of guano, came to his rescue, took over the contract, completed the purchase and gave the ruined abbey and its grounds to the people of Leeds, for which generous gesture he was honoured as the first Freeman of the town (Leeds became a city in 1893).

The *Huddersfield Chronicle* was quick to praise both North and Wilson. Under the heading, 'Report on the meeting of the Yorkshire Archaeological and Topographical Association', the article continued:

> The well-known ruins of Kirkstall Abbey have recently been presented to the borough of Leeds by Colonel North, a native of that town. It is a matter for congratulation that so fine an abbey has become public property, and it is with much pleasure that the Council record the fact that the initiative in the matter was taken by one of their own body, Mr Edmund Wilson, of Leeds, who has shrunk from no responsibility that he might secure the abbey to Leeds. Colonel North, by his judicious liberality, has enabled this to be done, and he has thereby earned the gratitude not only of the inhabitants of Leeds and of Yorkshire, but of all archaeologists throughout the length and breadth of the land. [*HC*, 26 January 1889]

The Corporation was keen to preserve, as much as possible, the fabric of the buildings and it called upon W H St John Hope, a distinguished architect and archaeologist, to make recommendations in pursuit of this aim:

> One of the first acts of the new owners on obtaining possession was to carry out the recommendation to free the ruins from ivy and other destructive vegetation, and to remove carefully the many large elm trees which not only encumbered the buildings, but were a constant source of danger. Some judicious excavations were also made under the writer's superintendence, and resulted in several interesting discoveries. [Hope & Bilson, *TS*, Vol.XVI 1907, p.7]

Wilson married rather late in life and when his wife died in December 1902 he felt the loss keenly. She had been actively associated with the work of the Yorkshire Ladies' Council of Education.

He died on 25 November, 1914 aged 76. His funeral took place at Lawnswood on 27 November, the service being conducted by the Rev. Canon J R Wynne Edwards, Headmaster of the Grammar School. Attending the funeral were several members of the Territorial Army, the Lord Mayor of Leeds, J E Bedford, and representatives from the university, the Thoresby Society and the Leeds Law Society. His obituary in the local paper records that he was

> A man of cultured tastes, and possessed of much administrative ability, [but] he nevertheless made no conspicuous success of the rough and tumble of ordinary public life…Yet he could be the most courteous and

courtly of men, as his commanding presence and imposing bearing betokened…Into nothing that he attempted in life did he throw so much energy as this Volunteering business. [Source not verified]

In his will, he left many of his books and MSS. to the Thoresby Society. The Annual Report of the Leeds Philosophical & Literary Society for 1914-15 has the following entry:

During the year the Society lost by the death of Col. E. Wilson and the Rev. J.H.D. Matthews, M.A., two former Presidents of the Society. Col. Wilson had been President 1896-7 and 1897-8. His paper on "Slums" was one of the factors which influenced public opinion as to the dangers of the insanitary properties in Leeds. The citizens of Leeds should ever hold him in grateful remembrance for the part he played in securing the transference of Kirkstall Abbey to the citizens of Leeds by Col. North. [KC, p.123]

It is interesting to note that other headmasters of Leeds Grammar School were elected President of the Society. Joseph Holmes held the post from 1835 to 1837, Alfred Barry from 1859 to 1861 and J R Wynne-Edwards from 1909 to 1911.

Bibliography
Bradford, Eveleigh, Thoresby Society, *Notes from the Library* (No.1, November 2009), 'Colonel North's £10,000 cheque for Kirkstall Abbey'
Dyson, Robert, email communication to the author
Hope, W H St John & Bilson, John, *Architectural Description of Kirkstall Abbey*, Thoresby Society Publications, Volume XVI (Leeds: 1907)
Huddersfield Chronicle dated 26 January 1889
Kitson Clark, E, *The History of 100 Years of Life of the Leeds Philosophical and Literary Society*, Jowett & Sowry Ltd (Leeds: 1924)
Leeds Intelligencer, 22 December 1861, article entitled 'Leeds Grammar School Amateur Theatricals'
Leeds Mercury dated 21 November 1882 and 25 June 1900
Singleton, James, *Colonel Edmund Wilson*, in Thoresby Society Publications, Volume XXIV, Miscellanea, pp. 25-30, Thoresby Society (Leeds: 1919)
Sitch, Bryan, *Kirkstall Abbey*, Leeds City Council (Leeds: 2000)
Thoresby, Ralph, *Ducatus Leodiensis*, 1st Edition
Wilson, Edmund, *Leeds Grammar School Admission Books from 1820-1900*, Thoresby Society Publications, (Leeds: 1906]
Wilson, Edmund, Thoresby Society Publications, Volume IX, *Miscellanea* (Leeds: 1899)
Wilson, Edmund, Thoresby Society Publications, Volume XI, *Miscellanea* (Leeds: 1904)

Field Marshal William Gustavus Nicholson

7

Field Marshal William Gustavus Nicholson KCB, Baron Nicholson of Roundhay 1845-1918 Chief of the Imperial General Staff and Military Engineer At LGS 1857-1862

Contributed by Mr John Davies, Archivist, The Grammar School at Leeds

WILLIAM GUSTAVUS NICHOLSON attended Leeds Grammar School from 26 January 1857 until July 1862 and is arguably the School's most illustrious Old Boy. His time at the School is quite unusual in a number of respects, not least that he was at the School at both the John Harrison building in Vicar Lane and also at the newly opened building on Woodhouse Moor.

He had been born on 2 March 1845 in the Mansion House, in what is now Roundhay Park, the fifth son of Mr William Nicholson Nicholson and his wife Martha. The family lived in Park Cottages until William Nicholson Nicholson inherited the estate from his uncle in 1858.

Life in his home was quite austere and regimented especially after a tragic incident in May 1840 when his father accidentally shot and killed their gamekeeper whom he had mistaken for a burglar. When WN Nicholson died the estate had to be sold off in order to pay the death duties and to allow his thirteen children their share of his remaining estate. A group of prominent Leeds men, including the Lord Mayor of Leeds, John Barran, bought it for £139,000. Having obtained an Act of Parliament Leeds Council then purchased the land and turned it into a public park, Roundhay Park.

William came to Leeds Grammar School under the headmastership of the great Rev. Alfred Barrry, who had been appointed to the headmastership in 1854.

Field Marshal William Gustavus Nicholson – Chief of the Imperial General Staff

William's younger brother, Charles Langdon Nicholson, was admitted to the School on 2 August 1858 but left that Christmas to go to a private tutor. William was to have a very successful career at school and excelled as a student. As a consequence, Dr Barry tried to persuade him to follow a university career but William, despite his undoubted ability, had his mind set upon a career in the military, even though there was no family tradition of service in the army. Perhaps his greatest contribution to the life of the School was with regard to the formation of an embryonic Rifle Corps.

The School had one of the first Rifle Training Corps (Cadet Corps) of any of the country's Public Schools, being founded in 1860 at a similar time to those at Eton, Harrow, Rugby, Marlborough and Winchester, although Rossall School probably had the earliest, being founded on 1 February of that year. The foundation of the corps at the School was due entirely to the resourcefulness and drive of Nicholson, who was to become its first officer. In this as in all things Nicholson showed himself to be extremely able, astute, determined and an exceptional administrator with outstanding leadership skills.

Nicholson left the School in July 1862 to compete for a place at the Royal Military Academy, Woolwich. In the examination, which was very competitive, he emerged at the head of the list. Even though he was to spend most of his military career in outposts of the Empire he kept in touch with the School and he had the opportunity to visit, when he was Chief of the Imperial General Staff, on 11 July 1910 when he came to Leeds to receive an honorary degree from the University. He never forgot his home city and when he was raised to the peerage upon his retirement he took the title Baron Nicholson of Roundhay.

Again, at Woolwich he proved to be a most successful and able cadet and, at the end of his time there, he graduated on 22 December 1864, again at the head of

Mansion House

the list and was awarded the Pollock Sword and Medal. He also showed his other qualities; for example, one of his contemporaries spoke about William's kindness and consideration towards a forlorn "snooker" (new cadet) at a time when discipline at the RMA was lacking in those qualities.

He received his commission into the Royal Engineers on 21 March 1865 and was posted for two years' further training to Chatham. During his time there he was selected, unusually for an engineer, on behalf of the government to make observations and prepare a report on the guns on display at the Paris Exhibition of 1867, especially the new German Krupps 50-ton gun. Following the successful completion of that assignment he was posted to Barbados, one of the largest garrisons in the colonies to assist in the construction of the defences of the dockyard there. During this time, he also served at Demerara in British Guiana, where he met and married Victorine (Victoria) Dallier. The marriage was recorded in the *Army and Navy Gazette*: "7 June at Georgetown, Demerara. By the Reverend Father Wilson, Lieutenant William Gustavus Nicholson, Royal Engineers to Victorine, only daughter of the late Dominique Dallier, of this colony."[1] To be married at such an early age (24) was generally regarded as a hindrance to promotion in the Army and indeed Nicholson was to remain a Lieutenant until March 1878.

In October 1871 he volunteered for service in India, not least because, despite his father having been a wealthy man, his financial resources had not been sufficient to further his son's career and Army pay went further in India than at home. Nicholson was to spend the next thirty years serving mainly in India but also in other parts of the Empire. During his early years there, he proved himself a very able engineer and was responsible for one of the first uses of concrete in the subcontinent while constructing the major water works system at Peshewar.

The Afghan War broke out in the autumn of 1878 and three columns of British troops invaded Afghanistan via the Khyber pass, through Kurram and via the Bolan Pass. Nicholson was appointed Field Engineer to the latter column which had to follow an exceptionally difficult route as there was no bridge over the Indus river and over 100 miles of desert had to be crossed. Nicholson's task was to build the roads and ensure an adequate water supply to the troops. He was with the advanced troops that entered Kandahar and was Mentioned in Despatches for his efforts.

Following the massacre of the British envoy at Kabul, Sir Frederick Roberts (later Field Marshal Lord Roberts) was assigned the task of taking Kabul and he chose Nicholson to be his Field Engineer. At the end of the campaign Nicholson spent the early part of 1880 constructing the defences of Kabul and received a

---

[1] *Army and Navy Gazette* 21 August 1869. In other sources his wife's surname is recorded as Dillon and the date of their marriage as 1871.

Field Marshal William Gustavus Nicholson – Chief of the Imperial General Staff

special letter of congratulations from Roberts for his construction of the road to Lataband which allowed the advance of the relief column. Nicholson was then taken "under Roberts' wing" and became one of his protégés. He took part with Roberts in his famous March to Kandahar, again as Field Engineer. His reputation as a man of capacity, resource and knowledge was now established.

After a short period of leave he returned to Simla as Secretary of the Defence Committee, which had been constituted shortly before, to consider all the problems connected both with coast defence, frontier defence and internal arrangements for the safety of India. His relationship with Roberts became very close and indeed he became known as Roberts' "Golden Pen", writing many of his speeches, articles and despatches for him and advising on Roberts' books. Following a brief interlude, during which Nicholson took part in the Battle of Tel-el-Kebir in Egypt, he remained as Secretary of the Defence Committee for a number of years. Later on, in 1885, Lord Roberts was appointed Commander-in-Chief in India, and took great personal interest in the very important work of the Defence Committee. He left on record that, "it was in a great measure due to Colonel Nicholson's clear-sighted judgment on the many knotty points which came before us, and to his technical knowledge, that the schemes for the defence of the frontier, and for the ports of Bombay, Karachi, Calcutta, Rangoon, and Madras were carried out so rapidly, thoroughly and economically, as they were".

This high opinion of Nicholson's ability resulted in his being selected, in 1890, to become Lord Roberts' Military Secretary. In 1897 Nicholson was appointed as Chief of Staff and second in command to Sir William Lockhart for the extremely difficult campaign against the Afridi tribes in Tirah around the Kyber Pass. Lockhart had the highest opinion of Nicholson and, like Lord Roberts, trusted his sound judgment and clear grasp of affairs. In this campaign Nicholson occupied a position of the greatest influence. His knowledge of frontier warfare was now far-reaching, and he had studied the problem of mountain warfare with the best experts. Despite all this the campaign was not a great success, although Nicholson was again Mentioned in Despatches and made a KCB. In 1898 he was promoted to be Adjutant General in India, at that time the highest appointment on the Staff.

Following early disasters in the Second South African War Lord Roberts was sent for to command the British forces. He immediately sent for Kitchener from the Sudan and Nicholson from India to assist him. A particular problem was one of transport, which had proved to be in urgent need of complete reorganization. Nicholson had initially been brought in as Robert's Military Secretary and he was one of the very few officers to whom Roberts' plan of campaign had been revealed. Nicholson was subsequently made Director of Transport but fell out with Kitchener because he believed that the latter took all the glory for himself and didn't give Nicholson enough credit. Indeed, Sir Arthur Conan Doyle felt that this was the case and wrote that, 'Sir William Nicholson has not received that credit which is his due for his supervision of the transport'.[2] Nicholson, in a conversation with Lady Curzon[3] on 18 May 1901, said of Kitchener, 'I have worked two years with Kitchener, he is not a clever man – can't write a dispatch – his knowledge of administration is puerile and his only quality to praise is his relentless determination to advance himself, in that he is the best worker I have ever known'. He also said that Kitchener did not know the elementary rules of administration and his telegrams, which had to go through Nicholson, were quite astoundingly ignorant, unmethodical and lacking in clarity. Lord Curzon and Winston Churchill, the latter of whom had become a good friend of Nicholson, both expressed similar sentiments. Nicholson also, while in South Africa, had the opportunity to work closely with another Leeds Grammar School old boy, Colonel Frank Henderson (GFR Henderson, the distinguished military historian) who Roberts had appointed to his staff as Director of Intelligence.

In October 1900 both Roberts and Nicholson left South Africa; Roberts to return home and Nicholson to return to India. Roberts was then appointed Commander-in-Chief of the Army and immediately sent for Nicholson to join him at the War Office to the newly created post of Director of Military Intelligence and Mobilization. Nicholson was an immediate success and quickly became the most influential person within the Army. He believed that the Intelligence Department should be a controlling and governing power and that the policy and training of the Army should be based upon its reports and information. He believed that the military policy of the Army should be settled in broad outlines by the Cabinet and that it was the business of the Director of Intelligence to furnish the Cabinet with such information that would enable them to determine what their policy should be. It was clear that he was making his mark as a great administrator. Lord Esher, who was asked to head up a commission to investigate War Office reform, believed that Nicholson was the most intelligent man in the army and the most powerful personality – perhaps even too powerful.

Possibly for that reason Nicholson was sent for a time, early in 1904, as Chief Military Attaché to the Japanese army in Manchuria during the Russo-Japanese War, where he remained for just over a year. To a man of his wide experience and keen intelligence that proved to be of the greatest value because the operations which he witnessed were of a war on a greater scale than anything he had seen before. The Japanese army had been eagerly assimilating from all European sources every possible lesson that was of value.

---

[2] Conan Doyle A, The Great Boer War.
[3] Mary Curzon the wife of the Viceroy of India.

Field Marshal William Gustavus Nicholson – Chief of the Imperial General Staff

Nicholson was granted the Japanese War Medal and the Grand Cordon of the Rising Sun. On his return he was offered the post of Governor of Gibraltar but turned this down, preferring to wait for an appointment at home. He was soon offered the position of Quartermaster General, which carried with it a place on the Army Council. He was now able to influence directly the policy of administration. Following the performance of the British Army in the South African War it was clear that reform was needed, and Nicholson had learned a great deal from his observations of the Japanese army in the Russo-Japanese War.

Nicholson had a very sharp mind. Indeed, R B Haldane, the Secretary of State for War, described him as, 'one of the cleverest men I have ever come across'. He also had a very sharp tongue and did not suffer fools gladly; he soon gained a reputation as an acerbic, self-opinionated and uncongenial colleague to those unfortunate enough to differ from him in opinion. He did possess a great degree of talent and was able to see solutions where others only saw problems.

The British Army, together with its organization, that fought in World War One was largely the result of Haldane's Army Reforms of 1906-12. The main part of the reforms with regard to structure was the work of Nicholson, who had been appointed a full General in 1906 and who worked very closely with Haldane. Initially, Nicholson had considered the idea of conscription but in the end the reforms, which bore Haldane's name, devised a force composed of three elements. The first was a Regular Army composed of Regiments with two battalions in each, one for overseas duty and one at home.

The second element was the Special Reserve, composed of experienced former active-duty soldiers. The third was the Territorial Army, built from the Yeomanry and the Militia. This was the structure of the British Army that entered the war in 1914. 'With the Expeditionary Force organised, the Territorial Army in being and General Staff principles being applied to both, there remained one further field in which a burst of Haldane's cerebral energy was urgently required – the welding together of all the Armed Forces of the Empire into a coherent whole. The Minister [Haldane] turned to Haig and Nicholson to work out proposals whereby this might be achieved; he tells us…Haig worked out the details of the plan, and Nicholson embodied them in admirable drafts for the assistance of the Colonial and India Offices. I could not have had finer help than I got from these two.'[4]

At that time the concept of a General Staff was new, but it was widely felt that the British Army needed a "thinking" department along the lines of the Great General Staff in Germany if it was to be prepared for any forthcoming war. It fell to Nicholson to develop and strengthen this General Staff and indeed Sir Henry

---

[4] J Terraine, *Douglas Haig: The Educated Soldier* 1963 pp 43-44

Field Marshal William Gustavus Nicholson was also Baron of Roundhay, and Chief of the Imperial General Staff

Wilson (himself later to be the Chief of the General Staff) said that without Nicholson the General Staff would not have existed. In 1908 Nicholson succeeded Sir Neville Lyttleton as the second Chief of the General Staff, in other words the head of the British Army. The following year this post was re-designated as Chief of the Imperial General Staff (CIGS) as it embraced all the staff operations of the Colonial and Indian Armies as well as those of Britain. Nicholson became therefore the first CIGS.

The General Staff at this time was a more or less amorphous body, composed of many capable and brilliant men but they lacked the power and influence that united action would provide. This Nicholson supplied. He possessed a great knowledge of character and the ability to select good men and he wielded this ability with vigour and impartiality. He was not always an easy person with whom to work and men might fear him but they all had respect for his decision, capacity and impartiality. He welded together those divers elements of the General Staff while at the same time organizing units into divisions and other commands, supervising training and keeping in touch with the civil power in order to subordinate the military to its recognized policy.

Field Marshal William Gustavus Nicholson – Chief of the Imperial General Staff

Nicholson was, therefore, largely responsible for the creation of the modern General Staff and was promoted to Field Marshal in June 1911. He retired from the Army in 1912 (although of course Field Marshals never officially retire) and was raised to the peerage as Baron Nicholson of Roundhay.

As CIGS he had sat on the Committee for Imperial Defence and this continued after war broke out in 1914. As a member of the Committee of Imperial Defence his role was to represent the Army's views. He regularly clashed with Admiral Sir John Fisher, the Navy's most formidable champion. Fisher found to his cost that Nicholson was a disagreeable opponent who could strike back with telling effect.

The following exchange took place during the Agadir Crisis of 1911: 'The First Lord (McKenna) backed him [Fisher] up. I [Sir Henry Wilson[5]] said at once that the mode of employing troops and their numbers and places of operation were questions for the War Office General Staff and that we [the British] had worked them out with the French. The results had been periodically approved in the Committee of Defence itself. Sir William Nicholson [CIGS] asked Sir Arthur[6] whether they had at the Admiralty a map of German strategic railways. Sir Arthur replied that it was not their business to have such maps. 'I beg your pardon,' said Sir William, 'if you have meddled with military problems you are bound not only to have them, but to have studied them.' The discussion became sharp; I [Haldane] of course, agreeing 'ex animo' with the utterances of the CIGS. He had a rather too sharp tongue, and I remember that on a previous occasion Sir John Fisher had said to me that he wished I would enjoin 'Old Nick' not always to stamp his hoof on his [Sir John's] toes.'[7] Nicholson certainly was, as Haldane said, "the most powerful personality in the Army".

Nicholson was regarded as a progressive within the Army and was, along with Sir Henry Wilson, responsible for preparing it to meet the growing threat from Germany. He espoused the cause of conscription although came to recognize that it would not be supported in the country at large. He was enthusiastic about the development of field artillery and automatic rifles but did not believe that

---

[5] Field Marshal Sir Henry Wilson was sub Chief of Staff to the BEF and in 1917 was appointed as Military Advisor to the Prime Minister, Lloyd George. In 1918 he was appointed CIGS. On retiring from the Army he became a politician and was assassinated by the IRA in 1922.

[6] Sir Arthur Wilson was First Sea Lord from 1910-1911 and was a member of the Committee for Imperial Defence

[7] Nicholson enjoyed a brilliant yet unusual career. He was a gifted staff officer and military administrator, but he had a reputation of being hard to handle and his sobriquet "Old Nick" was certainly well earned. Despite never having commanded a unit in action (indeed he never commanded an infantry, artillery or cavalry unit), or having passed Staff College, he uniquely rose to the rank of Field Marshal and Chief of the Imperial General Staff through sheer hard work, intelligence and ability.

aeroplanes would have any part to play in warfare except for the purpose of observation and reconnaissance.

When he retired he was sent to India to head up a commission (the Nicholson Commission) to investigate the issue of Indian Army expenditure. With considerable impact, in 1916-17, he acted as the military member of the Dardanelles Commission, established to investigate the debacle of the Gallipoli Campaign.

He was also the Chairman of the London Territorial Force Association. He died at his home, 51 Pont Street, London on 13 September 1918, less than two months before the Armistice, aged 73, and is buried in Brompton Cemetery.

Colonel Frank Henderson

8
•
George Francis Robert Henderson CB 1854-1903
Military Strategist and Historian
At LGS 1862–1874

G F R HENDERSON WAS born on 2 June 1854, the eldest child of the Rev. William George Henderson, at that time the first Headmaster of Victoria School, Jersey, and his wife, Jane Melville. There followed thirteen siblings, seven of whom were to attend Leeds Grammar School during their father's headmastership from 1862. It was here that young Frank's 'education commenced, and he gradually worked his way to the top of the school'. [LRM, p.xiii]

This large Victorian family lived in the spacious Headmaster's house, within the 1859 buildings, grand enough, but it must at times have felt a little cramped. William George Henderson left Leeds in 1884 to become Dean of Carlisle Cathedral.

A contemporary pupil paints a glowing picture of young Henderson at school. 'As a boy he possessed many of the qualities which go to make a great leader, and I can readily believe that his personality acted largely in his influence as a teacher.' [quoted from LRM, p.xiii] He was very keen on games, especially rugby and cricket, and another contemporary recalled, 'I served under him…when he captained the cricket eleven, and in those early days he was no ordinary boy; by his own example he made us all feel that we must play the game'. [quoted from LRM, p.xiv]

This characteristic flair for bringing the best out in his team is amply demonstrated in his later career as a teacher and professor at the military academies, where he loved to organize competitive sports in order to encourage esprit de corps among his students. However, he was no mere hearty, for in one year he won the English Prize for an essay on Alexander the Great, possibly an indication of the direction in which his interests and enthusiasm would later take.

In his final year (1874) at Leeds Grammar School, when he was appointed Captain (Head) of School, according to one authority [*Leodiensian*, October 1904, p.79], Henderson won a History Scholarship to St John's College, Oxford. As an open scholar, he gained entry to the university by the relatively new process of examination rather than having been a pupil from one of the favoured schools. His father had always intended that he train for the church, but from the start of his university education he pursued his ambition to take up a military career. At St John's he devoted a great deal of time to competitive games and preferred physical fitness to academic study. He joined the recently founded Vincent's Club, which admitted only the very best college sportsmen. He was a member of the King Charles Club, a college dining society for the social élite there, much in the same vein as the better known Bullingdon Club, satirised by Evelyn Waugh in *Decline and Fall* as the Bollinger Club. [MR] As a result, in 1876, he left the university without a degree and immediately entered Sandhurst and spent two years there, again indulging in much sport, before being gazetted Second Lieutenant to the 65th Foot (the York and Lancaster Regiment) at Dinapore, near Patna in the Indian state of Bihar. He was then aged of 24 – at that time considered rather old to enlist. After a short stay in India, he returned to England as a full Lieutenant in the Second Battalion, the 84th Foot, and was stationed at Dover.

In 1882 he accompanied his regiment, the York and Lancaster (65th/84th – that is, both battalions) to Egypt to take part in the first campaign there. With typical Victorian middle class solicitude, he wrote to his mother:

> The route [to Egypt] has not yet actually arrived, but we are nearly all packed and ready to start…. It is a great bore for us being kept in suspense like this. Of course it is alright for us fellows, we have the voyage and all the excitement and novelty to look forward to, but it is sad work for the women…. I hope we shall do our duty and come back safe and sound. [quoted from LRM, p.xv]

In fact, he and his battalion arrived at Alexandria on 17 August 1882. The previous year, Colonel Ahmed Arabi Bey, a native officer of the Egyptian army, launched a revolt against the Turkish-appointed Khedive, recognised by Britain and France as the legitimate leader of the country. This was, in effect, a nationalist uprising against what Arabi and other Egyptians saw as intolerable interference in the running of the country. His master plan was to seize the Suez Canal and then capture Cairo. Alexandria was bombarded on 11 July 1882 by the British Admiral, Seymour, in response to serious rioting in the city and fears for the security of the Canal. There followed an inevitable period of hiatus, which Henderson used to study Arabic. When the British and Indian forces moved to the Front, under the overall command of Lieutenant-General Sir Garnet Wolseley, Henderson distinguished himself by his bravery and his concern for his men. He commanded a half company in action at El Magfar and Tel-el-Mahouta. At Kassassin, he commanded a full company and a few days later, on 13 September, took them into action at Tel-el-Kebir, strategically placed between Alexandria and the Suez Canal, where he led his men in a dawn raid into a redoubt, occupied by the enemy, at great personal risk. The battle was won convincingly, and following it, the Cavalry Division secured Cairo and on the next day Arabi surrendered. For his bravery, Henderson was awarded several medals and was Mentioned in Despatches. He then returned with his battalion to England.

The Battle of Tel-el-Kebir became so famous that the incorrigible poetaster Sir William Topaz McGonagall – he of the Tay Bridge disaster fame – was inspired to write in his inimitable style a panegyric to Sir Garnet Wolseley:

> *He [Sir Garnet] has gained for himself fame and renown,*
> *Which to posterity will be handed down;*
> *Because he has defeated Arabi by land and by sea,*
> *And from the battle of Tel-el-Kebir he made him to flee.*

In late 1882 Henderson was posted to Ireland and the following year he married Mary, the daughter of Mr Pierce Joyce of Galway. She proved to be a huge support to Henderson, always encouraging him to pursue his ambitions and comforting him when the pressure of work, especially his writing, became intolerable. They did not have any children.

Between 1883 and 1885, they enjoyed a posting to Bermuda and later to Halifax, Nova Scotia. It was while he was serving in Bermuda that he conceived the idea of writing a history of the American Civil War. He met a number of American military personnel and, talking to them, he realised that there was an opportunity to write the definitive history of that war. So, in 1885, he took Mary with him to Virginia and Maryland and saw for himself the sites of the great battles and campaigns, especially those of the American Confederate General he most admired, Thomas "Stonewall" Jackson.

In 1885 he joined the Ordnance Department at Fort George as Deputy Assistant Commissary General, a promotion if not in rank then certainly in remuneration, and this enabled him to concentrate on organizing the mass of material he had accrued on the American Civil War and the Franco-Prussian War of 1870. According to Roberts, he, unlike some of his fellow officers, was dedicated to his professional duties as well as the task in hand, namely writing his first book.

George Francis Robert Henderson – Military Strategist and Historian

Victoria College, Jersey, courtesy of Victoria College

He read widely, mostly military history, and studied the battle plans of the great commanders of history. When not writing, he engaged his men in all manner of sporting activities and treated them with scrupulous fairness in all aspects of their work and duties. As Lord Roberts writes, 'His consideration and his absolute fairness in his dealings with his men endeared him to them….he was, in fact, a favourite with all ranks…' [LRM, p.xix]

Whilst stationed at Fort George, he worked assiduously on his material for his first book, *The Campaign of Fredericksburg, a Tactical Study for Officers*. This was his first published work, albeit anonymously, written chiefly for the edification of his students, most of who belonged to the local Volunteers, and it was very well received both by the military tacticians and the general reading public, selling in quite appreciable numbers. Happily for him, at this time he received his brevet majority; that is he was, in 1886, made Captain but given the rank of Major as a courtesy only.

Buoyed by the success of his first book, he turned to the Franco-Prussian War and the Battle of Spicheren. He absorbed the astute tactics and strategy employed by the Prussian General Staff and was able to identify those crucial aspects of military conduct that worked so favourably against the French. By now, he had

Leeds Grammar School

Harrison window in St John's Church depicting him overseeing construction work
[photo by author]

John Harrison's statue in City Square [photo by author]

St Mary's Church, Whitkirk, left, and the Smeaton memorial, below [photos Pam Hargreaves]

Charles West Cope's portrait of his sponsor and friend, Prince Albert [photo courtesy of royal.uk]

The Cope altar-piece in St George's Church, Great George Street. [photo courtesy of Alasdair Elmes)

Hawkshaw's Lockwood viaduct, above, [photo by News from Nowhere], and Holyhead Lighthouse, below, [photo by Pam Hargreaves]

Joseph Chamberlain, left, helped George Dixon set up the National Education League [photo courtesy of Wikiwand.com]

Edmund Wilson helped procure the Kirkstall Abbey estate, below, for the people of Leeds [photo courtesy of the Thoresby Society]

Edward Barry's new school at Woodhouse, above, as it might have been had funds not run out [drawing courtesy of the British Architectural Library, RIBA, London]

The Henderson plaque at GSAL, left

The Battle of Tel el Kebir, below, at which Col. Henderson fought bravely [photo courtesy of Royal Museum, Greenwich]

John Ireland was inspired by landscapes such as Chanctonbury Rings, left, [photo courtesy Google]

Ernest Bristow Farrar's grave, is pictured right, [photo courtesy of CWC]

become the foremost expert on strategy and, when he joined Sandhurst and, later, the Staff College at Camberley, he was to put this research to good use. Unlike his study of the American Civil War battlefields, written in English, Henderson found that all the most accurate accounts of the 1870 War were written in German so, undaunted, he set about teaching himself that language – further evidence of his commitment to accuracy and authenticity. He produced *The Battle of Spicheren* in which he noted the similarity in the terrain over which that action took place to the range of heights between London and the Channel. As he told his Volunteer students, they would do well to note those similarities in the event of an invasion from across the Channel.

The main lessons learned from this study were, 'the absolute necessity for initiative, the ready acceptance of responsibility by even the most subordinate officers, the discipline of self-reliance and the fact that self-reliance could only be gained by the most careful education and training'. [LRM, p.xxii] It was this ability to employ initiative and respond to fast-changing circumstances on the battlefield that gave the Prussians the edge over their French adversaries. The key to success was sound and thorough training. As Lord Roberts (later Field Marshal Roberts) pointed out, Britain may be guarded by her navy but India, considered by British politicians and the ruling class to be the most important part of the Empire, was vulnerable to land attack from Russia.

There were other factors to consider and Henderson gave them careful thought. He realised at once the importance of rail communications in moving huge numbers of soldiers to the front line. This the Germans achieved, employing six railway lines over a period of three weeks to transport almost half a million men. Moreover, once at the Front, senior officers were encouraged to respond to constantly changing circumstances in the field. According to Archer et al in Cassell's *World History of Warfare*,

> German tactics (*Auftragstaktik*) were simple but effective. Front-line commanders were given leeway within the general strategic design to march to the sound of the guns, which indicated the decisive pressure point. Moltke's strategic genius lay in his ability to adjust to conditions as they presented themselves, rather than in readjusting his armies to fit into a prearranged plan; in short, in his brilliant opportunism. [CIA, p.432]

Henderson, still a Brevet Major, had been posted to Gibraltar in 1887 but what he ardently sought was a position at Sandhurst so that he might put into practice that disciplined training he had so astutely promoted through his writing. Luckily for him, he had been noted by senior officers in the Army and in September 1889 he was sent to the Staff College by Lord Wolseley to teach Tactics, Military Administration and Law. Here he advocated those principles that were stated at length in his books, not only in the classroom but also in the field during practical exercises. Once again, he promoted physical fitness through a variety of sporting activities.

Importantly for him, he was able to devote more time to his writing. He produced in 1891 the third edition of the Fredericksburg book, wrote numerous letters to the *Times* and contributed essays and articles to the *Edinburgh Review*, for which he was paid. So industrious was he that his health began to suffer, but despite this he now concentrated on his masterpiece, *Stonewall Jackson and the American Civil War*. This took him eight years to complete and is testament to his determination to produce the most comprehensive and accurate treatment of the American General. He was still working on the book when he was transferred to the Staff College at Camberley to take up the post of Professor of Military Art and History, in succession to Colonel F Maurice. Here he was able to engage the best minds the Army had to offer, by no means all young students; many longer-serving professional officers benefited from his teaching. Away from the classroom, he took his students out into the field and conducted tours of those battlefields he thought best illustrated his ideas.

The Commandant of the College, Lieutenant-General Sir Henry Hildyard, wrote of him: 'He showed great clearness of thought and perception, simplicity and correctness of demonstration, a practical mind that discarded at once methods impractical in war, and untiring industry and patience'. [LRM, p.xxix] Hildyard noted that Henderson was able to draw on a wealth of material, in particular the memoirs of those senior officers who had fought in previous campaigns and all this represented 'a severe labour, gone through with indomitable perseverance and pluck which always characterised him'. [LRM, p.xxx] However, there was a price to pay for all this hard work; his health continued to suffer.

Lord Roberts met Henderson, now promoted to Major, for the first time when the latter had been invited to lecture on Wellington to the Dublin Military Society in 1897. The two men immediately struck up a friendship and enjoyed mutual respect. Roberts was particularly impressed by Henderson's ability to organize and collate huge amounts of disparate source material into a coherent and succinct lesson. Even more impressive was the book on Stonewall Jackson that was published at this time (1898), by far the best biography of the American and still regarded to this day as the authoritative and standard work on strategy. As the *Times* wrote, it was a literary triumph 'which for most ordinary readers, and indeed for most military men, came almost as a revelation of the real meaning of strategy. The influence that work is destined to exercise on the future of our Army is one that can hardly be overrated.' [*Times*]

Beyond A Little Learning

The Henderson plaque in the reception corridor, courtesy of Steve Tootill

Field Marshal Wolseley, who wrote the "Introduction" to the book, warmly congratulated its author:

> I can cordially recommend Colonel Henderson's delightful volumes. From their perusal I have derived real pleasure and sound instruction. They have taught me much; they have made me think still more; and I hope they may do the same for many others in the British Army. They are worth the closest study, for few military writers have possessed Colonel Henderson's grasp of tactical and strategical principles, or his knowledge of the methods which have controlled their application by the most famous soldiers, from Hannibal to Von Moltke. [H, Intro, pp.vii-viii]

Wolseley went on to stress the importance of training and of having a Reserve of trained men in readiness should war break out. True to his military background and experience, he decried the interference by politicians in the strategic conduct of a campaign. The latest edition appeared in 2016.

An illustration of Sir Henry Hildyard, during the South African War, courtesy of The Boer War

There followed another book, *The Battle of Woerth* (Worth), published in 1899, yet another valuable treatise on the importance of planning, training and tactical flexibility.

He was also mainly responsible for the revision of the Drill Book, the tactical portion of the last edition being written by him. At the same time, he was contemplating a life of General Lee, which would have been a sequel to the Stonewall Jackson book but this was never written.

With the outbreak of the Second South African War (1899-1901), for which the country and the Army was ill-prepared, Henderson was now called upon to put his theories into practice. Roberts, who was appointed Commander-in-Chief in 1900, had read Henderson's approval of Stonewall Jackson's swift and unexpected movements against the enemy, and this encouraged him to march on the capitals of the Orange Free State and the Transvaal, thereby dividing the Boer forces.

In 1900, Henderson, now substantive Lieutenant-Colonel, accompanied Roberts, who gave him the post of Director of Intelligence, a trust he amply repaid by producing maps of the Orange Free State, admittedly rather sketchy but a big improvement on no maps at all. Even better, he discovered excellent maps of the Transvaal lying in the Post Office awaiting collection by the Boers, but Henderson relieved them of that responsibility by appropriating them for use by the British.

Once more his state of health gave cause for concern but he kept this to himself. 'It was far better to accept [my poor health]. I could not have stood waking up every morning and thinking that I was one of the few soldiers who were doing nothing for the country; I should never have felt like a man again.' [LRM, p.xxxvi]

In February, Henderson moved up to the Front to the Modder River and he knew that he was in more danger than he had been since the Egyptian Campaign of 1882. Many of the serving officers made a point of visiting Henderson and talking over those points of strategy that he had elucidated upon in the classroom with them. But within a few days his health deteriorated so badly he had to withdraw to Cape Town and so missed General Piet Cronje's surrender on 27 February after the Battle of Paardeberg. Ironically, Cronje's innovative deployment of his infantry at the base of the hill-line rather than along the top in order to increase the effectiveness of their rifles' flat trajectories, would have earned him a place in Henderson's studies.

He returned to England and over the course of the next months recovered sufficiently to take up his duties once more. In August 1900, he was tasked with writing the official history of the South African War, the prevailing view being that he was by far the best man for the job. He was made a Companion of the Order of the Bath (CB) on 29 November 1900.

In the autumn of 1901 he returned to South Africa to study the battlefields and survey that portion of the country affected by military action that he had not seen for himself. He worked assiduously to such an extent that in February 1902 his health broke down again, almost certainly suffering from a bout of malaria, so once more he returned to England.

A partial recuperation allowed him to resume his writing, but by June he was so ill he was ordered to Egypt in the belief that another English winter would be the death of him. Sadly, he never recovered and a sudden decline set in from which he did not rally, dying at Assouan (Aswan) on 5 March 1903. He was buried in the Roman Catholic cemetery in Cairo, where there is a memorial to him. His history of the South Africa War was never finished and no part of it, even the completed first volume, was ever published. Many believed it would have been a most accomplished and literary work.

Andre Wessels, Professor of History at the University of the Free State at Bloemfontein, writing on Henderson for the *Oxford Dictionary of National Biography*, gives a very fair assessment of his reputation:

> Henderson had rare gifts as a lecturer, historian, and writer, and was also an able staff officer. He had a fascinating and pleasant personality. He has been described as the most scientific British strategist of his time; through his lectures and person he exerted a profound influence on young officers, and in that respect has been compared with Prussia's Helmuth von Moltke…. By influencing Roberts's strategy in South Africa, Henderson helped shape the course of the war. [AW, ODoNB]

It is only fitting that Henderson should have the last word regarding his thoughts on the importance of strategy. As he writes in the "Preface" to his masterpiece

> It is impossible, then, to estimate the ability of any general without considering his strategy. Moreover, in this age of inventions, of rapid movement, and still more rapid communication, the science is more complicated and even more important than heretofore; and it is deserving, therefore, of far closer attention, from both soldiers and civilians, than it has hitherto received. [H, Intro to *Stonewall Jackson*, p.xxii]

Following his death, a number of Old Boys of the Grammar School contributed to the purchase of a fine brass memorial tablet which was placed in the Chapel at Moorland Road, and is now found in the main corridor immediately outside Reception at Alwoodley Gates.

The inscription concludes, 'This Memorial was placed here by his friends and school fellows'. There is a second commemorative brass plaque in the Chaplaincy Centre at the School.

The Henderson family distinguished itself in other ways.

His grandfather, George, was an Admiral in the Royal Navy. His younger brother, Charles (1866-1935), also rose to be an Admiral. He was given command of HMS Crescent in 1907 and ten years later was appointed Captain of the Dockyard and Deputy Superintendent and King's Harbour Master at Rosyth Royal Dockyard.

He was promoted to Rear Admiral on 25 August 1918. He retired the next day and all five Sea Lords voted he be retired on promotion to Flag Rank.

Another brother, Ralph, served with the 96th Regiment of Foot. Ralph's son, Ralph Anstruther, had a distinguished career in the Army, rising to the rank of Brigadier.

Bibliography

Archer, Christon I et al., *World History of Warfare*, Cassell (London: 2003)

Henderson, George Francis Robert, *Stonewall Jackson and the American Civil War*, Longman, Green and Co. (New York and Bombay: 1903)

The *Leodiensian*: The magazine of Leeds Grammar School; December 1891, p.124; February 1894, p.19; October 1898, p.90; February 1900, pp. 16-17; October 1904, p.79;

Riordan, Michael, FSA, Archivist, St John's and the Queen's Colleges, Oxford, email communication dated 15 June 2017

Roberts, Frederick Sleigh (Lord Roberts), "Memoir" to *The Science of War*

Times [date not discovered]

Wessels, André, *Oxford Dictionary of National Biography*, entry on G F R Henderson

John Ireland

9

John Nicholson Ireland FRCM 1879-1962
Composer
At LGS 1893

JOHN NICHOLSON IRELAND was born on 13 August 1879 at 'Inglewood', Bowdon, near Altrincham, Cheshire. His father, Alexander, who was aged 60 at John's birth, was a newspaper proprietor, the business manager and publisher of the *Manchester Examiner* until the newspaper failed in the 1880s. His mother, Annie, 30 years younger than her husband, was a published author and an excellent pianist. John started his piano lessons with her, spending hours in her bedroom where she was often confined as a result of her serious angina. Sadly for him, both parents died when he was relatively young, his mother on 4 October 1893 when John was 14, and his father on 7 December in the following year. He had what the *New Grove Dictionary of Music* describes as an 'unhappy childhood' [Hugh Ottaway, Volume 12 p.568]; he later claimed that he was dominated by his sisters, even punished by them for infant misdeeds, and that this made him uncomfortable in the presence of most women for the remainder of his life. One enduring memory of his childhood as a toddler was the occasion when, on entering the house from the garden, he dropped a handful of daisies into an upturned top hat which he saw in the hall. The top hat belonged to Ralph Waldo Emerson, the American poet best known for his monumental work *Leaves of Grass*.

At the age of seven he was sent to a dame-school in Altrincham and underwent the traditional education involving the three "Rs", enlivened on occasions by visits to the local park for recreation and nature study. Towards the end of his life he was able to recollect those visits and believed them to be the earliest nurturing of his life-long love of nature and landscape. He moved dame-school several times, ending up at Colwyn Bay.

He joined Leeds Grammar School in January 1893. He stayed with a Mr Phillips at 1 Balmoral Terrace, Headingley. There is no record of his achievements at the School, not surprising given his short stay of only two terms. However, already there was evidence of a lonely, introspective side to his personality. It was during this time of his schooling that he made his first public appearance as a pianist, playing Raff's "Cavatina" on the piano of a Harrogate hotel, much to the delight of his appreciative audience. From Leeds Grammar School he went, in September 1893, to the Royal College of Music and the circumstances of his enrolment are almost incredible. He had already confided to his mother that he wished to be a concert pianist and he knew that he must receive the very best tuition that England could offer, and that meant attending the RCM.

It seems extraordinary that he did not tell his parents that he was travelling to London for an audition at the College. He was, at the time, in the habit of going off for a whole day to a local automobile exhibition – he was fascinated by cars - and he used this as a cover for his trip to the RCM, *aged thirteen*, unaccompanied by any adult, in order to be auditioned for a place there. In this he was instantly successful. On returning to Bowdon, his mother was at first shocked at this display of highly uncharacteristic independent assertiveness, but then expressed her approval of his determined ambition.

For the following four years he concentrated his efforts on the piano, studying with Frederic Cliffe, and on the organ with Walter Parratt. He was becoming increasingly attracted to composition and from 1897 he joined Charles Villiers Stanford's (Sir Charles from 1901) classes. Stanford was harsh and demanding towards his pupils and John, being sensitive and prone to feelings of inadequacy, suffered more than his fellow pupils. Stanford was a great fan of Brahms at a time when musical tastes seemed to be polarised between Brahms and Wagner, a situation which had developed on the Continent at the time Bruckner was falling foul of the influential music critic, Edouard Hanslick, himself a Brahms man and who was severely critical of Bruckner's symphonies. Unlike Hanslick, Stanford did not insist that his pupils slavishly follow Brahms, something that Ireland must have found satisfying. In 1895 Ireland became a Fellow of the RCM aged 15, at the time the youngest ever recipient of the honour.

Ireland was continually in straightened financial circumstances whilst at the College, mainly due to the fact that, on the death of his parents, his two guardians, both lawyers (one of which was his uncle, Edmund Kell Blyth), were parsimonious when it came to paying his day-to-day living expenses from his legacy.

They were quite happy to quibble over the slightest matter, even querying the need to purchase two pen nibs rather than one. The situation only eased when,

St Luke's Church, Chelsea

in 1900, he reached the age of twenty-one and could say farewell to his miserly guardians.

When he left the RCM in 1901, he eventually supplemented his income mainly as an organist and choirmaster, first at St Luke's, Chelsea from 1904 to 1926, during which time he began to establish his reputation as an important English composer. From 1920 to 1939, with the title of professor, he taught composition at the RCM and his pupils included Benjamin Britten and Humphrey Searle. He was living at Gunter Grove, Chelsea, in the company of a close circle of friends, whose support was invaluable following a disastrous marriage that ended in divorce after only one year in 1928. The circumstances of this failed union are interesting; he was in the habit of taking on private students and one, in particular, was not making sufficient progress. Dorothy Phillips tearfully explained that her father was cruelly dominant and that she needed to escape from his bullying nature. Rather quixotically, he offered to marry her and so bring about her release from parental torment and this he did on 17 December 1926, he aged 47 and she 30 years younger. Needless to say, it all ended in tears and the marriage – never consummated – was annulled in September 1928. He then entered into a relationship with Helen Perkin to whom he dedicated the *Piano Concerto* of 1930, only to withdraw the dedication when that relationship failed. It is certain that his concerto was influenced by Prokofiev's *Third Piano Concerto* which Perkin performed at the RCM with Malcolm Sargent conducting.

Another friend at the time was Arthur Machen, a writer much given to works of pagan mysticism and whose influence may be detected in some of Ireland's compositions such as *The Forgotten Rite* and especially *Mai-Dun*.

Ireland was influenced by places as much as by friends. Possibly, he was

John Nicholson Ireland – Composer

driven by a need to find the idyllic English pastoral landscape that inspired his and much other contemporary British composition. From Chelsea he resided at Deal, where he rented the top flat of an attractive house called 'Comarques', then a house close to Chanctonbury Ring, an Iron Age Fort above Worthing, Sussex, and overlooking the Findon Valley, and eventually to the Channel Islands, where he chose to retire until the German occupation of 1940. His final years were spent at Rock Mill, Washington, Sussex, in the company of his personal assistant and companion, Mrs Norah Kirkby. Rock Mill was built in 1823 and converted to domestic use in 1919. Ireland moved there in 1953. Although Grade II Listed, the building is now [2021] derelict and close to collapse.

Ireland was not a prolific composer but his published works span a lengthy period of time, from the two string quartets of 1897 to the overture *Satyricon* in 1946. An eclectic variety of influences is discernible. According to Ottaway, 'The solid workmanship insisted on by Stanford provided a lasting foundation: in Ireland's best work a firm structural sense is combined with a deeply personal poetry.' [Ottaway in *Grove*, p.569] His early works were certainly influenced by Brahms, but he soon fell under the sway of more modern composers like Debussy, Ravel and Stravinsky. His later output shrugs off these mentors and, particularly in his piano music, he established a deeply personal, rather English, lyricism.

John Masefield

He came to the attention of the British musical establishment and concert-goers through his chamber music, especially the *Phantasie Trio* of 1906 (third prize in the 1907 Cobbett Competition), and the *Violin Sonata no.1* of 1908-09, which won the Cobbett Prize, coming 1st out of 133 international entries. The Cobbett Prize had been established in 1905 by Walter Willson Cobbett, an industrialist with a passion for chamber music. The *Violin Sonata no.2* of 1915-17, which is a first-class composition, was submitted to a competition organized to assist musicians in wartime. The jury for this included the violinist, Albert Sammons, and the pianist, William Murdoch. They gave the work its premiere performance at the Aeolian Hall, New Bond Street, London, on 6 March 1917. Ireland later recalled that, 'It was probably the first and only occasion when a British composer was lifted from relative obscurity in a single night by a work cast in chamber-music medium'. [quoted from Wikipedia] The sonata was highly acclaimed and the first edition, published by Winthrop Rogers, was sold out even before it had been printed. This was followed by works of equal merit: the *Cello Sonata* of 1923 and the *Fantasy-Sonata for clarinet and piano*, written in 1943. His *Piano Trio no.2* (1917) is the most distinguished example of that format composed by him.

Sir Charles Villiers Stanford

Among his more technically sophisticated works are the shorter pieces for piano, which are either contemplative (*For Remembrance* (1921)) and *Soliloquay* (1922)), Impressionistic (*Amberley Wild Brooks* (1921) and *Le Catioroc* (1940-41)), or sanguine (*Merry Andrew* (1918) and *Ragamuffin* (1917-20)).

The Piano Concerto in E Flat (1930) is regarded by some, including Hugh Ottaway, as a work of great merit. It is 'one of his richest and most rewarding works...a classic of 20th-century English music and its posthumous neglect can only be deplored'. [*Grove*, p.569] Others dismiss it as weak. Ireland dedicated the work to one of his young students, Helen Parkin, herself a pianist and composer, and she gave the premiere performance. Whether or not Ireland was romantically attached to her is not clear, but she subsequently married George Mountford Adie, and as a result, Ireland withdrew the dedication.

The choral work, *These Things Shall Be* (1937), was commissioned by the BBC to mark the coronation of King George VI. It formed part of the programme of music broadcast as a Coronation Concert. It is scored for Baritone Solo, Choir and orchestra and is Ireland's sole substantial choral work. It is a setting of eight verses from "A Vista" by John Addington Symonds and the prevailing sentiment is one of hope that mankind will live in harmony and employ science for the improvement of Nature, sentiments that were given a body blow by events in Europe and the

John Nicholson Ireland – Composer

onset of the Second World War. [from Programme Notes by Stuart Brown] Its style is reminiscent of Parry and Walton:

These things shall be! A loftier race
Than e'er the world hath known, shall rise
With flame of freedom in their souls
And light of science in their eyes.

And the hope is that:

New arts shall bloom in loftier mould,
And mightier music thrill the skies
When every life a song shall be
When all the earth is paradise.

From his childhood, Ireland had been appreciative of the beauty of poetry and many of his compositions betray this deep affection. His setting of John Masefield's "Sea Fever" is very moving, with its anticipation of a long sleep after a busy life:

I must go down to the seas again, to the lonely sea and the sky
And all I ask is a tall ship and a star to steer her by;
And the wheel's kick and the wind's song and the white sail's shaking,
And a grey mist on the sea's face, and a grey dawn breaking.

I must go down to the seas again, for the call of the running tide
Is a wild call and a clear call that may not be denied;
And all I ask is a windy day with the white clouds flying,
And the flung spray and the blown spume, and the sea-gulls crying.

I must go down to the seas again, to the vagrant gypsy life,
To the gull's way and the whale's way where the wind's like a whetted knife
And all I ask is a merry yarn from a laughing fellow-rover
And quiet sleep and a sweet dream when the long trick's over.

His last years were more tranquil. In 1949, to celebrate his 70th birthday, the Piano Concerto was performed at the London Proms, the soloist being Eileen Joyce who had been the first to record the concerto in 1942. In 1953, he retired to Rock Mill in Sussex where he lived for the remainder of his life. It was at Rock Mill that he met and befriended the young pianist, Alan Rowlands, whom Ireland chose to record his complete piano music.

John Ireland died of heart failure at Rock Mill aged 82 and he is buried at the church of St Mary the Virgin in Shipley, West Sussex.

Ireland was, above all, a modest man. Sir Eugene Goossens, who studied under Stanford at the RCM, and who knew Ireland well, wrote that 'a life-long friendship with him has been a rewarding experience. If the humility and artistic sincerity of a modest artist find their best expression in that artist's work then John Ireland's contains the deepest known to me.' [quoted from Norah Kirby, "Appreciation and Biographical Sketch", in Foreman (ed.), p.355]

Bibliography
Brown, Stuart, Programme Notes for the concert including "These Things Shall Be"
Foreman, Lewis (ed.), *The John Ireland Companion*, Boydell & Brewer (Martlesham: 2011)
Longmire, John, *John Ireland: Portrait of a Friend*, J Baker (1969)
Ottaway, Hugh, in *The New Grove Dictionary of Music and Musicians*, Volume 12, (Grove, Macmillan (London: 2002) pp.568-570
Richards, Fiona, *The Music of John Ireland*, Ashgate Publishing (Farnham: 2001)
Searle, Muriel V, *John Ireland: The Man and His Music*, Midas Books (Tunbridge Wells: 1979)
Wikipedia entry on John Ireland

Ernest Bristow Farrar

10

Ernest Bristow Farrar 1885-1918
Composer
At LGS 1895-1903

ERNEST BRISTOW FARRAR was born at Lewisham, London, in 1885. Two years later, his father, a clergyman, moved to Micklefield near Garforth, West Yorkshire. Charles Druce Farrar had been appointed vicar of the Church of St Mary the Virgin there, quite a culture shock because Micklefield was essentially a village of two contrasting halves, a newer mining community adjacent to an older core that contained most amenities like the church, public house and school. The whole community was plunged into mourning and a state of shock as a result of a terrible pit disaster that occurred in April 1896 in which 63 men and boys died out of a total workforce of 300. Ninety children were rendered fatherless and this must have been a difficult time for all concerned.

Ernest's mother was Rose Alice (née Handyside) and she and her husband had three children in total: Ethel Rose, born in 1883; Ernest; and Cecil Francis, born in 1889. Both boys attended Leeds Grammar School: Ernest from 1895-1903 and Cecil from 1898-1906. Cecil was to follow in his father's footsteps and become a clergyman with a reputation for fierce rectitude. Ernest was taught music and organ by Bernard Johnson (music master at LGS from 1892 to1904) and was possibly given coaching lessons by the Leeds city organist, H A Fricker, who was associated with the School. He was, unsurprisingly, appointed organist at his father's church at Micklefield.

Ernest passed his Associateship Diploma of the Royal College of Organists in July 1903 and in the following year became an unattached member of Durham

Ernest Bristow Farrar – Composer

University, a connection which lasted for most of the remainder of his short life. It is likely that he read for a degree in music as an external student. He passed the first examination there in autumn 1904.

In May 1905 he was awarded a scholarship to the Royal College of Music (RCM), where, like John Ireland [q.v.], he studied composition under Sir Charles Villiers Stanford. Farrar, like Ireland, found Stanford to be a hard taskmaster; and, again like Ireland, he studied the organ under Walter Parratt. He won the Arthur Sullivan Prize in 1906 and the Grove Scholarship in 1907. In the same year, 1907, he had published his cantata, *The Blessed Damozel*, which Stanford conducted at a Leeds performance in the following year.

It was at this time, whilst at the RCM, that he became a member of the "Beloved Vagabonds", and this was to have a major influence on Farrar's development as a student of music. In *Frank Bridge: A Life in Brief*, Trevor Bray wrote that a group of musicians and instrumentalists, including James Friskin, Harold Samuel and Ernest Tomlinson

> belonged to an informal club called "The Beloved Vagabonds", founded by Audrey Alston, entrance to which was granted only to *musicians*, not mere performers. The Club meetings were held two or three times a term at a studio in Holland Park and the club members simply performed music for the love of doing so. Between each item there was much talking and friendly discussion, and on occasion, according to the singer, Clive Carey, 'Harold [Samuel] would go to the piano and throw off a brilliant nonsense in improvisation, or the quartet would join him in some exquisite impromptu fooling which seemed to me to be as near as could be to perfection in comedy'. [quoted from Trevor Bray, *Frank Bridge: A Life in Brief* (Internet)]

Membership of this club was to have a profound effect upon Farrar. The word "vagabond" became a favourite of his and he was, later, to compose 'Vagabond Songs for Baritone and Orchestra' in 1913. He even named himself "Vagabond" on the manuscript of his choral setting of Shakespeare's 'It was a lover and his lass' [Bodleian Library], possibly intended as a pseudonym.

Another major influence on his work was the American poet, Walt Whitman, whose epic collection of poems, *Leaves of Grass*, written between 1847 and 1854, was published in 1855. Farrar may well have been attracted to Whitman's poetry in view of its contentious explicit exaltation of the human body and sexual love, as well as its free verse in long rhythmical lines. One of the poems, 'Song of the Open Road', expresses what must have been for Whitman as well as Farrar, a rapturous delight in Nature and freedom:

Afoot and light-hearted I take the open road,
Healthy, free, the world before me,
The long brown path before me leading wherever I choose.
[from "The Open Road"]

In 1909, the year he left the RCM, Farrar wrote his *First Orchestral Rhapsody* 'The Open Road'. How ironic that he was to be led inexorably along the path leading to the First World War and the Somme Valley. A later composition by Farrar, the choral suite *Out of Doors*, owes much to Whitman's spirit of free will and joie de vivre.

The poetry anthology, *The Open Road*, published by E V Lucas in 1899, offers another inspiration for Farrar's compositions. Lucas' anthology was very popular, influential and successful, being reprinted several times. One of its avowed aims was to encourage people to experience the beauty of the English countryside, and possibly watch a game of his beloved cricket. Farrar set a number of his poems to music, including the short poem 'Brittany' which became one of Farrar's better known songs.

Christ Church, Harrogate

Ernest Bristow Farrar – Composer

Whilst at the RCM, Farrar entered into a relationship with the musicologist and violinist Marion Scott, who was nine years older than him. This association continued after he left the College in 1909, having decided to accept the offer of a post as organist at All Saints Anglican Church on Weiner Strasse in Dresden in February. The church was built in 1868-69 to serve the English community living in the city, then a magnet for artists and musicians. He was there for six months and then moved to St Hilda's Church at South Shields to be organist, remaining in post there until 1912. His remuneration was pitifully small, 'less than the caretaker' [RW] and his impecunious position was recognised by none other than Ralph Vaughan Williams, who wrote to him: 'I suppose I must congratulate you on your appointment – I certainly congratulate them – but it's a beastly job being organist and unless one is very careful lowers one's moral tone (not to speak of one's musical [tone] horribly'. [quoted in RW]

There followed a curious incident whereby, despite still ostensibly in a relationship with Marion Scott, Farrar took up with, and became engaged to, Olive Mason, a member of the congregation at St Hilda's. Inexplicably, he did not take the trouble to inform Marion of the change in his circumstances, so that when she travelled to South Shields to perform the incomplete *Celtic Suite for Violin and Piano*, written for her, she discovered for herself the altered situation. She was devastated, played the piece, then left hurriedly and never spoke to Farrar again.

Ralph Vaughan Williams

Farrar married Olive in 1913 and for his best man he chose Ernest Bullock, later to be the organist at Westminster Abbey. Olive was a friend of the author Elinor Brent-Dyer (1894-1969), who was living at South Shields at the time and whose *Chalet* series of books contain many references to the song 'Brittany'.

From South Shields, Farrar moved to Harrogate to be organist at Christ Church, founded in 1749 and built in the austere Early English style. The church was well received by the local press: 'a prominent and beautiful object of admiration from all the surrounding parts of this celebrated watering place'. [The *Leeds Intelligencer*, quoted from the Christ Church Internet site] Farrar was able to display his skills on a new Norman and Beard organ installed as recently as August 1908. Although slightly better off in his new post, he was forced to supplement his meagre income by taking on private pupils, one of whom was Gerald Finzi, who started lessons in 1915 at the age of 13.

Farrar and Finzi became close friends, with Finzi frequently visiting the

Farrars' home at Hollins Road, Harrogate. They attended concerts together and visited Stanford in London with a view to gaining for Finzi a scholarship at the RCM, though in this he was unsuccessful.

Harrogate was enjoying something of a musical renaissance at this time and Farrar became heavily involved. He conducted the Harrogate Orchestral Society and performed with the Municipal Orchestra, then conducted by Julian Clifford, who was happy to premiere some of Farrar's compositions. These included the *Orchestral Rhapsody no.2 'Lavengro'*, the score of which was subsequently lost. Other works given a first performance by Clifford were *The Forsaken Merman* of 1914 and the *Variations on an Old British Sea Song* of 1915. *English Pastoral Impressions* was dedicated to Ralph Vaughan Williams, and a measure of its quality may be ascertained from a report in the admittedly provincial newspaper, the *Leeds Intelligencer*, dated 25 May 1916:

> Included in the programme of the Symphony Concert at the Harrogate Kursaal yesterday afternoon was a new suite, "English Pastoral Impressions" (Op.26), by Mr. Ernest Farrar.... The first movement is lyrical in style, and has for its second subject the old English tune, "Sumer is i-cumen in" which is scored for string quartette, and the 16th century melody of the Angelus is also employed. The second movement is very impressive, and in the last movement a horn call ushers in the principal theme upon which the work is built. The orchestra gave a very artistic interpretation to a suite of great merit and attractiveness, which was loudly applauded by a large audience. Mr. Farrar conducted.

Benjamin Britten uses the same round or rota, 'Sumer is a-cumen in' to introduce his *Spring Symphony*.

Clifford did not hesitate to promote Farrar's music whenever the opportunity arose. Later, Farrar's death moved him deeply and he was keen to perpetuate his memory. An entry in the *Musical Times* of November 1919 recorded: 'A tone-poem, 'Lights Out', by Julian Clifford, was performed under the composer's direction by the Harrogate Municipal Orchestra on September 17. It was written in memory of Ernest Farrar, whose 'Variations in G for Pianoforte and Orchestra on an old British seasong' were also in the programme'. [*Musical Times*, Vol.60, 1 November 1919, p.621]

During this period at Harrogate, Farrar composed a number of smaller-scale works, including a choral part-song *Margaritae Sorori* ('The Late Lark'). For him, this was a happy and fulfilling period in his life but the ominous threat of war was to intervene.

Ernest Bristow Farrar – Composer

The works of EV Lucas provided inspiration for Farrar's compositions – particularly via a shared love of cricket

He enlisted in the Grenadier Guards in 1915 and undertook the usual initial officer training. He was commissioned Second Lieutenant in February 1918. Despite the demands of his military service, he was able to write his last major orchestral piece, the *Heroic Elegy (For Soldiers)*, which he personally conducted in Harrogate whilst on leave. It was to presage his own fate. Called back to France in September, he was attached to the British Fourth Army under General Rawlinson, who was keen to attack the Hindenburg Line. He was killed by machine-gun fire on the first day of the Battle of Epehy Ronssoy on 18 September after only two days at the Front. His grave reference is B.27, Ronssoy Communal Cemetery, France. [John Davies, LGS Roll of Honour]

Stanford, who – like Ralph Vaughan Williams – had considered Farrar to possess the potential to become a great composer, wrote in his obituary of Farrar: '[He] was one of my most loyal and devoted pupils. He was very shy, but full of poetry, and I have always thought very high things of him as a composer, and lamented his loss both personally and artistically.' [*Durham University Journal*, quoted in RW] Again, he wrote that Farrar was to be 'recognised as one of the most promising of the young British composers, and had he lived would have undoubtedly made a great name'. It was Stanford who worked hard to keep Farrar's name in the public mind and he was the driving force behind the publication of many of the organ and vocal works.

Musical tributes to Farrar included Frank Bridge's *Piano Sonata* (1921-24) and

Finzi's *Requiem da Camera* (1923-25). The most important posthumous accolades were the selection of the orchestral *English Pastoral Impressions, Three Spiritual Studies for Strings* and the choral suite *Out of Doors* for the Carnegie Trust awards which led to their publication. Sadly, after Stanford's death, Farrar's work suffered from the general decline in appreciation of Edwardian music and many scores were lost, including the *Orchestral Rhapsody no.2 'Lavengro'*, which went missing when the Harrogate Municipal Orchestra was disbanded in 1930. Oddly enough, the work appears to have been re-discovered. A report in the *Yorkshire Evening Post* of 29 July 1953 refers to a broadcast performance of *Lavengro*:

> An item in last night's radio concert by the B.B.C. Northern Orchestra, conducted by Mr. Maurice Miles, was Lavengro, by the late Ernest Farrar.... This work was first performed at the Royal Hall, Harrogate, in 1913... and this revival, from manuscript, was due to the efforts of Gerald Finzi, the composer, who as a boy studied under Farrar at Harrogate.... Other works by Farrar exist in manuscript and Mr. Finzi and Mr. Miles are interested in possible performances of some of them. Last night's concert revealed Farrar's work, Lavengro, to be a highly sensitive work, the product of an original mind. [*YEP*, 29 July 1953]

That seems to be an appropriate eulogy to a man who, like many of his generation, was cut off in his prime by the horrors of war.

Bibliography

Banfield, Stephen, *Grove Dictionary of Music*, Volume 8, pp. 579-580
Bray, Trevor, *Frank Bridge: A Life in Brief* [internet]
Davies, John G, *Leeds Grammar School Roll of Honour*, Leeds Grammar School (Leeds: nd]
Holmes, Martin, *The Oxford Dictionary of National Biography*
The Leeds Intelligencer 25 May 1916
Weedon, Robert *War Composers – the music of World War 1, A Biography of Ernest Bristow Farrar*, 2013
Yorkshire Evening Post 29 July 1953; article headed "Ernest Farrar"
Whitman, Walt, *Leaves of Grass*, 1855

William Potts, courtesy of Michael S Potts

11

William Potts and Sons Clockmakers

Five members of the Potts family attended Leeds Grammar School: William Edgar (OL06) and his brother Cecil Middleton (OL06), grandsons of William Potts; Robert Gowland (OL03) and Charles Harold (OL06), two further grandsons; and William Anthony (Tony) (OL43), a great grandson of William Potts.

WILLIAM POTTS (1809-87), third son of Robert and Faith Potts, founded the firm of clockmakers, having inherited skills in horology from his father. He left school aged twelve and worked alongside Robert at Keighley until 1830, when he was sent to be an apprentice to Samuel Thompson, a clockmaker at Darlington, at a cost of £40. Three years later William moved to Pudsey and set up in business making and selling domestic clocks. He was helped by his father until the latter's death in 1839.

William Potts (1809-87), third son of Robert and Faith Potts, founded the firm of clockmakers, having inherited skills in horology from his father. He left school aged twelve and worked alongside Robert at Keighley until 1830, when he was sent to be an apprentice to Samuel Thompson, a clockmaker at Darlington, at a cost of £40. Three years later William moved to Pudsey and set up in business making and selling domestic clocks. He was helped by his father until the latter's death in 1839.

William married Elizabeth Banks, who possessed a flair for business, so the pair quickly developed a thriving enterprise with a growing clientele. They prospered to such an extent that they were soon able to move into a fine house in Chapeltown, Pudsey, and in 1847 William won the contract against stiff opposition to install a new clock for Ilkley Parish Church. Before being awarded the commission to carry out the work he was called upon to describe the technical aspects of his proposed design and he so impressed his rather daunting interviewer,

William Potts and Sons – Clockmakers

Edmund Beckett Denison, later Sir Edmund Beckett, a keen amateur horologist who designed the famous Houses of Parliament clock, Big Ben, that the two struck up a friendship and a business association. It is, perhaps, worth pausing for a moment to give due consideration to this clock. Denison was canny enough to encourage the church authorities to sign up to an agreement with Potts to provide a sort of after-sales care package. In a letter to Potts dated 21 September 1847, Edmund wrote:

> I believe a clock made in this way will go as well as it is possible for a turret clock to go, without a compensation pendulum or some other refinements which would be out of place here, provided of course that it is properly looked after; and I have told the people [the church authorities] that they ought to make an agreement with you to look after it, after the end of the first year, for which period you will of course look after it. [quoted from Michael S Potts, pp. 19-20]

The clock mechanism has survived in its original form, though the dial fell out of the tower in 1947 and it may still be found in the grounds of the churchyard just below the tower. The current dial, made of copper, was installed and the original hands re-fitted. Their design is rather different from the usual 'signature' Potts hands, and this may be explained by the fact that Denison, in conjunction with the church authorities, insisted on incorporating the Maltese cross upon the hour hand.

Thereafter, William's reputation grew apace and, with an ever-expanding order book for work in the Leeds area, in 1862 he moved from Pudsey to Leeds, into premises at 13 Guildford Street (later re-named as The Headrow), between the entrance to Butts Court and Green Dragon Yard, close to the Town Hall. The company was employing a score of workers and further expansion took place. In 1865, he won the contract to supply clocks to the Great Northern Railway, the first of many similar appointments. The maintenance and servicing of existing clocks became an important part of the business. Demand for turret and public clocks grew at an astonishing rate with orders coming in from churches, schools, markets and even stable blocks. Perhaps the clock which gave William greatest cause for pride was the one installed at Lincoln Cathedral in 1880. This clock has a plate with the names of William Potts and Edmund Denison inscribed in Latin upon it.

Three of William's four sons joined the company: Thomas (known as Robert) (1842-1917), James (1847-1910) and Joseph (1859-1937), and the company traded as William Potts & Sons. Both Thomas Robert and Joseph sent sons to Leeds Grammar School. The heyday for the company lasted from 1870 to 1900. In part, the business was stimulated by the Golden (1887) and Diamond (1897) Jubilees of Queen Victoria, and the Coronation of Edward VII (1902), with an upsurge in demand for public and turret clocks commemorating all three occasions. Following the installation of the garrison clock at Windsor, the company was awarded a Royal Warrant, the gold badge being awarded to Joseph. This was displayed for many years at the Cookridge Street works.

Many commissions for Potts clocks came from the recommendation of Sir Edmund Beckett, now Lord Grimthorpe, who modestly described himself as 'the greatest authority in the World on clocks and bells'. [quoted from *MSP*, p.153] When, in 1887, William died, his sons moved the manufacture of turret clocks to 19 Cookridge Street, Leeds, the retail shop and other works remaining at Guildford Street.

In the early years of the twentieth century, as demand for public clocks declined, James and Thomas Robert became principal shareholders in their own limited company, retaining the original name, while Joseph (with his son, Cecil Middleton) left to start his business, Joseph Potts & Son, following a disagreement between the brothers. Things got worse when the value of shares in the main company fell and Thomas Robert's son, Thomas Edmund, was dismissed for mismanagement. Eventually, after more acrimonious disputes, William Potts & Sons was sold to John Smith & Sons of Derby in 1934. Charles Harold Potts, another of Thomas Robert's sons, who had left the business in 1930, began trading under his own name for a while. He was more successful, selling clocks world-wide and modernising a number of the ageing Potts clocks, but on his death in 1958, the business was sold to The Synchronome Company Limited and managed for a time by his son, William Anthony (1926-2016), known as Tony. The last clock manufactured by the company was installed in 1962.

SOME FAMOUS POTTS CLOCKS

Leeds Town Hall: There is a persistent belief that William Potts supplied the clock for Leeds Town Hall, but the contract was given to Frederick Dent of London, an unfortunate choice because not only was the clock delivered very late, but it proved to be annoyingly unreliable. As a result, Potts was called in to make the necessary repairs and alterations, in particular on the winding and regulating gear, a process that took a considerable amount of time. Denison, who was called in by members of Leeds Corporation to investigate the problems, wrote to Potts complaining that the architect had rejected the need for iron beams to carry the motion workings of the clock and that such beams could not be retrospectively fitted. Denison made several recommendations, including altering the centre bevel wheels. For over a year, Potts worked on the clock until eventually he managed to correct all the faults, and it is the extent to which parts were replaced and major adjustments were made that may justify the clock being more attributable to Potts rather than to Dent.

William Potts and Sons – Clockmakers

W E Potts (standing third from left) and C H Potts (standing fourth from left) training for World War One, image courtesy of Michael S Potts

Leeds Covered Market Clock: This is certainly the work of William Potts & Sons and its history is fascinating. A tower clock was commissioned in 1904 for the new covered market and certain conditions were laid down by the Leeds councillors. It was to be an hour-striking piece with four dials and it must occupy a commanding position. The market was opened by Gerald Balfour MP and the honour of setting the clock in motion was given to Alderman Knowles on 1 July. However, in 1912, a new entrance to the market was created on Vicar Lane and as a consequence the clock had to be removed and the site chosen for its new home was Oakwood Corner. Over the years it suffered some deterioration, though a little restoration work did take place in 1977. With the help of a public subscription organized by the Oakwood Traders and Residents Association, along with a generous grant from the Heritage Lottery Fund, part of the clock and the tower were tastefully renovated in 2013 and today it may be enjoyed in pristine condition, especially attractive when illuminated at night.

The Arcade Clocks: Three of Leeds' shopping arcades boast a Potts clock: Queen's, Thornton's and the Grand. The Market Street Arcade with its Potts clock was subsequently demolished. The Queen's Arcade, named in honour of Victoria, was built on the site of the Rose and Crown Yard in 1887. The clock was installed in 1890 at the Briggate entrance. It has since been reduced in size and is now electrically operated. Thornton's Arcade was built on the site of the Old Talbot Inn in Briggate by Charles Thornton, the brewer and owner of the Leeds Varieties Music Hall. Its clock boasts a group of wooden figures – Richard the Lionheart, Friar Tuck, Robin Hood and Gurth the Swineherd - created by the Leeds sculptor, John Wormald Appleyard, whose studio was in Cookridge Street close to the Potts factory. It was converted to automatic winding in 1955 by Charles Harold Potts and further restored in 1997. The Grand Arcade clock was installed in 1898, probably at the request of Arthur Greenhow Lupton, the Leeds woollen merchant. He had seen and admired automaton clocks in Germany and the Potts firm took great delight in creating two copper bronze knights in armour to strike the quarter hours, while on the hour five figures emerge, including a guardsman and a kilted Scot.

Leeds Grammar School: not quite so famous but remembered with affection by many Old Leodiensians, this clock was commissioned in 1889 at a cost of £100 and is hour-striking with two prominent dials. As James Marshall, author of *Floreat per Saecula, A History of Leeds Grammar School* writes,

The Potts clock at Oakwood

The tower [on which the clock was placed] ceased to be used for ventilation purposes, the ventilation pipes connecting the rooms to the tower were ripped out, and the clock weights and mechanisms were placed there instead, in one central shaft. On the outside, two clock-faces were attached, on the north-east and south-west sides of the tower, and were painted green…. Later, the dial was painted white with the hands black, which made it far easier to read. [JWDM, p.35]

A C Price, a senior master at the School, ruefully commented in his *History of Leeds Grammar School*, 'The placing of the clock in the tower in 1889 may seem a small thing but it was a great blessing to the school; its value would have been still greater if two other faces had been added and the dial had been white with the hands black.' [ACP, p.253]

Anyone wishing to view the finest examples of Potts clocks in Leeds city centre should pick up a copy of Leeds City Council's *Potts Clocks Heritage Trail* leaflet (available now as a pdf file) which gives a brief history of the firm and then provides an easy walking route.

Bibliography

Dyson, Peter & Grady, Kevin, *Blue Plaques of Leeds*, Leeds Civic Trust (Leeds: 2001)
Marshall, James W D, *Floreat per Saecula, From Age to Age Excel, A History of Leeds Grammar School*, Smith Settle (Otley: 1997)
Potts, Michael S, *Potts of Leeds: Five Generations of Clockmakers*, Mayfield Books (Ashbourne: 2006)
Price, A C, *A History of Leeds Grammar School*, Richard Jackson (Leeds: 1919)
Wade, Stephen, *Heroes, Villains & Victims of Leeds*, Breedon Books (Stoke on Trent: 2007)

THE POTTS FAMILY at Leeds Grammar School

William Edgar Potts MM: He was born on 4 November 1890, the son of Joseph Potts and Sarah Anna Burton (née Middleton) of 21 Regent Park Terrace, Headingley. William attended Leeds Modern School for a time before entering Leeds Grammar School in 1903 and leaving in 1906. He later moved to 26 Estcourt Avenue, Headingley. In 1909 he joined the West Yorkshire Regiment (Leeds Rifles). He then emigrated to Canada in April 1913 and by August 1914 was farming in Alberta and serving in the Alberta Hussars. In January 1915 he returned to England when he heard that the Alberta Hussars were not destined to participate in WW1. He served with the British Army in the First World War, initially as a Private with the 2nd/8th Battalion (Leeds Rifles TA) and was awarded the Military Medal in 1917 while with them. The citation read, 'He successfully held a forward outpost against heavy shelling and continuous attacks by the enemy'. [JGD, *A High Ideal*, p.117]. Soon after, he was promoted to Sergeant. The citation in the regimental war diary stated

> On the morning of February 19, 1917, in front of Beaucourt Trench, this NCO was in charge of an advance post which was attacked by the enemy which, however, he successfully defended with the loss of the raiders. Throughout the whole incident he showed great coolness, judgement and initiative and so saved the situation. [MSP, correspondence by email to *YEP* 13 April 2018]; [also entry in the Genealogists' Magazine, p.460 submitted by Michael S Potts.]

Then, in January 1918, he returned to England to be married to Winifred Middleton on 27 March 1918. After receiving officer training, he returned to France in April 1918 as a Second Lieutenant with the 5th West Yorkshire Regiment attached to the 15th Battalion (Leeds Pals). He was present at the Lys offensive (Operation Georgette) on the Western Front and it was in this capacity that he was killed in action. His entry in the School's Roll of Honour reads,

> William Edgar Potts, 2nd Lieutenant 5th Battalion, attached 15th Battalion West Yorkshire Regiment. He was killed in action on 13th April 1918, aged 27. He was awarded the Military Medal. He was the son of Joseph and Sarah Anna Burton Potts of 9 Estcourt Avenue, Headingley, Leeds and the husband of Winifred Middleton [who subsequently in 1923 married Arthur Scipio Mussabini] of 20 Merton Avenue, Chiswick, London. Grave reference: Ploegsteert Memorial, Comines-Warneton, Hainaut, Belgium.

The circumstances of his death suggest that he was a very brave soldier, determined to do his duty. He led his platoon into action against a heavy German attack and at a critical moment, whilst operating a Lewis gun, he was killed by an enemy shell. He has no known grave. He is remembered on the Leeds Rifles memorial in St Peter's Church and on the Headingley War memorial in addition to the Leeds Modern School Roll of Honour.

Cecil Middleton Potts: the brother of William Edgar. He was born on 17 September 1894 and attended Leeds Grammar School from 1904 to 1906. It is assumed he left the School early because he contracted scarlet fever. His father, Joseph, left the family firm in 1906 after a disagreement with Robert and James Potts, who bought out his interest for £7000. Subsequently, Joseph set up in business with his son Cecil as Joseph Potts & Son. After Joseph died in 1937, Cecil continued with the firm until he joined his cousin's company, Charles H Potts & Co. Ltd in 1943. In 1956, Cecil was appointed a director and oversaw the production of the last clock to be manufactured by the Potts family and installed at Shincliffe Parish Church, near Durham, in 1962.

Robert Gowland Potts: the brother of Charles Harold, who also attended the School. His parents were Thomas Robert Potts and Jane (née Clarke). He was born in 1886 and was at the School from 1897 to 1903. He chose not to join the clock making firm in a hands-on capacity but instead became a Chemist, initially with Mr Overend on Harehills Road. He would later become a Dispensing Chemist at Stonegate Avenue, Meanwood.

Like William Edgar, he saw service with the Army during the First World

William Potts and Sons – Clockmakers

War. He joined the 15th Battalion of the West Yorkshire Regiment (Leeds Pals) and was quickly promoted to Corporal. Shortly afterwards, he was commissioned as Second Lieutenant into the 3rd Battalion, the Yorkshire & Lancashire Regiment. He married Elsie Lake, who was appointed Company Secretary of William Potts & Sons Ltd in 1924, and he acted as a manufacturer's agent for the firm whilst continuing to build up his own business as a Chemist. He died on 15 February 1959.

Charles Harold Potts: of the five Potts offspring who attended the School, Charles Harold was certainly the most involved in the business set up by his grandfather, William. The brother of Robert Gowland, he was born on 30 June 1889 and was at Leeds Grammar School from 1903 to 1906. He joined William Potts & Sons Ltd in 1907, aged 18, in the small clock-making department and was not required to serve any sort of apprenticeship. He later confided to his son, Tony, that he was required to produce domestic clocks for stock as sales were disappointing. As he settled into the firm, he began to think strategically about the future of public clock sales and came to the conclusion that it would benefit all turret clock manufacturers if they were to form an association and so keep prices at a financially viable level. In this, he was unsuccessful, so during the early years of the First World War, he floated the idea that the company could diversify into the munitions market, but in this he was opposed by his father, Thomas Robert. He joined the Royal Garrison

The Potts clock in Thonton's Arcade

Artillery and survived the War, returning to Leeds in 1919. He lived at 3 Grosvenor Mount, Headingley, and married Evelyne Cork at St Michael's Church, Headingley, on 21 July 1921.

He very quickly saw that the firm was not being run efficiently and put the blame firmly on his elder brother, Thomas Edmund, who had also served in the Armed Forces during the War. The problem was the very same one he had previously identified: that prices were set too low and profit margins were negligible. He took on the task of travelling around the country promoting the Company's reputation, was appointed Company Secretary in 1923 and then made a Director in the following year. However, further fractious infighting eventually forced him to resign from the Company on 1 April 1930 and he traded under his own name until forming his own business, Charles H Potts & Co. Ltd. in 1933, specialising in turret clocks. Sadly, this meant that two Potts companies were now competing with each other, producing identical clocks. He gradually built up a thriving business restoring, reconstructing and servicing older clocks, modernising the mechanisms by converting to electrical motors and auto-wind systems, one example being the clock in the Grand Arcade in Leeds. In 1943, he was joined by Cecil Middleton Potts, who specialised in the small clock department. The 1950s saw a dramatic increase in orders, especially from abroad. Charles became ill in 1957 and died a year later, having handed over control to his son, William Anthony (Tony).

William Anthony (Tony) Potts: the son of Charles Harold and Evelyne Cork, he was born on 21 March 1926 and attended Headingley Kindergarten before entering Leeds Grammar School in 1934, joining Form JI. By this time, the family had moved to 46 Spennithorne Avenue, Spen Lane, West Park. He remained at the School until 1943, leaving from Form Classical VI, having passed his Northern Universities Joint Matriculation Board School Certificate and Higher School Certificate. The School was pretty impressed with him: his report included the comments 'A good sound fellow' and 'Very good in the House'. He joined the Junior Training Corps, forerunner of the Combined Cadet Force, played for the Second XV and represented the School Swimming Team.

During the Second World War, he served with the Royal Electrical and Mechanical Engineers (REME) and, later, the Royal Army Education Corps (RAEC), before joining Charles H Potts & Co. Ltd, succeeding his father as MD in 1957. When the Company was taken over by the Synchronome Co. Ltd in 1958, Tony was appointed Manager of the Leeds branch, but in 1961 he resigned, aged 35, and took up a post as Lecturer at East Ham Technical College, living at 54 Elmfield Road, North Chingford, London in 1969. He remained in further education for the remainder of his working life. He died on 2 July 2016.

Bibliography
Davies, John G, *A High Ideal. Leeds Grammar School and the Great War*, The Old Leodiensian Association (Croft Publications) (Boroughbridge: 2015)
Davies, John G, *Leeds Grammar School: Roll of Honour* (Leeds: undated)
Leodiensian magazine, various volumes
Potts, Michael S, letter by email to the *Yorkshire Evening Post* dated 13 April 2018
Potts, Michael S, entry under the heading 'They shall not grow old…' in *Genealogists' Magazine*, p.460
Potts, Michael S, *Potts of Leeds: Five Generations of Clockmakers*, Mayfield Books (Ashbourne: 2006)

Geoffrey Kennedy

12

Geoffrey Anketell Studdert Kennedy MC 1883-1929
Clergyman: Vicar and Royal Chaplain; Army Padre; Pugilist; Poet
At LGS 1898-1901

GEOFFREY ANKETELL STUDDERT KENNEDY was the living embodiment of Christ's instruction to give all to the poor. He was capable, quite literally, of giving the coat off his back – on another occasion giving up his bed – to those parishioners who were destitute, much to the alarm of his wife and friends. But he is best known for his scintillating, riveting oratory through which he could engage the attention and sympathy of soldiers preparing to go over the top in the First World War. He was a man suffused with love for his Christ and for his audience and that love drove him remorselessly to his early death.

He was born on 27 June 1883 in the vicarage at St Mary's, Quarry Hill, Leeds, then an area of slum housing and desperate poverty. The church was one of three built and consecrated between 1826 and 1827 using funds from the First Parliamentary Grant set up under the Church Building Act of 1818. The cost of building, £10,809, was provided by the fund and two other Leeds churches benefited in the same way, Christ Church and St Mark's. The seating capacity of St Mary's was huge – 1207, most of them free, that is, reserved for the poor. [HWD, pp. 90-91] Geoffrey's father, William, served a congregation that included a large number who simply could not manage on their paltry incomes and who, in many cases, were to end up in the Poor House. His church was rarely filled with worshippers, hardly surprising given its huge capacity, but those he attracted stayed loyal to him. His deep affection for the poor and needy was passed on to Geoffrey at an early age.

Geoffrey Anketell Studdert Kennedy – Clergyman, Padre, Pugilist and Poet

William married twice and his two wives produced 14 children between them. This was a large family even by Victorian standards. Geoffrey's siblings were later to write that, even at a very early age, he exhibited a gentle, loving and forgiving nature. His brother later wrote, 'Mother always said he was the best baby she ever had. When he was about two years old (or less), a storm one night blew down a chimney, and some bricks fell through the ceiling close to his cot. I remember him being carried down into the nursery – and his chubby face one big smile.' [JKM, p.13] Later, he especially loved the countryside around Leeds, enjoying bicycle excursions into Wharfedale. He was an avid reader, a habit inculcated into him by his mother, Joan, and he immersed himself in diverse literature. His sister, Rachel, recollected, 'He was always very fond of reading, and even before he could read himself would sit still as long as anyone would read to him'. [JKM, pp.14-15] Perhaps as a consequence of this he was also very absent-minded, easily forgetting to carry out quite important duties. Much later, in his capacity as vicar, he was known to forget he was engaged to carry out a funeral service.

He started his formal education aged nine at Mr Knightley's private school where he was coached for entrance to Leeds Grammar School and to Trinity College, Dublin. He joined the Grammar School at a time when the Headmaster, John Henry Dudley Matthews, was improving the curriculum and facilities and, as a consequence, increasing the number of pupils. When Geoffrey joined in 1898 the school roll was 161. He quickly settled in, despite the fact that he frequently went to Dublin to engage in the curriculum there, and joined a number of extra-curricular activities, notably boxing and the Literary and Debating Society. One of his contemporaries later wrote that Geoffrey was, 'a very valuable member of the school, a fellow with a really good brain, a hardworking and intelligent Rugger forward with plenty of strength and grit, and a good long distance runner'. [quoted from JKM, pp. 22-23] His best friend at school, J K Mozley, himself later to become a distinguished theologian and scholar, remembered a debate on the motion "That England has mainly herself to thank for her unpopularity abroad": 'He [Geoffrey] made an excellent speech, which again took the debate out of the domain of hard fact to the region of abstract ideas'. His biographer, William Purcell, speaking of Studdert Kennedy the impassioned clergyman, adds, 'He could never be ignored, as the words poured from him and the eyes glowed and the Irish voice went on. It is true that he became dangerously adept at playing upon crowds as on an instrument'. [WP, pp.32-33]

Is it possible to trace Studdert Kennedy's later oratorical skills as a Padre back to his involvement in the school's Literary and Debating Society? He appears to have been gifted with an unusual fluency of expression coupled with a fervour and intensity that captivated his audience. That he was capable of eliciting fear or awe in others due to the passion he sometimes evinced is evident from the reaction of the Secretary of the Society who, when he learned that Geoffrey was to be joined as a member by his brother, promptly threatened to resign! Geoffrey was not afraid to tackle contentious subjects like Irish nationalism; on 5 February 1901 he read a paper on *Irish Peasant Life* in which he stated that 'although he did not defend the action of tenants in promptly dispatching landlords whose demands for rent were too pressing, yet, considering the Irish character, he wondered there were not more proceedings of that nature'. [JKM, p.26] Here, perhaps, are the seeds of a restless mind conjuring up disputatious views and expressing them with a dynamic, forthright and unassailable certainty.

Regarding his school career in a more general sense, Mozley added:

> Leeds Grammar School meant a great deal to Geoffrey. He worked hard and he played hard and entered fully and gladly into the school's corporate life. It would not be true to say that he made many close friends, but it was always natural for him to like and admire people, just as I think it has always been impossible for anyone who has come to know him at all well not to like and admire him. To his school contemporaries he was always probably a bit of a wild Irishman but I think that those of us who knew him best realized something of the intellectual ability which lay behind his oddities. And from quite an early stage in my friendship with him I was struck with the fineness of his character. [JKM, p17]

Purcell, in his biography of Studdert Kennedy, *Woodbine Willie*, notes that, 'Geoffrey was happy at [LGS] and it says a good deal for the civilised nature of the place that his almost theatrical Irishness caused little friction'. [WP, p.30]

Alfred Thompson, Captain of Rugby at LGS from 1900-1902, and later Vicar of Holy Trinity, Wimbledon, recalls a Classics lesson in which Geoffrey was translating Socrates' *Apology*:

> Kennedy was translating. There are some rather long sentences in Socrates' speeches which, if not broken up, seem rather involved. Kennedy, without taking any liberties with the Greek, rolled out sentence after sentence of perfect English. The master, the excellence of whose degree was not at that time equalled by practical good sense,

said: "That's a very good translation, Kennedy. Are you using a crib?" I was sitting next to Kennedy and I feared an explosion. It was interesting to see the look of fury on his face, and to hear his indignant protest. Both however gave way to his sense of humour, and a general laugh closed the situation so far as we were concerned. [quoted from JKM, p.22]

A C Price, Senior Master from 1918-1919, wrote affectionately of Studdert Kennedy:

Whatever L.G.S. may have done for him, Kennedy's real development was later, and at school he scarcely stood out from the ranks of his contemporaries. My memory of him is of a singularly good-tempered boy with an Irish brogue, a roguish twinkle in his eye, and a pleasant smile, who gave no trouble to his master, and never got into hot water, but was liked both by masters and boys; interested in all the School life, both in work and games, but without (I think) any conspicuous distinction in either. I seem to remember – but I may be mistaken – that when he came to me he had considerable ground to make up in work, and I certainly remember thinking it a pity that he was bent on going to Dublin as I fancied he might have got a scholarship or exhibition at Oxford or Cambridge, though whether he would have distinguished himself in the schools is doubtful. [Source not known but quoted from Mozley, pp. 18-19]

In his last year he entered the Headmaster's poetry prize competition and showed the poem to Mozley, who considered it had merit; he did not win the prize but perhaps it was a harbinger of those *Rough Rhymes* that later earned him fame. Mozley recalls that he was an all-too-frequent visitor to the St Mary's Vicarage, engaging in fervent, even febrile, discussions on such arcane matters as the nature of God as well as subjecting the Gospels to intense intellectual scrutiny. Again, there is evidence here of the nurturing of that passionate advocacy of God's unremitting love for mankind that formed the basis of his sermons and lectures during and after the Great War.

At the end of 1901, he left the Grammar School and entered Trinity College, Dublin, for which he had been carefully prepared as an external student, having passed his first year examinations at that institution whilst in his final year at Leeds Grammar. He was eventually awarded a first class degree in classics and divinity.

From Trinity College he went to Calday Grange Grammar School at West Kirby in Cheshire. He taught general subjects there for two and a half years. Away

Trinity College Dublin (Arcadia Study Abroad)

from the academic curriculum, he took games and coached boxing. His schoolmaster duties permitted him time to engage in a great deal of wide reading, in particular psychology, especially Havelock Ellis and Sigmund Freud. He had maintained contact with Mozley, who went up to Pembroke College, Cambridge, and eventually became a Fellow there, and they continued their discussions. Mozley was convinced that Geoffrey was destined for the Church and this turned out to be the case.

The Anglican Church at that time was going through a troubled period, especially regarding the alienation of the working class, who saw the Bishops and clergy as remote figures catering to the needs of the upper and middle classes. At the same time, the number of capable entrants into the ministry was falling alarmingly for a number of reasons and not solely because of growing doctrinal doubts. For Geoffrey, these considerations counted for nothing: he was perfectly at ease with the essential message of the Gospels.

Accordingly, he entered the Ripon Clergy College, then very much at the forefront of training clergy to minister to the working class. Its founder, William Boyd Carpenter, a gifted orator of immense talent, was particularly keen to develop the speaking abilities of would-be priests. He saw in Geoffrey just what he was looking for: 'Here was something different; here was something, in this Irish voice, this intensity of real power. One thing, however, was clear: the man was unique, could be fitted into no mould. As regards instruction in the art of preaching, Studdert Kennedy, in fact, was best left alone to develop in his own way.' [quoted in BH, p.18, taken from WP, p.46] As part of the course, he was tasked with taking the service in a neighbouring mission church and a fellow student, who witnessed Geoffrey preaching, recalled that 'he seemed to be able to forget himself, the place and the clock; and to make the congregation of tired children and women on a hot afternoon do the same, as both were jointly carried away'. [WP, p.47] He completed the one year course and in 1908 was ordained Deacon in Worcester Cathedral and then sent to work in Rugby. He was assigned to St Andrew's, then an admirable parish church, and was taken in hand by the Rector of Rugby, A V Baillie. His opinion of Studdert Kennedy is interesting: 'K was one of the strangest characters I ever knew. An Irishman, with brains, he had infinite charm, complete devotion to his work, and a fine sense of humour. But mentally he was incredibly undisciplined.' [WP, p.57]

Rugby had more than its fair share of social problems and poverty. The Poor House was full and there was rampant unemployment. But for Geoffrey, these challenges were welcome. He was happy to concentrate on helping the poorest in the community, and was at ease working in the slums. He would happily give out money from his own pocket and even the clothes off his back. He would walk into the mean public houses and stand at the bar to sing "Nazareth", and many of the hardened men there learned to love him because they knew he loved them. He set up a children's club in an abandoned Nonconformist chapel and soon had between 200 and 300 youngsters attending to sing songs and chant prayers. At the same time he took services in Holy Trinity Church, upsetting some of the regular worshippers but attracting many more newcomers. Baillie was so impressed with him he recommended Geoffrey for the priesthood. Geoffrey was ordained as priest on 29 May 1910 in the Collegiate Church of St Michael, Coventry, by the Bishop of Worcester.

He returned to St Mary's, Leeds, which in 1910 was a very different church. The area around it had changed in character: many of the older folk had died off and there was a strong influx of Jews, mainly from what were to become the Baltic States, who naturally shunned the Christian churches. William Anketell Kennedy was still Vicar and his son, Geoffrey's brother, Cecil, was curate under him. Cecil turned to the Christian Scientists and joined them so Geoffrey was parachuted in to replace him. He continued to work among the poor as he had always done and he stayed at Leeds until the death of his father in 1914. On several occasions he visited the School or preached in the School Chapel. The local congregation requested that Geoffrey be allowed to replace his father but the church authorities refused. By this time, Geoffrey had fallen in love with and married Emily Catlow. It was time to move on.

So he went to St Paul's, Worcester, which held a great attraction for him: 'St Paul's has the smallest income and the poorest people – go and look at the house and, if you think you can manage it, I will accept,' he said to his new wife. So she looked, and he accepted the post with a £300 a year salary and a parish of over 4,000 people, mostly living in abject poverty. He was installed on 9 June 1914, shortly before the cataclysmic event that changed most lives forever.

He immediately made a stunning impression on the congregation – and added considerably to its numbers – solely on the strength of his dynamic preaching. Scores waited behind after the service had ended to speak with him. He turned none away. Whatever their problems, drugs, alcohol, poverty or promiscuity, he counselled them. He was suffused with love and understanding. He would visit the sick, give money to the penniless and bury those who had given up the struggle. It was here at St Paul's that he even gave the marital bed away to a destitute parishioner.

With the outbreak of war, Studdert Kennedy threw off any doubts and came down wholeheartedly on the side of military intervention against Germany. He immediately applied to enlist as an Army Chaplain but had to wait until his replacement at Worcester could be found. In the meantime he was encouraged to preach to the hundreds of volunteers at Norton Barracks, home to the Worcester Regiment. The Dean of Worcester, William Moore Ede, recalled, 'Each time he [Geoffrey] went into the pulpit and spoke to those two thousand unwilling listeners, he held them spellbound – not a cough, no shuffling of feet. What he said became the main topic of conversation during the ensuing week.' [quoted in BH, p.31]

He was appointed Chaplain on 21 December 1915 and on Christmas Day he was preaching to 400 soldiers in the pouring rain in a village square in France. A few days later he was posted to Rouen where he preached in a large shed that had been converted into a canteen. These were men who were to be despatched by train to the Front the following day. He listened to their problems, cautioned them against using the local brothels and helped them to write home to their loved ones and families. He saw them off at the railway siding, walking along the platform handing out New Testaments with one hand and Woodbine cigarettes with the other. He wrote, 'God only knows the hardships men endure on these journeys in packed and dirty carriages. No place to wash, no place to move, they sit and wait for eighteen hours or more until, I suppose, they hear far off the sound of guns and know that the end is near...' [quoted in WP, p.107]

He was posted to the Front immediately prior to the opening of the Battle of the Somme. He attached himself to soldiers carrying out a multiplicity of duties: marching, digging trenches and tunnels, cleaning kit, guard duty and inspections. When they did go over the top he went with them, always with his abundant supply of Woodbines, giving comfort to the dying or helping carry the injured back to the lines. When the fighting ceased, no matter how fatigued he was, he would call in at the makeshift hospital and hold men down who were undergoing amputations without anaesthetic. Even then, before collapsing into his bed, he would write letters home to families who were to know the ultimate grief of losing a husband, brother or lover. He quickly became proud of his nick-name. In fact, many soldiers knew him only as Woodbine Willie and were unaware of his real name. On one occasion, an officer was searching for him and approached a sentry:

"Has Captain Kennedy gone along?"
"No, sir."
"Have you seen the Chaplain, then?"
"No, sir."
"Have you seen the padre this way?"
"No, sir."
"Look," said the officer, "have you seen Woodbine Willie lately?"
"Yes, sir: just gone by." [quoted from WP, p.115]

Exposed daily to unremitting horrors at the Front, Studdert Kennedy found his attitude to the war had changed. For him it was a dreadful waste:

Waste of Blood, and waste of Tears
Waste of youth's most precious years,
Waste of ways the Saints have trod
Waste of Glory, Waste of God –
War!

Later, he was to write, 'War is only glorious when you buy it in the *Daily Mail* and enjoy it at the breakfast table. It goes splendidly with bacon and eggs. Real war is the final limit of damnable brutality, and that's all there is in it.' [GSK, "Glory of War" in *The Hardest Part* (1918)]

For him the war caused a re-evaluation of his own personal creed and he said to D F Carey, his senior chaplain, 'You know, this business has made me less cocksure of much of which I was cocksure before. On two points I am certain: Christ and his Sacrament. Apart from that I am not certain of anything.' [WP, p.113]

His *modus operandi* was quite simple. As he said to T B Hardy*, a chaplain on his first posting at Étaples:

Live with the men; go everywhere they go. Make up your mind you will share all their risks, and more if you can do any good. The [front] line is the key to the whole business. Work in the very front, and they will listen to you; but if you stay behind, you're wasting your time. Men will forgive you anything but lack of courage and devotion. [quoted from WP, p.118]

It was during the Battle of Messines Ridge in June 1917 that Studdert Kennedy won his MC. During an engagement, when he was assisting at a Dressing Station close to the fighting, the supply of morphine had run out and he volunteered to fetch fresh supplies from another Station. Despite heavy shelling and murderous machine-gun fire, he ran in a series of short bursts from shell hole to shell hole, collected more morphine, and returned safely. Having handed over the morphine he then volunteered to go into the fighting zone to bring in three seriously wounded soldiers one of whom was blown to pieces in the process. As the official citation stated, the award was

> For conspicuous gallantry and devotion to duty. He showed the greatest courage and disregard for his own safety in attending to the wounded under heavy fire. He searched shell holes for our own, and enemy wounded, assisting them to the Dressing Station, and his cheerfulness and endurance had a splendid effect upon all ranks in the front line trenches, which he constantly visited. [quoted in BH, p. 63]

One criticism levelled against him by the political establishment in these latter stages of the war was that he failed to adhere to the "conspiracy of silence" that had prevailed, by means of which the truth about trench warfare was being withheld from the public at large. To some extent this was aided and abetted by combatants themselves, most of who simply would not talk about their dreadful experiences. Studdert Kennedy in his letters home did describe the horrors that he witnessed daily, including gassing, from which he himself suffered and which almost certainly exacerbated his asthma.

It was through his writing that his fame began to spread more widely. Both during and after the war he had been inspired to write poetry and the result was *Rough Rhymes of a Padre* (1918). This collection of 30 poems, written between 1916 and 1918, is written in the language of the ordinary soldier, reflecting their thoughts, judgements, doubts and hopes. An excerpt from "A Sermon in a Billet" captures the flavour of these rhymes:

> *Ye remember old Billy Buggins, the sargint what lost his stripes,*
> *Well, 'e were a bloomin' 'ero, a daisy to scrap but cripes,*
> *That man was a blinkin' mixture o' all that were good and bad,*
> *'E broke 'is poor ole Mother's 'eart , the best friend ever 'e 'ad.*
> *But 'e died to save a pal at Loos, an' that were the other side,*
> *'E killed 'is Mother an' saved his pal, - that's 'ow he lived an' died.*

Geoffrey Anketell Studdert Kennedy – Clergyman, Padre, Pugilist and Poet

Military Cross (Gov.UK)

Literary purists will condemn his poetry as flawed and superficial but it was very popular with the fighting men and it sold well after publication in 1918. By 1922 over 400,000 copies of *Rough Rhymes* had been sold. Studdert Kennedy had clearly taken his style from Rudyard Kipling and refined it to suit the particular conditions of the Great War. That he could express himself in much more beautiful language is evidenced by his sermons and by some of his later poems in *War Rhymes*.

By the time he was demobbed in 1919 he, like the Ancient Mariner, was a sadder and wiser man. He did enjoy life as a family man at Worcester and continued his undifferentiated generosity to those for whom the war brought no relief from poverty. He noted the number of war widows and ex-soldiers horribly maimed and unable to work. This was no "land fit for heroes". There was no denying the nation-wide feeling of disillusionment and disenchantment. The Church made some attempt to reach out to the working class and initiated the National Mission for Repentance but effectively there was no religious revival.

But life was about to change for him if not for the church in general. His fame as Woodbine Willie grew rather than faltered after the War's conclusion. Moreover, he was invited by King George V to become a Royal Chaplain. As his fame and reputation spread, so the demand grew for him to preach and talk all over the world and one of his main themes was the futility and madness of war and this struck a chord with his audiences. He spoke scathingly of the vindictive nature of the Paris Peace Conference and with great prescience forecast another war. Mostly, however, he kept his distance from politics in general and the Labour Party in particular, again predicting accurately an era of social confrontation when he, perhaps unrealistically, wanted redemption and harmony through Christ. He wrote a number of books which developed his beliefs and hopes, each selling well and going into several reprints.

By September 1921 he had left St Paul's, Worcester and became the main messenger – or speaker – for the Industrial Christian Fellowship, an organization very much in sympathy with Studdert Kennedy's hopes for a consensus in Britain rather than a smouldering class war. It did argue for a fairer distribution of resources and wealth in a country where the gap between rich and poor was glaringly obvious. ICF missionaries visited the industrial centres throughout Britain; their aim was 'to present the Christian religion to the people of a town or district as a solution of the problems of modern social life as they see and experience it'. [BH, p.116] Studdert Kennedy toured the country with careless disregard for his increasingly fragile health. He visited, by invitation, the United States and Canada, but had to refuse requests from Australia and South Africa because he wanted to focus his energies on his mission to Britain.

His health finally began to fail, especially with the onset of the 'flu epidemic of 1929. He travelled to Liverpool with the intention of giving a series of Lenten lectures at the Parish Church. He arrived at St Catherine's vicarage and set about preparing his talks, but he felt so ill he had to retire to bed. Pneumonia was diagnosed; his wife, Emily, was called to be with him; and he died at 01.30 on 8 March 1929 aged only forty-five. His coffin rested in St Catherine's Church. The funeral took place at St Paul's, Worcester, with his brother, William, and J K Mozley officiating. Thousands turned out to pay their respects, not only in Worcester but around the country wherever he had preached. William Purcell, his biographer, commented, 'One thing became immediately apparent. Geoffrey had been a national figure to a degree which would probably have astonished him more than anyone else." [BH, p.141]

Perhaps, though, the most touching gesture, one that surely would have pleased Geoffrey more than anything else, was that, while his coffin was lying at Liverpool, some of the ex-soldiers who had been with him in the trenches placed packets of Woodbines on it in affectionate remembrance of 'our fallen comrade'.

* Three Army chaplains received the Victoria Cross in World War One but the only one to receive in addition the MC and DSO was Theodore Bayley Hardy who met Studdert Kennedy at Étaples in 1916. He was wounded crossing a plank bridge over the River Selle on 11 October 1918 and died a week later.

Bibliography
Dalton, Harry W, *Anglican Resurgence under W. F. Hook in Early Victorian Leeds*, The Thoresby Society (Leeds: 2002)
Grundy, Michael, *A Fiery Glow in the Darkness*, Osborne Books (Wokingham: 1997)
Holman, Bob, *Woodbine Willie. An Unsung Hero of World War One*, Lion Hudson (Oxford: 2013)
Mozley, John Kenneth et al, *G A Studdert Kennedy by his Friends,* Hodder & Stoughton (London: 1929)
Purcell, William, *Woodbine Willie*, Hodder & Stoughton (London: 1962)

Bishop A M Hollis

13

Arthur Michael Hollis 1899-1986
Anglican Bishop of Madras and Ecumenical Leader
At LGS 1910-1917

ARTHUR MICHAEL HOLLIS, the eldest of the four Hollis siblings, was born on 23 June 1899, and named after St Michael's Home in Axbridge, 'an old folks' home, founded – I do not know exactly how – by some Anglican charity'. [CH, *TSA*, p. 1] where his father attended to the spiritual needs of its clientele. On the family moving to Leeds, he was entered into the Leeds Grammar School Junior School at an early age. He travelled across town from Armley to Woodhouse on the electric tram. He clearly settled down to his studies and became engaged in a number of extra-curricular activities. These included Captain of Barry House, playing for the Rugby 1st XV, Captain of Running, a member of the Cricket 1st and 2nd XI and Hon. Secretary of the Literary and Debating Society. One of the motions to which he contributed was that a tunnel be constructed connecting England with France. He became Editor of the school magazine as well as a Sergeant in the Officer Training Corps.

Of all these activities, he was most successful in Running. On 20 January 1916 he won the Senior Paperchase, a competition whereby "hares" took the lead and "hounds" followed over a cross-country course of varying length. On 17 February, he and Guy Russell Willans (who was to die at the Front on 29 March 1918) acted as "hares", laying a trail that was made difficult by strong winds. On 24 February, he was placed in charge of the junior competitors and, possibly to his chagrin, his younger brother, Roger Henry, came last. Michael performed equally well in the inter-House running competitions, representing Barry House. On Sports Day, 18 April 1916, he won the Half-mile Handicap and the Open Mile race.

In Cricket, he was not quite so successful. He first played for the 2nd XI and was recognized as an able captain, and a little later joined the 1st XI, but he never seemed to reach his potential. In the review of the 1917 season, it is pointed out that he 'does not possess the invaluable cricket quality of patience. Has a fair idea of batting, but too often throws his wicket away. With perseverance he would make a good slow bowler. He has a nice easy action. Must improve his fielding.' [*Leo*, Vol. XXXVI, No. 5, November 1917, p.70]

In Rugby, he first represented the School at 2nd XV level and then became a reserve player for the 1st team, finally becoming a full member. The *Leodiensian* report on the 1916 season notes that he is 'a rather sleepy forward who does not make enough use of his size. Must learn to tackle and follow up properly. Dribbles well.' [*Leo*, Vol. XXXVI, No. 1, February 1917, p.149] He must have improved considerably because he was awarded his full Colours twice before leaving the School

He was a loyal and industrious member of Barry House. He rose to be Captain and was always encouraging the younger members to join in the full range of activities. The previous Captain, G R Willans, in his report for the Michaelmas Term, 1915, writes, 'My very best thanks are due to Hollis and Stross whose help and advice as regards House matters have been invaluable'. [*Leo*, Vol. XXXV, No. 6, December 1916, p.146] In his first report as House Captain, Michael starts by saying, 'I must first say how sorry we all were to lose Willans after Whitsuntide, and wish him all good luck in the Army', words that may well have caused him great sorrow when news of Willan's death reached the School. [*Leo*, Vol. XXXVI, No. 4, July 1917, p.52] In his last report for the House, he expresses concern for the degree of apathy shown by some of the boys. 'To come to more modern events, the House is larger than ever before, and this naturally makes it harder to deal with slackers but I hope that more boys are getting really keen on the House. It is very little use turning up merely from fear of punishment. It is only by keenness all round that a House can achieve anything.' [*Leo*, Vol. XXXVI, No. 6, December 1917, p.28]

The Literary and Debating Society chose a range of interesting, topical subjects for motions, including giving the vote to women and teaching Esperanto rather than French and German. On debating the motion "That school-work should be adjourned for the duration of the War", 'A.M. Hollis…feared that the buildings would decay unless occupied, and opined that boys were too indolent to do more than a negligible amount of war-work [such as helping farmers gather in the harvest]'. [*Leo*, Vol. XXXV, No. 3, June 1916, p.65] Under the same report, Michael is described as a 'copious speaker, but his speeches are somewhat unsubstantial. The effect of his words, generally sensible, is spoilt by delivery and enunciation, the latter of which is improving. Is a fertile inventor of private business.' [*Leo*, ibid, p.67] When the motion, "That in the opinion of this House the War must lead to

Disarmament" was debated, Michael spoke in favour in keeping with his pacifist views.

Academically, he was very successful: he won several prizes, including the Hook Classical Prize, the Classical Composition Prize, the Hook Theological Prize and the Senior General Knowledge Prize. He passed his Oxford & Cambridge Higher School Certificate, with a distinction in Divinity, gained an Open Classical Scholarship to Trinity College, Oxford and was awarded a Leeds Senior City Scholarship. Years later he admitted that he envied his brother, Christopher, who was lucky enough to have his fees paid so that he might go to Eton, but added that he was quite sure he had received a better academic education at Leeds Grammar School than he would have received at Eton. On leaving Leeds Grammar School in 1917, he could not immediately go up to Trinity College, Oxford, as the Great War was still in progress. Accordingly, he was drafted into the Army as an Officer Cadet and then commissioned as Second Lieutenant into the Guards Machine Gun Regiment in January 1918. He remained with his unit until April 1919, but was fortunate not to be sent to the Front.

By this time, his father had been appointed Residentiary Canon at Wells as well as Principal of the Theological College there. After the Armistice of November 1918, Michael went up to Trinity College to read Classics (Greats). He was a diligent student, shunning most of the distractions with which college life can beguile the unwary. He gained a First in 1922 and immediately entered the Theological College

Theological College, Bangalore

Arthur Michael Hollis – Anglican Bishop and Ecumenical Leader

St Andrew's Church, Huddersfield, courtesy of Geograph

at Leeds, which was to some of his acquaintances a surprising choice, but for Michael Leeds offered an opportunity to engage with urban parish work. Interestingly, the Principal there was John Kenneth Mozley who had attended Leeds Grammar School from 1898 to 1902.

He was ordained a deacon into the Anglican Church in 1923 and was sent as Curate to St Andrew's, Huddersfield, where he stayed for two years. From there he went to Hertford College, Oxford to be Chaplain and to lecture in Theology. He was appointed a Fellow of the university in 1926. He placed great emphasis on the intellectual foundations of Christianity whilst at the same time endearing himself to those students with whom he came into contact. He wrote a thesis entitled *The attitude of the Roman Government towards the Christians down to A.D. 200*, for which he was awarded a Bachelor of Divinity degree (BD).

In 1931, he approached the Society for the Propagation of the Gospel in Foreign Parts (SPG) to become a missionary in South India. He was posted to teach at the Bishop's Theological Seminary in Nazareth, in the Diocese of Tinnevelly (now Tiruneveli), Tamil Nadu State, in the south-east of India. During his early days there, he may well have come into contact with, or worked alongside, Francis Bernard Jameson, who was at Leeds Grammar School from 1902 to 1904, and who was an SPG missionary at Tinnevelly from 1917-1933.

He met and married Cordelia Burn, a nurse who had assisted in the operation to remove Michael's tonsils at the Van Allan Hospital in Kodaikanal. The wedding took place on 5 January 1935 and she proved to be a great support to him in his work as a missionary. In 1936 they returned to England for some well deserved leave and while there they expected their first child. Sadly, the boy was born prematurely and died after a few hours. They were unable to have other children.

In May 1937, he resigned from the SPG, chiefly because returning to India would be injurious to Cordelia's health.

He was appointed Perpetual Curate at St Mary's Church, Charlton Kings near Cheltenham. Cordelia's health improved slowly and Michael gave a great deal of thought to his overwhelming desire to unify the various Protestant denominations in India into a coherent whole. He was aware of the growing demand in India for independence and the implications for evangelism there. During the course of the Second World War, he became an Army Chaplain briefly before he was elevated, in succession to Edward Waller, to the post of Bishop of Madras, in which capacity he served from 1942 to 1954. As bishop, he chose a simple way of life and the comparison with Woodbine Willie [q.v.] is interesting:

> He [Michael] did not wish to be thought of as a remote figure of wealth and power, far removed from ordinary Christians. He planned to have a simple lifestyle that would bring him closer to people than had been possible for previous bishops when they were part of the Establishment…He practised simplicity and even rode a bicycle in Madras, a fact not pleasing to everyone! [CMM, pp.57-58]

He even had the odd habit of cleaning the sandals of his Indian guests.

He, more than any other Bishop preceding or succeeding, worked hard to achieve some sort of agreement between the various Protestant doctrines and traditions. There were many hurdles to overcome and all too often meetings and conferences ended in acrimony and recriminations.

Throughout this difficult time, he persevered patiently and doggedly, arguing that only by unifying could the different Churches work effectively to evangelise and retain the loyalty of the Indian people disposed towards conversion.

Armley Parish Church, courtesy of Wikimedia Commons

Arthur Michael Hollis – Anglican Bishop and Ecumenical Leader

As Lesslie Newbigin, a later Bishop of Madras, put it in his Foreword to Constance Millington's book

> Michael Hollis played a decisive part in the bringing into one body of the Anglican, Methodists and Reformed Christians in South India to form a single church, the Church of South India. The inter-church discussions which led to the inauguration of the union in 1947 had been going on for nearly 30 years. It seemed, during the latter part of this period, that they were doomed to failure, because it was always possible to propose further matters for 'clarification' and thus postpone the moment when decisions had to be made. Those decisions would be costly, for – once taken – they were irreversible, and there was strong and sometimes bitter opposition to the proposed union on the part of influential bodies in the Church of England. It was Bishop Hollis who had the courage to cast the decisive casting vote which settled the matter. He earned thereby the deep and lasting displeasure of many and he had to live with this for the rest of his life. But he made possible the birth of the Church of South India. [Lesslie Newbigin, Foreword to Millington, p.vii]

Once the CSI came into being, there was always the possibility that dissent and strife would break out again. To avoid this happening, Hollis concentrated on liaising with all the differing parties and was at great pains to reassure them that unity could work and that it would bring untold advantages in promoting the Christian religion in South India. Again, Bishop Newbigin expresses this with admirable succinctness:

> The same qualities of clarity and courage ensured that he played a decisive part in the early years of the united Church. He did, I think, more than anyone else to create an atmosphere of mutual trust without which even the best church constitution cannot work. He understood the feelings of those who came into the united church from other traditions and, more than any other single individual, he made sure that they were never ignored or over-ridden. He had a transparent honesty which, sad to say, is not always the most obvious character of those of us who have to engage in protracted and difficult negotiations on ecclesiastical matters. [Ibid, p.vii]

In 1954, he was succeeded as Bishop of Madras by David Chellappa. He was also Moderator of the Church of South India. Staying in India, he was then asked to

Arthur M Hollis's AR entry

become Professor of Church History at the Theological College of Bangalore. In 1961, aged 62, he again returned to England where he received a cool reception from the Anglican Church authorities, chiefly because of his strong views on the ecumenical movement, opinions that offended some sections of the Church. He was not offered a prestigious appointment but instead became Rector of Todwick, near Rotherham, while at the same time acting as Assistant Bishop within the Diocese of Sheffield. These positions were not commensurate with either his undoubted intellect or his illustrious service to Christianity and the Church in India. He died on 11 February 1986 aged 86.

Bibliography:

Hollis, Christopher, *The Seven Ages. Their Exits and Entrances*, Heinemann (London: 1974)
Leodiensian, The Magazine of Leeds Grammar School, various issues
Millington, Constance M, *Led by the Spirit, a Biography of Bishop Arthur Michael Hollis, sometime Anglican Bishop of Madras and later First Moderator of the C.S.I.*, Asian Trading Company, (Bangalore: 1996)

Christopher Hollis

14

•

Maurice Christopher Hollis 1902-1977
MP, Author and Publisher
At LGS 1910-1911

CHRISTOPHER HOLLIS WAS born on 19 March 1902 at St Michael's Home in Axbridge, in the Cheddar Valley, Somerset. After about a year, the family moved to Wells, where they lived for the next four years. Wells was unusual at that time because it was primarily an ecclesiastical city with little industry or commerce. The Theological College there trained graduates for ordination into the Church of England.

Christopher's abiding interest as a child was cricket and particularly the Somerset County team. His daily routine, however, was dominated by religious observance. He recalls in *The Seven Ages*:

> We began the day with family prayers – which, I fancy, had been universal in Victorian times and which, now virtually unknown, were still common enough in the first decade of the century. The maids, in their little white caps, trooped demurely in to hear a collect or two, recite the Lord's Prayer and listen to a passage from the Bible. Of course, we were regular attendants at the Cathedral. [*TSA*, p. 6]

On moving to Armley and then Headingley, Christopher joined Leeds Grammar School under the Headmastership of John Rosindale Wynne-Edwards. Christopher's chief delight in living in the vicarage of St Michael's Church was that he was close to the cricket ground where, in most years, a test match was played.

At eight years old, he was the youngest boy in the School, something he resented and about which he felt rather ashamed; though there was little shameful in his marks and assessments, it was perhaps more unbecoming in the means by which he gained high marks. He explains that his bright performance in class tests had little to do with academic prowess:

> There was in fact nothing to be proud of in my place in form, for we acquired marks by writing down on slips of paper the answers to the questions which we had prepared in Home Work and which the master asked us the next morning. We then handed our slips to our next-door-neighbour whose duty it was to mark them as the master read out the correct answers. The boy who shared the desk with me suggested that we should each always mark the other's answer as 100 per cent correct. I agreed and followed this plan. We were never detected, though why it was that the master so lamely accepted such results I cannot guess. [*TSA*, pp. 10-11]

Christopher claims in *The Seven Ages* (page 10) that he was there for only two terms (September 1910 to April 1911), but the Admission Register states that he joined the School on 5 June 1910 and left on 31 July 1911, making it just over three terms. This would account for his memories of the cricket season. Writing in 1974, he does give an insight into the daily routine at the School:

> Leeds Grammar School was, and is, an admirable school. My brother [Arthur Michael] stayed there for his full scholastic career and won from it academic success a great deal better than mine. I have no doubt that I would have benefited had I remained there….The school was of course nominally an Anglican school and had, as most schools then did, a clerical headmaster. But its religion did not in the least impinge upon my life. We began the day every morning by an Assembly of the whole school and I suppose that on that occasion some prayer was said or hymn sung, but I have no memory of either. All that I can remember of it was an occasion for the headmaster to make announcements about forthcoming events and on one occasion for very full-throated applause for one of the prefects who had made a century in a match on the previous day. [*TSA*, p.11]

Whilst at the School, he went through a curious phase of claiming allegiance to the Irish Independent Nationalist cause and of being 'half-Irish'. There was no logical basis for this claim, although a long-dead relation had belonged to a Quaker family

Christopher Hollis's Admission Register entry

that lived in Cork. He was quite open about this political loyalty and voiced his views at school, much to the amusement of some of the masters and his fellow pupils:

> I got by my antics a certain amount of amused notoriety among some of the smaller boys at Leeds Grammar School, which I was then attending. Doubtless most of them thought – very reasonably – that I was half cracked. But others were more kindly. The master used, I remember, to discuss with me before the form the fortunes of my party with mock solemnity. Maurice Healey won for it a seat at a bye-election in County Cork at about this time, and I was formally congratulated by the master. I remember also batting one day in the summer of 1911. The wicket-keeper was a boy whom at the time I thought to be enormously old and big. He was in reality, I suppose, perhaps twelve years of age to my nine. I cannot now remember his name, but I remember that I had a passionate liking for him because, from his Olympian heights, he always spoke to me and ragged me in a kindly fashion. "He's an

Independent Nationalist," he explained to the rest of the fielding side. "He's the only Independent Nationalist in the school." [CH, *ATRTF*, p.16]

Christopher left LGS after only three terms and when the news of his imminent departure for Summer Fields Preparatory School at Oxford was broken to him by his mother he was very upset:

> I burst incontinently into tears….It was explained to me that, if I was to go to a public school, it was necessary because of my father's narrow means that I should get a scholarship, whatever that might be, and that, though the Grammar School was a very good school, it did not provide the early training in Latin and Greek which was necessary for a public school scholarship. [*TSA*, pp.16-17]

In the September of 1911 he went on to the private school of Summer Fields, near Oxford and was there until July 1914. Among his contemporaries were the two Runciman brothers, Steven (later author of the magisterial history of the Crusades), and Walter Leslie; and Anthony Asquith, the film director son of Herbert Henry Asquith, the Liberal Home Secretary.

Another was I J Pitman, who was to join Christopher in the Commons as MP for Bath. Whilst there, Christopher discarded his Irish Nationalist affiliation but retained his love of cricket. Towards the end of his time at Summer Fields he began to question the tenets of Anglicanism and in this he was influenced by the writings of Samuel Butler and George Bernard Shaw.

From Summer Fields, he went on to Eton in September 1914. The war impinged only a little upon his life. He remembered the blackouts, the rationing and the temporary cessation of cricket at Lords. He

Evelyn Waugh in 1923

recalled George Lansbury, the militant Socialist, addressing the inaugural meeting of the Political Society at the College, which included members whose leanings were definitely towards the Left.

His parents were still living in Headingley, and he was never loath to visit them whenever possible. In *The Seven Ages*, he admits, 'I have never had any love for any town except Leeds' [*TSA*, p.158] and on one occasion at home it was mentioned that some refugee children from Belgium and Serbia were now living in the city. A number of the Serbian boys were admitted to Leeds Grammar School and one Serbian girl attended Leeds Girls' High School.

In December 1920 he went up to Balliol College where he won the Brackenbury History Scholarship. On reflection, he considered his education at Eton to have been sufficient but not outstanding, and freely admitted that academic achievement there compared unfavourably with, say, northern grammar schools. One thing in Eton's favour was the amusing quality of its teachers.

When he went up to Balliol, he found that half the freshmen were ex-soldiers returning from the War and who were allowed to take shortened courses, and half had come up straight from school or college. One of the main distinguishing features between the two was the attitude to drink. Those straight from school drank with adolescent foolishness while the older returnees were more moderate in their consumption. Hollis' social life at College focused upon the Hypocrites' Club and Offal luncheons. The Club met in premises close to Folly Bridge in Oxford and modestly-priced food was served to its members. Febrile conversation tended to be its main function, but it attracted notoriety and was soon closed down by the authorities. Most of its members moved over to the New Reform Club. This, too, served reasonably-priced food that was easily affordable to those students of limited means.

'Offal' members lunched every day in Evelyn Waugh's rooms at Hertford. The menu consisted chiefly of bread and cheese and, of course, beer. Many of the members paid scant regard to their studies.

Hollis turned to Oxford journalism and for a time was one of the editors of *The Oxford Outlook* as well as briefly the first editor of the new *Cherwell* magazine. But perhaps his greatest contribution to the University was through the Oxford Union, where he made his maiden speech only weeks after joining Balliol. By the end of summer term 1922 he was elected Secretary and it was in this capacity that he was chosen as one of a team of three to visit east coast American universities and debate with them. Accordingly, he flew to Montreal and took the train to Maine and took part in debates at Harvard, Yale, Princeton and Columbia among other universities.

On returning to England, he had his first taste of political electioneering, holding meetings and speaking at various villages around Wells in support of Arthur Hobhouse, the Liberal candidate, who came second to the Conservative man. Later he was to support Frank Gray, another Liberal aspirant, this time for the Oxford constituency, and Gray was duly elected against all the odds. By this time Hollis was promoted to Librarian of the Oxford Union and then, eventually, President in 1923. That autumn, he was again electioneering on behalf of Arthur Hobhouse, this time successfully.

One very important cause that emerged in his later time at Balliol was support for Irish independence, an echo of his earlier, somewhat spurious sentiment whilst at Leeds Grammar School. This time he had an illustrious fellow-traveller by name of W B Yeats with whom he struck up an association. There was much celebration when the Irish Treaty of 1921 was signed. Ironically, there followed for him a period of political cynicism, during which he castigated the whole structure of party politics. In this atmosphere of disenchantment, he began to read Belloc and Chesterton and began to see the Catholic Church as a means of salvation. In the late summer of 1924 he was received into the Faith by Monsignor Barnes, the Catholic chaplain at Oxford.

That same summer, he set off on a second debating trip on behalf of the Oxford Union to America in the company of Douglas Woodruff and Malcolm Macdonald. Being free from the pressure of exams, they were able to travel across the continent, taking their leisure and sampling the American way of life. They visited the southern states and went on to Mexico, Australia and New Zealand. They found time to call on President Coolidge but he rather summarily dismissed them, claiming he was too busy. Prohibition, Christopher thought, was a quite extraordinary policy, yet it was supported by a majority of the population who regarded it as a profound moral and religious issue. He also found that most Americans placed no value on privacy, unlike the English. To his amazement, he discovered that public toilets simply did not exist. On a more serious note, the most popular debating topics were prohibition and the League of Nations. In those debates covering the ethics of Imperialism, he found that his hosts were resolutely opposed to the concept and the practice of annexing territories and countries with no inherent ties to the mother country. He found this rather inconsistent with the USA's annexation of Hawaii.

After Australia and New Zealand, they visited Java, Malaya, Burma and India. In the latter country he experienced quite a lot of antagonism towards the British but at the same time was impressed by the railway network built by them to facilitate economic development. He was made aware that the campaign for independence would advance apace.

On returning to England, he chose teaching as his vocation. He had gained a Third in Greats (*literae humaniores*) at the end of his university course and, in view of his conversion to Roman Catholicism, looked at the possibility of teaching in one of the premier Catholic schools. There was no vacancy at Downside so he applied

Summer Fields School, courtesy of the School

to Stonyhurst in Lancashire and was appointed as a teacher of history to start in September 1925. The school had about 250 boys in the main school and another 60 in the Prep department at Hodder close by. His teaching duties were not especially onerous and so he was able to spend a lot of time writing. He wrote and published his first books whilst there. These included *The Monstrous Regiment* (1929), a history of the reign of Elizabeth I, *Dryden* (1933), *Evelyn Waugh* (1934) and *The Two Nations* (1935). His old debating companion, Douglas Woodruff, had joined the staff of *The Times* newspaper and Christopher frequently visited him during school holidays. This was to facilitate his writing career.

He married Madeleine King in 1929. She was the daughter of the Revd Richard King of Cholderton rectory near Salisbury. At the time of their marriage Madeleine was an Anglican but by the time of the birth of their first child she converted to the Catholic faith. The college built a modest house for them a little distance away from the main buildings.

Maurice Christopher Hollis – MP, Author and Publisher

His book, *The Breakdown of Money*, was published in 1934. In it, he criticised the monetary system which seemed at the time to be stifling any reprieve from the enduring economic depression. On the strength of these views, he was invited to take up a temporary teaching post at Notre Dame Catholic University in Indiana

St Michael's Church, Headingley, courtesy of the Faith Team St Michael's Church Headingley

on a salary that far exceeded what he was receiving from Stonyhurst. He accepted the offer with some reservations, sad to be leaving the college and England. He found the educational system at Notre Dame to be very different from that in England. It was casual to a degree that beggared belief. Attendance at lectures appeared to be the sole criterion for success. There was, however, relief at discovering that prohibition had ended.

As a deeply committed Roman Catholic, Christopher was troubled by the Vatican's silence over the Italian invasion of Abyssinia. Mussolini's purpose, apart from a serious measure of vaingloriousness, was to settle some of Italy's 'surplus' population there. There could be no justification for the military action, and he came to the sad conclusion that, over certain matters, the Church was concerned with the rights of Catholics to practise their religion but was much less concerned about the rights of non-Catholics. He was even more distressed over the Church's concordat with the Nazi government in Germany after 1933.

Hollis returned to England in the summer of 1936 and viewed with horror the deteriorating situation in Europe. Mussolini had invaded Abyssinia; Hitler had re-occupied the Rhineland; and, perhaps most troubling of all, the Spanish Civil War broke out. He returned to North America in early 1937, visiting Ottawa before going on to Indiana. He found himself being challenged by the students there on the policy of appeasement by Britain and discovered that most Americans supported their government's insistence on isolationism.

When war did break out in September 1939 Hollis returned to England. In the late summer of 1940 he was sent on a mission to America but, with the Battle of Britain raging, he desperately wanted to return to his wife and children back home. As soon as he achieved this, he put his name down for the Officers' Emergency Reserve, but was not called up so he joined the local Home Guard at Mells. This had all the slightly farcical qualities of *Dad's Army*. His abiding memory of the time was manning a post at the summit of a local hill watching out for German paratroopers without having the least idea what to do should such a situation arise. Eventually, in May 1941, he was commissioned into the RAF and summoned to report to Uxbridge. After three weeks' square bashing he was sent to Blackpool to train recruits on the sands there, a task for which he was entirely unsuited, and from which he was saved by an irascible Sergeant. After a further few weeks he was transferred to a department of the Air Ministry entitled, somewhat mysteriously, A.I.6. He had two duties: to compose communiqués which were issued each day on Allied or enemy air activities; and to censor manuscripts submitted for publication by RAF personnel.

From A.I.6 he was moved to the Air Historical Branch whose main function was to prepare reports for Air Staff on the part played by the RAF in various operations. His special area of interest was the Eastern Mediterranean and to gain the necessary intelligence he travelled widely throughout the area, including Palestine. Towards the end of the war he was required to report on the SOE (Special Operations Executive) droppings over Europe.

Whilst President of the Oxford Union he had considered the possibility of a career in politics but at the time was drawn to education instead. On being discharged from the RAF at the end of the war his future career was by no means certain, so it was with some relief that he was asked to stand for the constituency of Devizes for the Conservatives. He was, against the run of things, duly elected and he retained the seat in both the 1950 and 1951 elections. He spoke out against the conditions imposed by the Americans in order to secure the post-war loan; and he seconded the clause of the Criminal Justice Reform Bill that called for the abolition of the death penalty – in contradiction of official Conservative policy. The Commons accepted abolition but the Lords rejected the Bill – it took another twenty years for capital punishment to be taken off the Statute Book. The public reaction to this attempt to abolish capital punishment took him by surprise – some of his constituents were angry and appalled and there were hints that some of them would like to murder him. Fortunately, they failed to do so and he was for a number of years one of the British Delegates at the Council of Europe in Strasbourg, but apart from that he held no office and was not unhappy when he left the Commons, having found it incompatible with a happy family life. Unlike many of his contemporaries, he never courted publicity or fame.

As part of his parliamentary duties whilst at Strasbourg, he was able to travel to many different countries and in January 1954 he visited Israel. For him, of course, a priority was to view the Holy Places but he was distressed to find that the Christian buildings were in poor order, especially the Church of the Holy Sepulchre (restored by King Abdullah). He was also saddened to find the region full of closed frontiers. Of the Balfour Declaration he was scathing:

> With the collapse of the Turkish Empire the problems of that part of the world were going to be sufficiently complicated anyway. To inject into them the further complication of Zionism was to render them utterly insoluble, and what will be the final price that the world will have to pay for that madness one trembles to think. [*ATRTF*, p.210]

Events may well prove him right. However, he did accept that, having created a homeland for the Jews, it was the duty of the United Nations to protect them.

On leaving parliament (he retired undefeated) he continued to take an interest in its proceedings by writing observant and knowledgeable articles on them in the satirical magazine *Punch*. He retired to Somerset, a county for which he had the highest regard, and followed the varying fortunes of the County cricket team there.

At home in Mells, he devoted much of his time to writing and his literary output was prodigious. Occasionally he wrote for the papers. He was also much involved in the publishing firm of Hollis and Carter, a subsidiary of Burns and Oates. On average he produced about a book a year. The last book he wrote was *Oxford in the Twenties*, published the year before his death on 5 May 1977. He also wrote articles for the *Tablet*, the Catholic paper, of which he was a director.

Hollis was a very popular character in all his varied employments. The most important single event in his life for him was his conversion to Roman Catholicism. Like many converts, at first he adopted a rather over-zealous defence of the Church, but as time went by his views mellowed and he was happy to accommodate the views of others. His love of cricket stayed with him throughout his life. His authorship betrayed a polymath knowledge ranging from economics through history to biography, with, of course, a heavy emphasis on his religious beliefs.

Bibliography:
Hollis, Christopher, *Along the Road to Frome*, George G Harrap & Co Ltd (London: 1958)
Hollis, Christopher, and Cummings, *The Ayes & the Noes*, Macdonald (London: 1957)
Hollis, Christopher, *Dryden*, Duckworth, (London: 1933)
Hollis, Christopher, *Evelyn Waugh*, Longmans, Green & Co. (London: 1934)
Hollis, Christopher, *The Monstrous Regiment*, Sheed & Ward (London: 1929)
Hollis, Christopher, *The Oxford Union*, Evans Brothers Limited (London: 1965)
Hollis, Christopher, *The Seven Ages*, Heinemann (London: 1974)
Oxford Dictionary of National Biography, entry on Christopher Hollis

Sir Roger Hollis

15

Sir Roger Henry Hollis KBE, Knt, CB, OBE 1905-1973
Intelligence Officer
At LGS 1915-1918

SIR ROGER HENRY HOLLIS was born at Wells, Somerset, on 2 December 1905, the third son of the Rev. George Arthur Hollis, a priest vicar and lecturer at the Theological College there, and his wife, Mary Margaret, a writer of Anglican histories and stories. According to Constance M Millington, the biographer of Arthur Michael Hollis, Roger's eldest brother, Wells 'was a wonderful place in which to live: the atmosphere of the Cathedral Precincts, the majestic grey stone Cathedral with its heavily carved West front, and the Bishop's Palace with its beautiful gardens and moat…' [CMM, p. 1] As Roger put it later, 'I grew up not merely as a clergyman's son, but in a cleric-inhabited society - in a sort of Trollopean world'. [CMM, pp.1-2] It must have been something of a daunting move when, in 1909, his father was appointed Vicar of St Bartholomew's Church, Armley, and then, a little later, Vicar of St Michael's, Headingley. Armley, a huge parish situated amongst rows of back-to-back houses, could boast few of Wells' refinements. All four of the Hollis sons attended Leeds Grammar School: Arthur Michael (1910-1917), Maurice Christopher (1910-1911), Roger Henry (1915-1918) and Hugh Marcus Noel (1916-1918). George Arthur Hollis later became Vice-Principal of Wells Theological College and then Bishop-Suffragan of Taunton.

According to Chapman Pincher, Roger 'was a sickly child and suffered from inferiority feelings with respect to his brother' [CP, p.38], and possibly because of this he was tutored at home at Armley before attending Leeds Grammar School in 1915 under the headmastership of the Rev. Canon Wynne-Edwards. He gives no indication of what life at the School was like, but his brother, Christopher, offers some vivid memories which are recorded under his entry.

In 1918 Roger was sent to Clifton College at Bristol and subsequently went up to Worcester College, Oxford, with a classical exhibition. He read English but contemporaries noted that he was more attracted to the social side of the college rather than academic rigour, joining the group of aesthetes and voluptuaries led by Harold Acton and including Evelyn Waugh. He was an excellent golfer and gained a half-blue whilst at college; tennis was his other favoured sport. He joined the New Reform Club and became friends with Claud Cockburn, who was a staunch Communist. He also became acquainted with Tom Driberg, a member of the British Communist Party, a notorious homosexual and, later, a left-wing Labour MP from 1942-1955. Chapman Pincher believed Driberg to be a double agent working for MI5 and the KGB. In view of his hedonistic tendencies, Roger left the College without taking his undergraduate examinations. This angered his parents to such an extent that they refused to finance his planned visit Mexico in the company of Maurice Richardson, another left-wing sympathiser and close friend. Richardson backed out of the proposed visit so Roger decided instead to go to China, assuming he could save sufficient money to fund the trip.

To do so, he worked for a year at Standard Chartered Bank in London and then left England to work as a journalist for a Hong Kong newspaper. This, too, proved a brief assignment, as he then joined the British American Tobacco Company in April 1928, where he stayed for eight years in the advertising department at Shanghai, witnessing momentous events in China, then being ravaged by war. He met, and became friends with, Agnes Smedley, an American left-wing journalist and dedicated agent of the Comintern, the movement for International Communism founded by the Russian Communists in 1919, with contacts with Soviet spy rings in the city. His work took him to a number of other major Chinese cities, including Peking (Beijing), Hangkow (Hangku) and Dairen (Dalian, formerly Port Arthur). He wrote with perspicacious authority on the complex situation brought about by the brutal Japanese invasion and the unavailing response of the Chinese war-lords. Sadly, an attack of tuberculosis caused him, in 1936, to return home to England via the Trans-Siberian Railway and he briefly joined the Ardath Tobacco Company. In the following year he married Evelyn Esme at Wells Cathedral, and there followed a son, Adrian Swayne, who was later to become a Fellow and Tutor in Classics at Keble College, Oxford, and an excellent chess player.

In October 1937, he gave a lecture to the Royal Central Asian Society in which he delivered a lucid analysis of the situation in China. He offered the following apology:

Before taking my plunge into the situation in China, it may be as well to present my credentials – very slender ones, I am afraid, for addressing so distinguished a gathering. I have lived for nine years in China, first as a journalist in the south, and later I travelled fairly extensively through Central and North China on business, and have been resident at one time or another in most of the important cities of this part. I make no pretence to having the inner knowledge of a diplomat, or close personal acquaintance with Chinese leaders and officials. Consequently, I shall not attempt to make any *ex cathedra* pronouncements upon the policy and secret aims of either side, though I shall in all humility advance my own suggestions of these aims, based on my reading of a situation which I have studied closely. [RCAS *Journal*, p.24]

After an initial rejection, Hollis joined the Security Service, MI5, in 1938, a vocation to which he was particularly suited. His first role was that of assistant to Jane Sissmore (later Jane Archer), a highly respected member of the organization, especially in the field of interrogation. He was put to work in Section F, the department of MI5 responsible for overseeing Soviet and Communist operations

Spies – Anthony Blunt, left, courtesy of Wikimedia Commons, and Kim Philby, below, courtesy of You Tube

Sir Roger Henry Hollis – Intelligence Officer

Worcester College Oxford, courtesy of Andrew Shiva

in the United Kingdom and the Colonies. He was a diligent and conscientious worker, able to grasp complex situations with astonishing ease, and always able to view matters objectively. His early work for the organisation was in the field of international communism and in this he quickly established himself as an astute authority. In 1940 he was promoted to be Head of Section F. His remit during the years of the Second World War was to monitor and assess the dangers of Russian-inspired communist initiatives and plans regarding the fate of Europe after the collapse of Nazism. He started as Assistant Director of Counter-subversion but was soon promoted to Director of C Branch, which gave him responsibility for all forms of vetting and protective security, such as document classification and the installation of security systems on all government buildings. He was, thanks to his meticulous organization, eminently qualified to monitor the ramifications of the Cold War and the West's troubled relationship with the Soviet Union and its Warsaw Pact allies. As a consequence, he was appointed Deputy Director-General of MI5 in 1953, becoming Director General in 1956, succeeding Sir Dick Goldsmith White, who went on to become Director General of MI6.

According to Peter Wright, Hollis took over at the helm of MI5 at a time when relations between it and the other intelligence services, especially MI6 and the newly formed GCHQ, were in crisis.

For the following nine years he master-minded MI5 policy at a time when the Cold War posed an enormous threat world-wide and particularly in Europe, where the Iron Curtain pointedly reflected a divided continent frequently assailed by rebellion and strife. Soviet espionage was ubiquitous in its tentacle-like presence, and the decade 1955-1965 was infamous for its plethora of sensational spy cases. The Old Bailey witnessed the trials of some of the most notorious agents: George Blake, Ethel Gee and Gordon Lonsdale among them. Others escaped trial: Kim Philby, Guy Burgess, Donald Maclean and Anthony Blunt. The Profumo scandal of 1963 caused great consternation, leading to nothing less than national anxiety over the threat of communist infiltration and a possible putsch directed from Moscow. Some of this fear may well have been disproportionate to the actual menace but in the period of the Cuban Missile Crisis, some degree of hysteria was understandable. Throughout this turbulent time, Hollis fulfilled the duties of his post with admirable efficiency.

He was even more aware of the dire threat from the Soviet Union when a number of defectors arrived in Britain bringing with them what were, in some instances, exaggerated accounts of the danger posed by communist-inspired infiltration. Successive governments sought to allay fears by putting the Security Services through a series of official inquiries and it must be stressed that Hollis conducted himself with great acuity and acquitted his department in unequivocal terms. The Denning Inquiry in particular praised him for his inspirational leadership. He left MI5 in 1965, having being made OBE in 1946, CB (Companion of the Order of the Bath) in 1956, knighted in 1960 and was later created KBE (Knight Commander of the Order of the British Empire) in 1966. He enjoyed an enviable reputation among those in the intelligence services, though some junior officers did find him reserved and aloof. He himself was of a retiring nature and never promoted himself to the exclusion of others, and he would have been delighted to retire into relative obscurity. In this he was to be thwarted by the unfortunate circumstances of later allegations, chiefly brought about by the writings of Chapman Pincher, W J West and Peter Wright.

On retirement, he moved to Wells for two years but his personal circumstances changed when his first marriage was dissolved and he married his erstwhile secretary, Edith Valentine Hammond. As a consequence, he moved to Catcott in Somerset, enjoying his favourite sport, golf, in which he was very proficient. It was at this time that he was called in to MI5 to be told that he – and others – were to be investigated regarding possible collusion with the Soviet authorities. He was interrogated under conditions of the utmost secrecy given the seriousness of the accusations and the sensitivity of the matters under discussion, but some of the details of the investigation were leaked after his death in October 1973, and this led to a number of people jumping to conclusions regarding his professional integrity. In view of the grave public concern this elicited, both in parliament and the media, Margaret Thatcher, Prime Minister at the time, was forced to set up an official inquiry. This was chaired by Lord Trend, Secretary to the Cabinet (1963-1973) and its conclusions were inconclusive, but on balance declaring Hollis innocent of all charges. Despite this, his family had been forced to endure a period of intense perturbation and this was only a little alleviated by the later evidence from ex-KGB agents, Oleg Gordievsky and Yuri Modin, in 2009, who exonerated Hollis.

Professor Christopher Andrew, in his seminal history of MI5, *The Defence of the Realm: The Authorized History of MI5*, published in 2009, *above*, concluded that there was no evidence to suggest that Hollis was a Russian agent. Professor Andrew devotes a chapter of his book to revealing the unprofessional ineptitude of the Secret Service when investigating those agents considered to be the most plausible suspects working for the Russians. He is especially scathing of Peter Wright, not because he was particularly ineffectual, but because he was too quick to draw false conclusions from selected evidence:

> The gaps in the Service's knowledge of the Five [Kim Philby, Guy Burgess, Donald Maclean, Anthony Blunt and John Cairncross] and their handlers provided increasing opportunities for its small but disruptive group of conspiracy theorists. It was possible to argue, for example, that the tip-off to Maclean [that he was to be charged with treason], instead of coming from Philby via Burgess, had been given

instead by an undiscovered Soviet agent inside the Security Service. In the imagination of Peter Wright the KGB became transformed into an agency of extraordinary operational subtlety and sophistication. As Wright began to descend into his conspiratorial wilderness of mirrors, Hollis warned him, "They're [the Soviet handlers] not ten foot tall, you know, Peter!" [Andrew, pp.434-35]

As it happened, the British Secret Service monitoring of their own agents was so inept that Wright and others believed that there must be an inside mole: 'The failure to identify STANLEY [Soviet code name] as Philby was so remarkable that Wright and others later claimed that the identification must have been deliberately suppressed and therefore pointed to possible Soviet penetration of the Service'. [Andrew, p.432] In fact, the Soviet handlers of the 'magnificent five' were equally inept, something that Wright and his fellow conspiracy theorists never took into account. Professor Andrew concluded that Hollis was innocent of all charges and exonerated him from all suspicion.

Bibliography:

Andrew, Professor Christopher, *The Defence of the Realm: The Authorized History of MI5*, Allen Lane, (London: 2009)

Hollis, Maurice Christopher, *Along the Road to Frome*, Harrap, (London: 1958)

Hollis, Maurice Christopher, *The Seven Ages –their exits and their entrances*, Heinemann, (London: 1974)

Millington, Constance M, *Led By the Spirit. A biography of Bishop Arthur Michael Hollis, onetime Anglican Bishop of Madras, and later first Moderator of the C.S.I.*, Asian Trading Corporation, (Bangalore: 1996)

Pincher, Chapman, *Their Trade is Treachery*, Sidgwick & Jackson, (London: 1981)

West, W J *The Truth About Hollis*, Gerald Duckworth & Co. Ltd, (London: 1989)

White, Dick, *Oxford Dictionary of National Biography*, revised on-line edition, (2016)

Wright, Peter with Greengrass, Paul, *Spycatcher*, William Heinemann, (Australia: 1987)

Geoffrey Crowther (Alchetron)

16

Geoffrey Crowther Bt, Kt 1907-1972
Journalist, Businessman, Educationist and First Chancellor of the Open University
At LGS 1915-1919

GEOFFREY CROWTHER WAS born at 16 Monk Bridge Road, Headingley, on 13 May 1907, the eldest son of Charles and Hilda Louise Crowther. Charles Crowther was a lecturer in, and then professor of, agricultural chemistry at the University of Leeds. By the time of the 1911 census, the family had moved to 169 Kirkstall Lane, Headingley. Geoffrey, who had an elder sister, Phyllis, and two younger brothers, Bernard Martin and Donald Ineson, attended Leeds Girls' High School in the early years section and then progressed to the Grammar School Junior Department in 1915 aged 8. From LGS he moved, in 1919, to King's School, Warwick for one year and then went on to Oundle School, Northamptonshire, which he attended from 1920-1925, his father being appointed Principal of the Harper Adams Agricultural College at Shropshire.

At Oundle, he won a scholarship to read modern languages at Clare College, Cambridge, switching to economics in his third year. He became President of the Cambridge Union in 1928 and gained a double first. Even at this early stage in his career, he seemed to stand out as a brilliant man with a remarkable career ahead of him. Donald Tyerman, editor of *The Economist* from 1956-1965 in succession to Crowther, said of him that his 'self-awareness and self-confidence were not so much asserted as taken for granted. But men who did well enough in life after Cambridge were in despair when they saw how sure it seemed that he would succeed in whatever he chose to do.' [quoted from Ruth Dudley Edwards, *The Pursuit of Reason*]

Geoffrey Crowther – Journalist, Businessman and Educationalist

Following this success at Cambridge, he was awarded a Commonwealth Fund fellowship and went on to study at Yale and Columbia universities between 1929 and 1931. He spent some time on Wall Street and formed a close affinity with the American people. Whilst in the USA, in 1932 he met and married, Margaret, the daughter of Edward Hallowell Worth and his wife, Anna Vail. The wedding took place at Claymont, Delaware. They had two sons and four daughters. Already highly regarded as a perceptive economist, he was recommended by J M Keynes to take up the post of economic adviser on banking to the Irish government. His report, written when he was only 25, was the first of many thorough and distinguished documents that he was to write during the course of his career.

In 1932, Crowther joined the staff of *The Economist* and six years later was promoted to editor, in which capacity his first issue was on the night of the Munich Agreement. He remained editor until March 1956, a longer stint than any of his predecessors. 'His writing was succinct, uncomplicated, sparing of polysyllables, and always brightened by wit. He composed in a neat small hand, and with seemingly effortless facility, pellucid leading articles on questions of great inherent complication...' [Roland Bird, *Oxford DNB*] As a result, the circulation of *The Economist* grew from 10,000 to 50,000 and its influence increased in proportion. His inspiring leadership was such that he attracted a number of gifted journalists, some of whom, unusually for the time, were women. Among his recruits were Donald Tyerman, Barbara Ward, Isaac Deutscher, Margaret Cruickshank and George Steiner. Towards the end of the Second World War, he introduced a series of articles concerned with economic and political aspects of American policy, which were aimed primarily at his British readers, but they became essential reading for many Americans, including presidents. Whilst at the helm, he transformed the journal from a publication of limited appeal to one of world-wide acclaim and authority. For this and other services to journalism, he was knighted in 1957.

During the course of the Second World War, Crowther was heavily involved in the Ministry of Supply (1940-41) and in the Ministry of Information (1941-42). He became deputy head of the joint war production staff at the Ministry of Production (1942-43). It was after the War that he became more and more attracted to business and succeeded Lord Layton as chairman of The Economist Newspaper Ltd, a post he held until his death in 1972. He was also deputy chairman of Commercial Union Assurance and he was a member of the team that set up the Trafalgar House property group, later becoming its chairman. He created the British Printing Corporation by merging Hazell Sun with Purnell, though he found himself embroiled in a bitter struggle to remove the Purnell chairman from the board. As chairman of Trust Houses he once again proved himself to be a tireless worker, improving and expanding the firm's interests until its merger with Forte Holdings in 1970. Again, he found himself opposing the principles and policies of the Forte

The Open University charter ceremony

Holdings board and, after an abortive attempt to invite Allied Breweries to take over the company, he and many of the old Trust Houses team resigned en masse. This turbulent time took its toll on his health and he collapsed and died on 5 February 1972 of a heart attack at Heathrow Airport following his return from Australia.

Although Crowther did not actively seek high public office, he was appointed chairman of the Central Advisory Council for Education and in this capacity recommended the raising of the school leaving age (ROSLA) from 15 to 16. This principle was enshrined in *The Crowther Report – Fifteen to Eighteen*, published in 1959. ROSLA was introduced in 1972. Its chief recommendations were: that extended courses be made available to all secondary modern school pupils; that less able pupils should not be automatically entered for external exams if deemed inappropriate; that all pupils possessing the ability to attempt subjects at GCE Ordinary level be allowed to do so and that secondary modern pupils, where appropriate, be entered for examinations at a level below GCE; a greater emphasis on school assessment rather that total reliance on examination results; the raising of the school leaving age to sixteen; revising the post-Ordinary level syllabi in order to cater for the increasing number of pupils who were likely to stay on into the sixth form; to attract highly qualified and motivated teachers to inspire sixth form pupils; to create more tertiary education places to cope with a spike in demand from those sixth form pupils; and – very importantly and perhaps relevant to today's employment requirements – to build many more secondary technical schools to encourage pupils who do not respond to an academic syllabus but who would much prefer a more practical, vocational education.

Geoffrey Lloyd, the then Minister of Education, wrote in his preamble to Volume I of the Report:

> …I am sure that we owe a great debt of gratitude to Sir Geoffrey Crowther and his colleagues on the Council [the Central Advisory Council for Education]. They have dealt with a reference which raised many difficult and complicated issues with great thoroughness and they have presented their findings in a very readable and interesting report. It will, I believe, come to be accepted as well worthy to take its place in the line of distinguished reports which have had so much influence on the development of education in England and Wales. [Foreword by Geoffrey Lloyd to the *15-18 Report*, HMSO, 1959]

According to the *Leodiensian* magazine, Volume 86, No.2 (Lent 1972), Geoffrey Crowther visited LGS at the time Charles Woodford was Headmaster [1954-62] to discuss the Crowther Report.

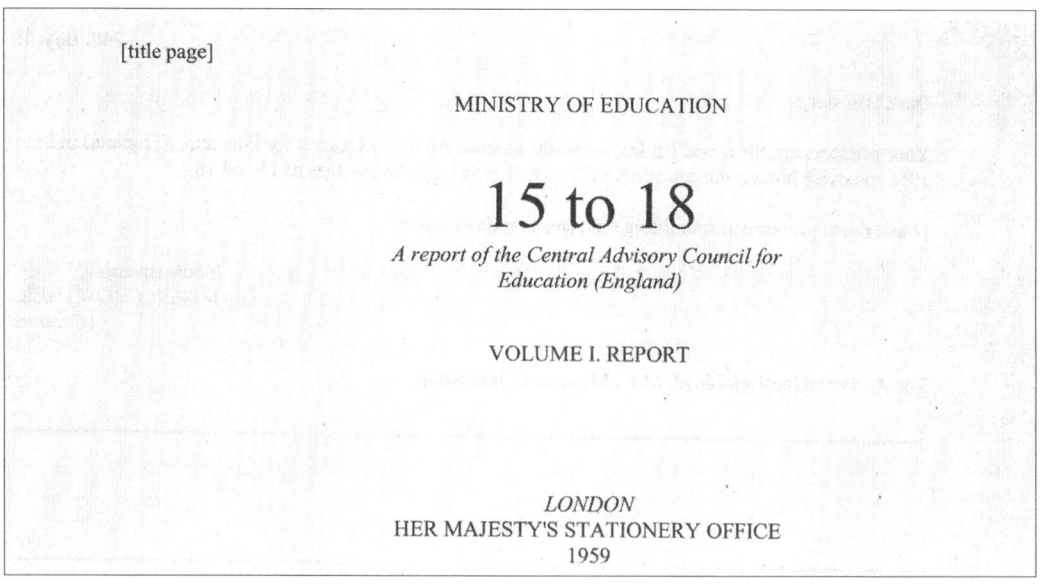

The Crowther Report – title page

Then, between 1968 and 1971 he was chairman of the committee on consumer credit and managed to modernize the law and practice of what was becoming a major and expanding business. This led directly to the Consumer Credit Act of 1974.

He sat on many more governing bodies; the one of which he was most proud was that of the Open University (1969-1972). He was installed as Chancellor at the first meeting of the Congregation of the University at the Royal Society. This was combined with the award of the Charter by the Privy Council on 23 July 1969, and was attended by the Prime Minister of the day, Harold Wilson, along with Jennie Lee and Walter Perry. Crowther used the occasion to give a speech, describing the new University as open to people, places, methods and ideas: the University's mission statement even today.

> The first, and most urgent task before us is to cater for the many thousands of people, fully capable of a higher education, who for one reason or another, do not get it, or do not get as much of it as they can turn to advantage, or as they discover, sometimes, too late, that they need. Only in recent years have we come to realise how many such people there are, and how large the gaps in educational provision through which they can fall. The existing system, for all its great expansion, misses and leaves aside a great unused reservoir of human talent and potential. [Taken from Lord Crowther's Inaugural address, Open University Digital Archive]

On 18 May 1970, Crowther welcomed Lord Mountbatten to the University for a ceremony to open officially the new buildings of the OU at the Walton Hall campus. Sadly, Baron Crowther was only able to serve as Chancellor for three years. Walter Perry, the first Vice Chancellor, wrote a fitting tribute to Crowther following the latter's death:

> In the difficulties of the early years my task as Vice Chancellor was greatly eased by his backing. He had a mind of exceptional quality, and seemed unfailingly able, having listened to garbled accounts of a complex problem, to isolate the critical issues and state them with complete clarity. I never heard him make an irrelevant comment. It was a privilege to have gained his friendship. It was a tragedy that his early death was to rob the University of his services after all too short a period of office. [Open University Digital Archive]

He was created a life peer in June 1968 with the title Baron Crowther of Headingley.

Open University programmes became a widely-recognisable presence on 1970s television sets

He received several honorary degrees from British and American universities: Hon.LLD (Nottingham, Swarthmore, Dartmouth, Michigan and Liverpool) and Hon. DSc (Econ.) from London. His most widely read book, *An Outline of Money* (1941) was for a long time the standard work on the subject.

Six years before his death, the *Illustrated London News* offered a succinct appraisal of his career to that point. Although to the general public his association with *The Economist* was his chief claim to fame, 'yet today, at 59, he is on the board of 36 companies, and more important, can fairly claim to be the biggest hotelier in Europe' [*ILN*, 3 September 1966] The article continues, 'The man who can extend such an all-embracing welcome to the world at large is a small, well-built, epigrammatic Leeds-born economic pragmatist…who has been described as a younger, better-looking Edward G. Robinson. He is a master of the apt phrase: at one time he defined the *Economist*'s political position (and by implication his own) as standing "at the extreme centre"; he also coined the expression "soft underbelly of Europe" which Sir Winston Churchill made famous.' [*ILN*, ibid]

Bibliography

Bird, Roland, "Geoffrey Crowther", in *Oxford Dictionary of National Biography*

Crowther, Geoffrey, *An Outline of Money*, Thomas Nelson & Son (London: 1949)

Crowther, Geoffrey, *Balances and Imbalances of Payments*, Harvard University (Cambridge, Massachusetts: 1957)

Crowther, Geoffrey, *Economics for Democrats*, Thomas Nelson & Sons (London: 1939)

Crowther, Geoffrey, *Free Enterprise Versus Planned Economy*, State University of Iowa (Iowa City, Iowa: 1954)

Crowther, Geoffrey, *The Morality of Discrimination in International Trade*, University of California (Oakland: 1957)

Crowther, Geoffrey, *Ways and Means: A Study of the Economic Structure of Great Britain Today*, Macmillan (London: 1936)

Edwards, Ruth Dudley, *The Pursuit of Reason*, Hamish Hamilton (London: 1993)

HMSO, *15 to 18. A report of the Central Advisory Council for Education (England). Volume I. Report*, HMSO (London: 1959)

Illustrated London News, 3 September 1966

Leodiensian magazine, Volume 86, Number 2, Lent 1972, p. 41

Godfrey Talbot OBE, courtesy of SWWEC

17

Godfrey Walker Talbot OBE 1908-2000
Journalist and Royal Correspondent
At LGS 1919-1924

GODFREY WALKER TALBOT was born on 8 October 1908 at West Leigh, Walton, near Wakefield. He was the fifth and last child of Frank Talbot, an agent for building materials, and his wife, Kate Bertha. Both parents were staunch Methodists. The family moved to 29 Inglewood Terrace, Hyde Park, Leeds when Godfrey was four years old. He attended Quarry Mount Council School. From a very early age, Godfrey was keen to become a journalist and on leaving Leeds Grammar School in 1924 after taking his School Certificate, he joined the *Yorkshire Post* as an office boy. Following a two-year stint in the commercial office, he was transferred to the editorial side, where he soon made his mark. At the early age of 20, he was promoted to assistant editor of the paper's weekly edition.

Two years later, he moved to Manchester to join the staff of the *Guardian*'s weekly edition, *City News*, and in 1932 was appointed editor of that paper, which unfortunately ceased publication in 1934. Talbot then moved to the *Daily Dispatch*, another *Guardian* publication, as its Lancashire reporter. Not long after, he left the newspaper world altogether because he had been accepted by the BBC as its north region press officer.

In the meantime, he married, on 7 October 1933, Bessie Owen, the daughter of the borough engineer of Wigan.

With the impending threat of war, the BBC decided to increase its news staff and, in the light of this, Talbot was called to London to take up the role of editing agency copy for the news bulletins. Fearing accusations of partiality, the BBC had in the past refused to employ its own reporters with the sole exception of the then promising Richard Dimbleby. However, the Corporation was acutely aware of the need to be able to provide comprehensive cover of the unfolding events of the autumn of 1939, and this meant sending reporters to wherever military action occurred at home and abroad. Talbot was initially assigned to the London Blitz, on which he reported with some distinction. After further assignments, he was made an official war correspondent and sent out to the Middle East to replace Dimbleby as the reporter embedded with General Montgomery, with whom he soon struck up a cordial relationship. Dimbleby had made himself unpopular with his lavish life-style, including a liveried chauffeur and a house-boat on the Nile; and he had been sending over-optimistic reports concerning General Auchinleck's achievements, something that annoyed Churchill who was seeking to replace him. Thanks to Talbot's more muted style, he got on rather better with Montgomery and he was in an excellent position to follow the British Eighth Army as it advanced from El Alamein to Tripoli. His broadcasts 'displayed a natural flair for descriptive detail, including the arrival of Churchill in Tripoli, the Fall of Monte Cassino and finally the entry into Rome'. [quoted from the Second World War Experience Centre]

In *Permission to Speak*, he describes the environment in which he found himself:

> And for the next year and more my scene of operations, the battlegrounds round which I crawled and ducked, the wide open spaces from which I spoke my dispatches, was the stony desolation of coastal Egypt and Libya and beyond, a hard, scorched region of duststorms and flies, mirages and minefields. A dry, astringent land, healthier than most, for all the dysentery and jaundice. A land in which we seemed to be isolated from the rest of the world; a land inhabited only by the warring armies. [*PTS*, p. 44]

Talbot was present at the commencement of the Second Battle of El Alamein. He broadcast his messages from an old truck he and his team christened "Belinda", a thirty hundredweight vehicle that he described as 'large and fat and friendly-looking; a bit slow, always over-burdened, long-suffering but great hearted'. An extract from his broadcast gives a flavour of his ability to create mind pictures for those avidly listening:

> I knew it [the opening barrage of the battle] was going to happen that night mind you, but it was dramatic all the same. Absolutely dramatic, absolutely quiet, when the signal was passed and somehow, at any rate,

Godfrey Talbot prepares to take off in a Mitchell Bomber ahead of the invasion of the south of France, August 1944, courtesy of SWWEC

it was passed straightaway, simultaneously, right along the Alamein front, until a voice, or whatever it was, some signal was given, "Fire", or whatever the word was, and then whether you were a soldier, civilian, whatever you were, suddenly all hell, absolutely cracked and nowhere in any war has there been such a barrage at dawn. Something like 900 field guns along miles and miles of front simultaneously burst into flames. The most dramatic, theatrical thing you had ever seen. [quoted from SWWEC]

Godfrey Walker Talbot – Journalist and Royal Correspondent

He did leave the Eighth Army for a short while and reported on the air-borne landings in the south of France in July 1944. His report included the memorable words:

> And then, one after the other, our gliders slipped their tow-ropes and slid and circled down to make excellent landings. I myself saw only one crash. It was most skilful – I saw 14 gliders land beautifully close together, in one not too big field, half grass, half ploughed. They raised a dust cloud and then they stopped and out came men. [quoted from *Guardian* obituary]

Talbot's reports had impressed the BBC's editor-in-chief, William Haley, who complained that there were only two correspondents he could consistently rely on, Dimbleby and Talbot. He deplored the fact that he was under pressure from the Government to make arrangements to be prepared to cover the proposed invasion of France on D-Day without suitably qualified reporters. Talbot was instructed to stay with the Eighth Army which was now moving northwards towards Monte

The reports of Godfrey Talbot were crafted from personal experience, courtesy of SWWEC

Casino and the fall of Rome. Once again, his accurate, succinct reportage was appreciated by both the military and his employers, and he was awarded a military OBE and was Mentioned in Dispatches.

The Italian peninsula campaign was very different from that of the North African desert:

> After the Messina strait crossing it was a case of inching forward up the mainland: Salerno, Naples, Cassino, Pescara, Rome, then on to Florence, Bologna, Ravenna and Milan – those were the mileposts of a bitter and often bogged-down campaign. But to the fighting soldiers it was not the towns but the country and the valleys which spelled the agony; and especially river after bloody river to cross: Volturno, Sangro, Liri, Arno and Po. [*PTS*, p.58]

On one occasion, in July 1944, in Italy, King George VI made a visit and was introduced to Talbot, who was later to write that the King said, 'Do you know, as a matter of fact I think Talbot, you, I shouldn't say this, you are about our favourite broadcaster. You broadcast very frequently in the news bulletins. I think you are our favourite, and then he paused and he said, You and Tommy Handley'. [quoted from SWWEC]

Talbot's broadcasts were appreciated by the general public. A Red Cross Nurse sent him a letter dated April 1943 in which she wrote:

> You cannot imagine how many people say to me, "Have you heard Godfrey Talbot" or "Do you listen to Godfrey Talbot?" and the many lovely things they say about you. I have an old friend who's [sic] boy is with the 8th Army, and who is now in hospital. She said I feel very happy and do not worry about him because of [your] broadcasts. So you see, we all think of you too – no doubt thousands of mothers, wives and sweethearts feel like we do. [quoted from SWWEC]

After the war, Talbot was called to the BBC's headquarters, made Chief Reporter of the News Division, and asked to organize a news-gathering team for BBC Radio. After covering the trial of "Lord Haw-Haw" and the reinstating of the flood defences at Rammekens in Holland in 1946, he settled into his new post. One of his recommendations to the BBC's top executives was that there should be a number of specialist correspondents covering a variety of news topics, among whom should be a Royal correspondent accredited to Buckingham Palace. Without actually canvassing for this particular post, he was promptly given the job and became the first BBC court reporter. He needed to approach his job with some caution and certainly a great deal of tact, because there were difficulties within the royal household that included Princess Margaret's private life and, even more delicate, the Queen's relationship with the Duke and Duchess of Windsor. As far as the general public were concerned, Talbot was most recognizable as the radio voice commentating on state occasions such as the wedding of the Princess Elizabeth and Prince Philip, and the frequent royal tours. In fact, not many years passed before Queen Elizabeth became the most travelled Head of State in the world. For him, it was not always straight forward. On one occasion, during the tour of Canada by the then Princess Elizabeth in 1951, the royal train made an unexpected stop at a remote station, so the ever-resourceful Talbot jumped off the train and sent his broadcast from a public telephone adjacent to a public toilet.

It was a period when royal affairs were given an absolute priority by the BBC. As far as the news department was concerned, the rule was that even minor news topics regarding the royal family were to be given top billing even if other momentous world events were unfolding. This, of course, meant that Talbot was constantly broadcasting to the nation. It was in many ways a very different time, with a greater emphasis on formality and an even greater adulation of the Royal Family, as witnessed by the occasion when the Queen announced on the concluding day of the Commonwealth and Empire Games at Cardiff that she was to create her son, Charles, Prince of Wales. For Talbot and many others, this was the broadcast of the year. 1958 was indeed a very busy year for him. He covered the state visit to Holland, the tour of Ethiopia and Somaliland by the Duke and Duchess of Gloucester, the World Fair in Brussels and Winston Churchill's golden wedding celebrations which took place on the Riviera. Then came de Gaulle's inauguration as President of France, accompanied by a wave of Algerian terrorism.

Just a taste of the frenetic pace of Royal Tours of those days is given by Talbot in *Permission to Speak*.

> Those tours were endurance tests. One of them lasted a whole 6 months, the first of the Queen's visits to Australia and New Zealand…..Journeying with the official party, broadcasting every day, I experienced some peculiar restrictions and personal difficulties. Every place visited was on holiday: it was always once-in-a-lifetime Royal Visit Day, an official and absolute pause for celebrations. Therefore no one worked, no shop was ever open wherever we were. I could never get laundry done, and it took me a fortnight to buy a toothbrush. [*PTS*, p.91]

To what lengths he went in order to broadcast from an advantageous position may be judged from his experience when covering the Royal Tour of Nigeria:

Beyond A Little Learning

I imagine the funniest sight I ever presented was when I was playing Broadcaster Afloat aboard a very different craft [from the Royal Yacht *Britannia*]: a war canoe. It was in Nigeria and I was crouching, with a portable recorder in my lap, at the sharp end of a huge canoe which was in a flotilla of overloaded tubs parading in front of royalty on the muddy waters of the [river] Bonny at Port Harcourt, in the region of deltas and mangrove swamps which are part of the Rivers Province. Behind me, all in our one frail craft, were forty armed paddlers, four drummers, a naked figure manning an old Portuguese cannon, and on a platform two chiefs carrying flags, one dressed in a funeral top hat and the other wearing a Victorian fire helmet. The voyagers in our canoe and others of the amazing fleet paddled up and down chanting and yelling and discharging hundreds of old rifles in a non-stop *feu de joie*. It was a remarkable sight. Best of all, for certain of the spectators on the river banks, was the spectacle of me, an incongruous figure in a sweat-stained bush shirt among all the undressed warriors, trying to talk and keep my balance in the din and the dithering of my rocking vessel. A great shout of laughter went up when we had a collision and I was shot off my perch and fell into the river, still talking. The recording machine suffered far more than I did. [*PTS*, pp.122-23]

BBC presenter Richard Dimbleby

Such minor vexations were gladly accepted as a small price to pay for the privilege of seeing a bewildering variety of places for which tourists would be only too happy to pay. And there was always the unintended and unpremeditated hitch to add a touch of humour to the overly elaborate formal occasions such as technical hitches or over zealous brass bands drowning out his broadcast.

Sadly, with the ever-increasing popularity of television, Talbot's radio reporting began to be subservient to the newer medium, and in the public mind it was the new generation of television reporters that captured the attention of a widening audience. Indeed, Richard Dimbleby himself was to become the familiar, almost venerated, voiceover of splendid royal occasions.

Godfrey was the castaway on Roy Plomley's *Desert Island Discs* on 29 August 1960 and chose as his favourite music Rachmaninov's *Second Piano Concerto*. His choice of book was Thomas Macaulay's *Critical and Historical Essays*, and for his sole luxury he opted for 'writing materials'. He later recalled,

> *Desert Island Discs* is hardly ever broadcast "live". But my edition was – from a studio like a goldfish bowl too: the programme went out direct and unrehearsed from a glass-walled room at the Radio and Television Show at the Earls Court exhibition centre in London. Plomley gracefully said he wouldn't have done it "live" if he hadn't had a "pro" as a victim. He had, in me, an old hand at the Hello Business. [*PTS*, p.129]

In *Who's Who*, he offered as his recreation 'keeping quiet'.

Godfrey Talbot was appointed Lieutenant of the Royal Victorian Order in 1960 and in 1969 he retired from his duties as royal correspondent. He lived for many years in a large detached house on Tinshill Lane, in Cookridge. He began a new career as a popular speaker on various lecture circuits, regaling his audiences with amusing anecdotes about royalty. He wrote several books on the royal family and two volumes of memoirs, *Ten Seconds from Now* (1973) and *Permission to Speak* (1976).

He became President of the Queen's English Society in 1982 and very occasionally reported for the BBC again on special occasions. On the fortieth anniversary of VE Day in 1985 he managed an interview with the Queen, during which she mentioned that during the celebrations on the day itself in 1945 she went out of the palace in disguise to mingle with the crowds.

Talbot lamented the fall in standards of written and spoken English. Commenting shortly after the death of the Duke of Norfolk in January 1975, and seeing in that august peer the quintessence of service to one's country, he wrote:

It is difficult to find leaders and patriots now. It is difficult to find England and the English. We are so cursed by trendy wreckers of tradition and loyalty, so invaded and infiltrated by alien people and foreign ways, that our motherland is in danger of becoming an abstraction and pride of country something to apologise for…. And if the nation has taken a beating, so has its tongue. Nasty things have happened to the English language. Yet spoken English, my business, has been enriched as well as eroded. Word-broadcasting has become a universal weapon and a way of life in my time. [*PTS*, p.169]

Talbot died on 3 September 2000 at Kenley in Surrey. He had outlived his wife, Bessie, and one of their two sons.

Bibliography
Purser, Philip, "Godfrey Walker Talbot", in *Oxford Dictionary of National Biography*
Purser, Philip, *The Guardian*, Obituary dated 5 September 2000
Rowley, Allen, *Memory Lane – a Second Look*, The Breedon Books Publishing Company (Derby: 1999)
Talbot, Godfrey Walker, *Permission to Speak*, Hutchinson (London: 1976)
Talbot, Godfrey Walker, *Ten Seconds from Now*, Hutchinson (London: 1973)

*Geoffrey Wooler pictured at his graduation,
courtesy of Peter Wooler*

18

Geoffrey Hubert Wooler 1911-2010
Consultant Cardiothoracic Surgeon at Leeds General Infirmary and a pioneer of open-heart surgery
At LGS 1920-1924

GEOFFREY WOOLER WAS born on 24 November 1911 at 35 Spencer Place, Roundhay Road, Chapeltown into a family with well established roots in Leeds and the surrounding area going back to the eighteenth century. His father, George Hartley Wooler, was a successful businessman in the sanitary ware trade, having taken over the firm from his father, Edwin. His mother was Ethel Pauline, the daughter of a quarry owner. Sadly, she went blind following the birth of her elder son, Edwin John Loy (who was later to be Lord Mayor of Leeds). A sister, Joyce, was born a few years after Geoffrey. To assist Ethel, a nursemaid called Winnie was employed to look after the children and she taught Geoffrey how to knit and crochet, skills he later claimed helped him as a surgeon.

Geoffrey attended a local private kindergarten, Priory College on Roundhay Road run by the Misses Newman, and then, following the move to Spencer House on Shadwell Main Street, from nine to thirteen he went to Leeds Grammar School. Both his parents were musical and Geoffrey distinguished himself in his first year at the Grammar School by playing Beethoven's First Piano Sonata at a school concert. Then, in 1924, he went to Giggleswick School whose headmaster, R N Douglas, was a distinguished academic and devout Christian. He was the youngest boarder but he was saved from most of the initiation activities by his elder brother, Loy, who was an excellent rugby player. Making the erroneous assumption that Geoffrey would likewise excel on the rugby field he was promptly given a place by the sports master in the Colts' First Team but he disliked the game and was soon

Geoffrey Hubert Wooler – Pioneer of Open-heart Surgery

dropped. However, the academic side of the school was excellent and he achieved 11 credits in the School Certificate (Matriculation) examinations.

From Giggleswick he went up to Selwyn College, Cambridge to read Law for the LLB course (following the example of his elder brother) but very soon found he took exception to the course, chiefly because of its insistence on teaching Roman Law (in Latin) ad nauseam and so, with his father's blessing, changed to Medicine. He graduated with a BA (Hons) in Medicine after three years and in October 1933 he went to the London Hospital at Whitechapel to learn clinical procedures. These included gynaecology, in which capacity he helped to deliver babies in and around Limehouse, an area very different from his home at Shadwell. He qualified in 1937 after passing the London Conjoint Examination and graduated Cambridge MB (Bachelor of Medicine), ChB (Bachelor of Surgery) in 1938.

His second resident appointment at the London Hospital was House Surgeon to the Ear, Nose and Throat Department under Norman Patterson, senior Consulting Surgeon in the ENT department, and in a short time he became resident to Tudor Edwards in the Thoracic Surgical Unit. His third appointment was with Russell Howard, the senior Consulting Surgeon.

Geoffrey Wooler while a Cambridge student, courtesy of Peter Wooler

In September 1938 Geoffrey joined the Royal Army Medical Corps (RAMC) of the Territorial Army (TA) which was being greatly expanded in view of the threat of war with Germany. He was appointed Medical Officer (MO) to the 2nd Battalion, the Queen's Westminsters, and when war did break out in September 1939 he decided to remain in the TA before he completed his training, much against the advice of his seniors. Earlier, in the autumn of 1938, he had had a brief taste of life under the Nazi regime when he visited Professor Sauerbruch, a bold and pioneering surgeon, at his clinic at the Charité Hospital at Berlin. He had spent two days in Hanover where he met an old friend, Hans Brink, and together the two men visited Sauerbruch. He attended some concerts given by the German State Orchestra; but the dreadful aura of fear was amply demonstrated when he witnessed the violence of Kristallnacht on 9 November 1938. A little later, after eating at a restaurant one evening, he was arrested by two Blackshirts, who falsely accused him of stealing from damaged Jewish shops, a situation made worse when they discovered he was a member of the TA. He was further questioned, fined and released. He fled Germany before more serious charges were made.

On returning to England he applied to re-join the London Hospital and in time gained his MRCS (Member of the Royal College of Surgeons (of England)). His new role in the TA (RAMC) was to check the health of new recruits to the Army. However, rather more urgent was the severe outbreak of 'flu in the winter of 1939-40 which led to many recruits being laid off sick and sent home. Having dealt with that, he undertook weapons practice and was soon ready to move with his battalion on to Glanusk's Park, near Crickhowell.

In December 1940, Tudor Edwards invited him to go to South Wales to deal with chest injuries sustained by men caught in the bombing of several English ports and airfields. By now he was a Captain and in 1941 he took his final examination and passed. With German air raids slackening off somewhat after Hitler invaded Russia in May 1941, he returned to his Unit and by May 1942 was transferred to the 70th General Hospital stationed at Oxford under Colonel Whelton. It was at this time that penicillin was being produced in small quantities and this was to have a major impact on the treatment of patients. He recounts an incident when a young serviceman was in a coma and was administered a small dose of penicillin, then in very short supply, which had no effect whatsoever so Geoffrey used his charm and managed to acquire a much larger dose which brought the young man round in double-quick time. [DVD interview supplied by Peter Wooler]

In November, Geoffrey received his movement order to join the British First Army in North Africa. Leaving Oxford, he entrained to Glasgow and on 22 November arrived off Algiers. From there he sailed eastwards to Bone where he was asked to form a small mobile surgical team from 70th General Hospital personnel in order to help surgeons working with Field Ambulances at the Front. He joined the Unit at Sedjenane where 185th Field Ambulance was billeted in an old tobacco factory. This was badly bombed by the Germans in February 1943 so he was transferred to 83 General Hospital at La Calle (El Kala) which was much closer to the savage fighting around Tunis. By late February the fighting was very severe and the number of casualties – British, Italian and German – grew alarmingly. For Geoffrey this meant working day and night with only brief snatches of sleep and rest. After a brief spell at Gafour, where he was temporary OC of 31 Field Surgical Unit, he returned to his own Unit at Thibar, but a major German offensive resulted in a flood of casualties, many of who died. The tide, however, was turning and with the Germans retreating from Tunis in May Geoffrey now had to deal mainly with Axis soldiers. Ironically, he was assisted by very competent Axis surgeons.

He was now assigned to No. 3 Field Surgical Unit and sent to the island of Pantelleria, south west of Sicily which had surrendered after a terrific aerial bombardment and this represented the first successful Allied landing in Europe. He was forced to perform complex surgical procedures in severely damaged petrol storage tunnels in appalling conditions: fleas and ordure were a constant problem. Soon, however, the Unit was quickly moved to a more hygienic site on the island.

With the invasion of mainland Italy under way, he flew to Taranto to take over the TB hospital there and was busy dealing with the casualties following a successful German air raid on Bari harbour which damaged several Allied ships. To his consternation, one of the ships was carrying mustard gas, a fact that was kept secret by the military authorities, and many of the victims died horribly because the RAMC doctors were not told of the gas poisoning until it was too late.

In December 1943 Geoffrey was promoted to Major and took over as OC 26 Field Service Unit at Torremaggiore in Apulia. From there he was sent to Cassino where the major battle commenced in March 1944. Working once more under dreadful conditions and constantly at risk of shelling and gunfire, he struggled with a fresh influx of injured soldiers; and when Cassino fell, he was appalled by the number of dead Germans and recalls spending days hurriedly burying them to ameliorate the stench. [DVD interview] Astonishingly, he was given no respite (apart from four days' leave to Positano) and sent north to the Gustav Line where the Germans were putting up a strong defence. Here, he learned that, for his unstinting work at Cassino, he had been Mentioned in Despatches. From the Gustav Line he moved to Rome and then Ceprano. It was at this time that he took his one and only German prisoner, a cook who thankfully offered no resistance and was probably only too glad to fall into Allied hands. After further spells at Lake Trasimeno, Pompeii and Rimini, always working under enormous pressure, he ended up in Bari. At last the relentless pressure ceased when the Germans surrendered in May 1945. It is estimated that, throughout the War, he treated around 3000 casualties, many of them very seriously wounded.

Potts clocks at LGI and Otley Market place, right [photos courtesy of Pam Hargreaves]

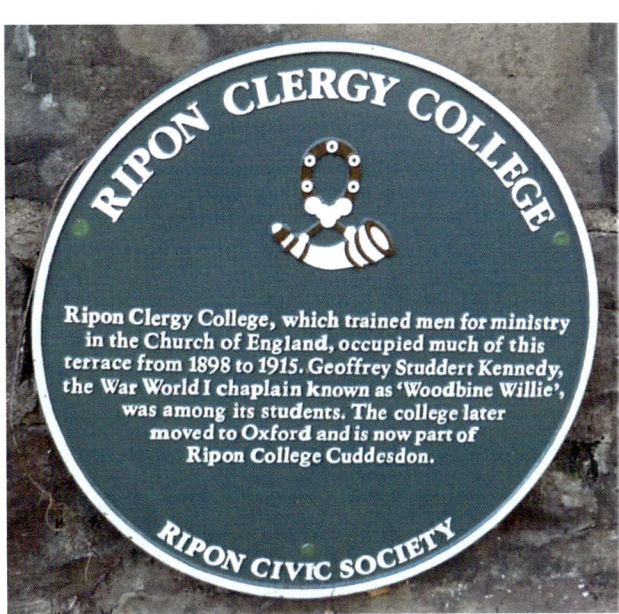

Plaque, left, commemorating Woodbine Willie's student days, [photo courtesy of Church Times*]*

The Cathedral Close at Wells, above, where the four Hollis brothers lived as children, [photo courtesy of Wikipedia]; Stonyhurst College, Clitheroe, below, where Christopher Hollis taught and wrote his early books, [photo courtesy of Stonyhurst College]

Robert (left) and Lord John Dyson wearing his robes of Master of the Rolls, above. Below: Robert (left) and John go boating on Roundhay's Waterloo Lake. It was normal for pupils to wear their school uniforms, even on an annual family holiday [photos courtesy of Robert Dyson]

The ruins of Monte Cassino, above. Both Geoffrey Wooler and Godfrey Talbot were horrified by the scale of casualties there. [photo courtesy of Military Times*]; Geoffrey Wooler's name, below, on the Honours Board inside the entrance to the LGI [photo by author]*

1924	MR . MICHAEL W.C. OLDFIELD	1938
1924	MR . ARTHUR J.C. LATCHMORE	1940
1926	MR . T McMASTER BOYLE	1946
1927	MR . HENRY S. SHUCKSMITH	1946
1930	MR . HERBERT AGAR	1946
1931	MR . JOHN M.P. CLARK	1946
1933	MR . GEOFFREY H. WOOLER	1948
1933		

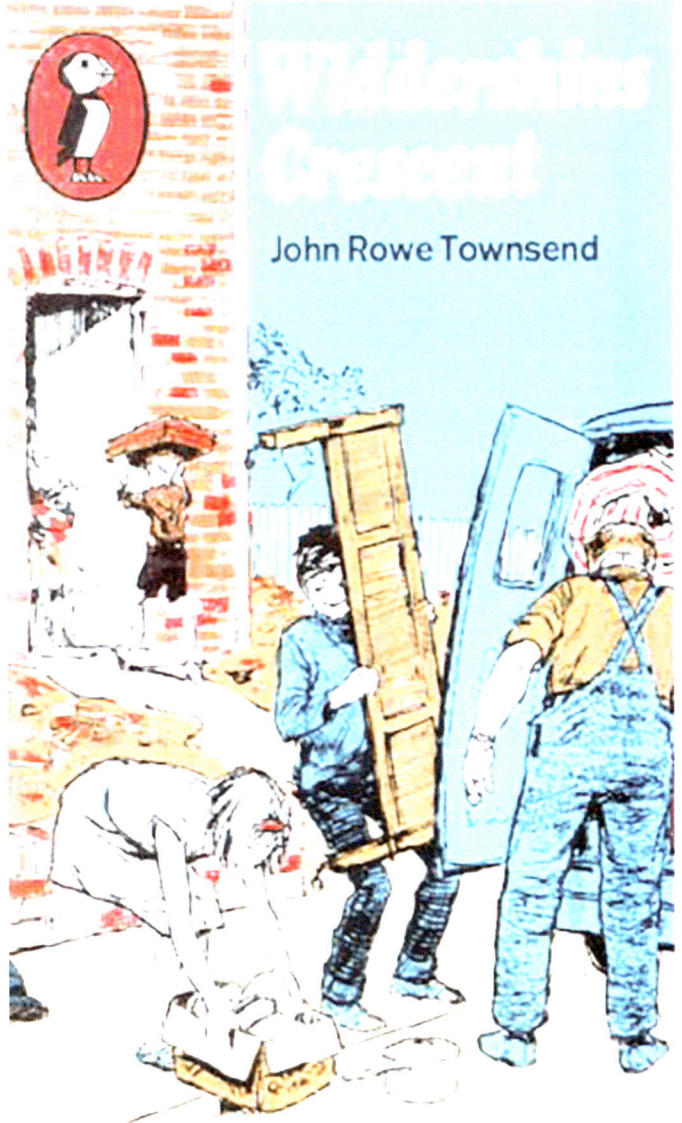

Hawker Hart plane, above, on which John Freeborn undertook flying training [photo courtesy of ww2aircraft.net]

John Rowe Townsend's Widdershin's Crescent, left, was praised for its gritty realism [photo of cover courtesy of Puffin Books]

Sir Gerald Bernard Kaufman was an MP for 47 years [drawing courtesy of Doreen Greenshields]

Barry Cryer has performed at the Leeds City Varieties, above, on many occasions [photo courtesy of Leeds City Magazine*]*

Clare College, Cambridge, above, where Geoffrey Crowther studied Economics
[photo courtesy of Clare College]

Two drawings by Rodney Hill. Rodney became a distinguished scientist specializing in Applied Mathematics

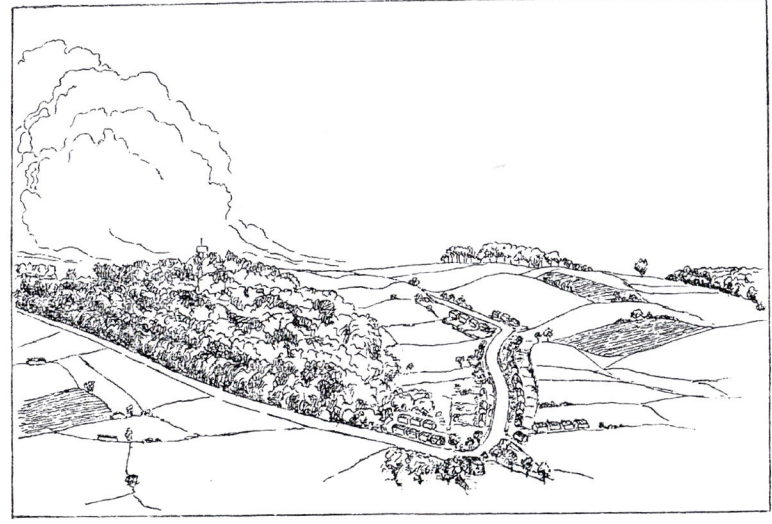

COOKRIDGE FROM THE WEST.   R. HILL.

A tour poster for Kaiser Chiefs with Ricky Wilson centre stage [photo courtesy of Ricky Wilson]

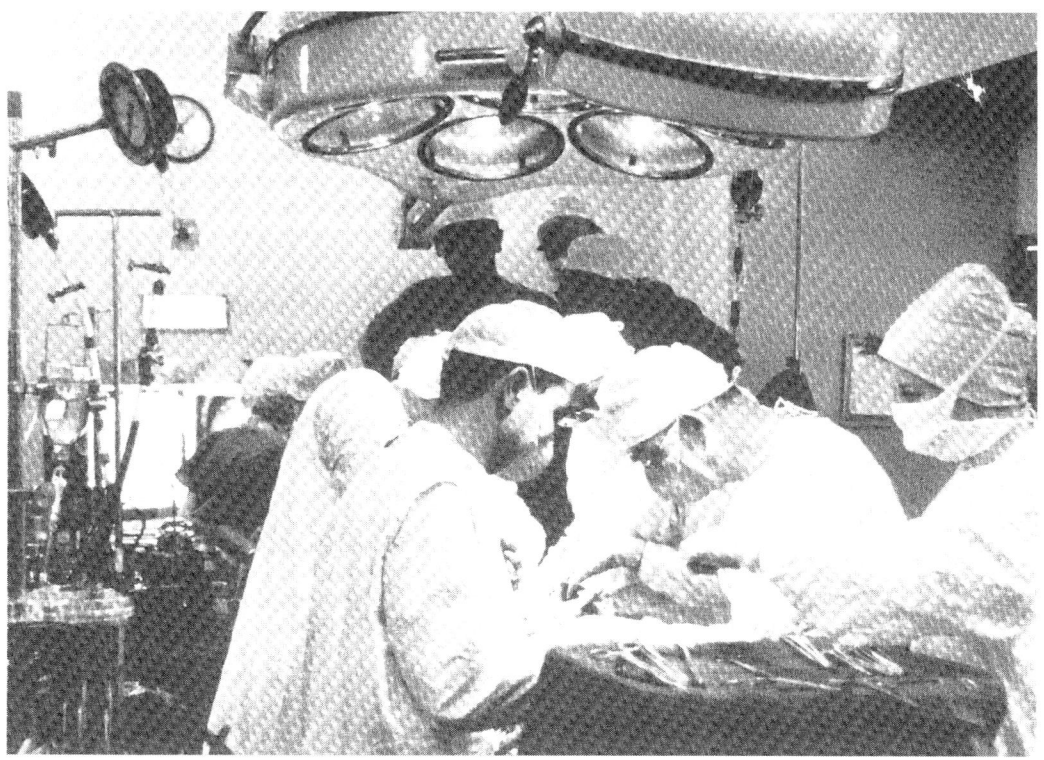

Geoffrey Wooler operating at LGI (second from right), courtesy of Peter Wooler

In January 1946 Geoffrey was discharged from the Army with the rank of Lieutenant-Colonel. He was war-weary and ready for a quieter life in England. He even felt that he had had sufficient surgical experience to last a lifetime. Back in Shadwell he met up with his brother Loy for the first time in four years. To his delight he learned that Loy had married and there was a son, Peter. Loy had received an MBE for downing a V1 rocket whilst commanding an AA Battery at Dover. He was later elected Lord Mayor of Leeds in 1963. Geoffrey enjoyed a quiet spell with his family and this so restored his vitality that he returned to the London Hospital as a Consultant. He was now a Surgical First Assistant to both Tudor Edwards and George Neligan.

He was gaining a great deal of experience delivering civilian surgery and he began to publish his results through the medical journals. He also wrote up an account of his war-time surgical exploits and for this he was awarded an MD from Cambridge University.

His reputation was spreading throughout the medical world and in October 1954 John Latchmore from the LGI in Leeds invited him to join the thoracic surgery team there. Geoffrey, always happy to be close to his family, readily accepted and

Geoffrey Hubert Wooler – Pioneer of Open-heart Surgery

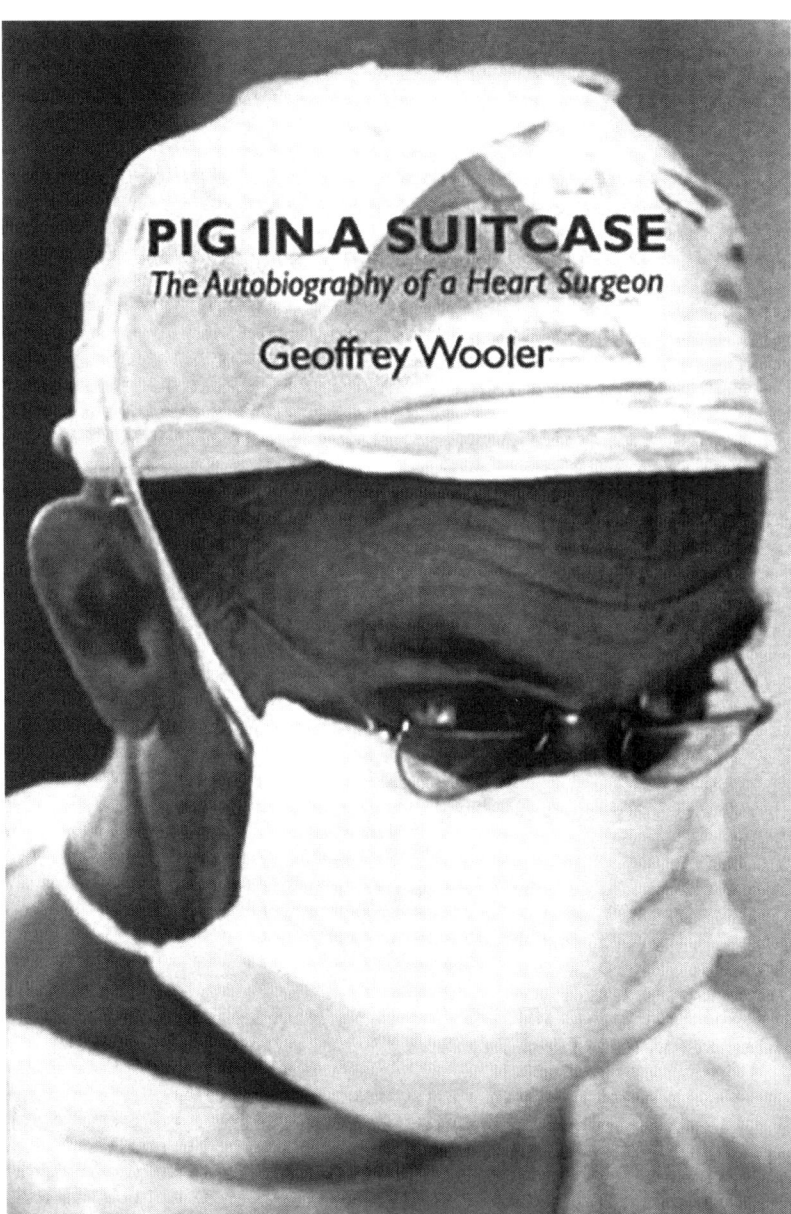

Geoffrey Wooler shared his own account of a remarkable career in an autobiography

started at the LGI in February 1947 with Philip Allison, who was appointed Professor of Surgery in 1953. Here, he became acquainted with the so-called "Leeds incision" which meant that surgery was not limited to the chest area, because the incision could be any length required by the operating surgeon. This allowed him to perform surgery for a much wider variety of conditions such as stomach cancers and in effect meant that he was a general surgeon rather than a specifically thoracic one. He was promoted to Consultant in 1948 and was elected as Fellow of the Royal College of Surgeons (FRCS).

Such was his reputation that when, in November 1952, Lord Woolton, President of the Queen's Council, became seriously ill at the Conservative Party Conference held in Scarborough, Geoffrey was called to the Belvedere Nursing Home to attend to him. He received a frosty reception from the other consultants and specialists who had misdiagnosed the condition, but Lord Woolton was delighted to see him. Geoffrey performed a bronchoscopy on him to release a build-up of phlegm from a ruptured abscess and a couple of days later removed part of a rib to allow the abscess to drain more freely. His lordship made a good recovery and was so grateful he recommended Geoffrey for a knighthood, an honour that was rejected by the College of Surgeons because they considered him too young and that his method was too dangerous.

Another patient of his in the same year, 1952, was Bob Appleyard, the Yorkshire County Cricket player who had contracted tuberculosis a year after he had taken 200 first-class wickets in his first full season.

Geoffrey carried out a life-saving operation on him: '…tuberculosis was correctly diagnosed, and…he underwent an operation to remove part of the infected lung. The surgeon, Geoffrey Wooler, showed exceptional skill in minimising the damage to his rib cage.' [*Daily Telegraph*, 17 March 2015] The two men became good friends. For many years, Geoffrey was to be seen at Headingley watching the cricket as Bob's guest.

In the years that followed, he undertook several more procedures similar to the one performed on Lord Woolton and his success rate was excellent. In 1964, the revised edition of *Clinical Surgery* by Professor Charles Rob and Lord Rodney Smith included his method so it had clearly been accepted as good practice.

In 1954 Geoffrey was appointed Professor of Surgery at Leeds assisted by John Alwyn. They worked on cirrhosis of the liver at a time when the first heart/lung machines were being developed by Denis Melrose, who was then working in the Department of Physiology at Hammersmith Hospital. Experimental work was carried out on dogs and, following some technical improvements to the cannula and the pump, the machine was ready for its first open-heart surgery patient in February 1957, repairing a leaking mitral valve. The whole procedure was in its infancy, so much so that there was no mechanical respirator to assist breathing. Nevertheless his team worked all hours to achieve greater efficiencies and the result was a growing number of successful repairs to faulty heart valves, despite the woeful lack of investment in technical apparatus.

This good work in open-heart surgery was interrupted when Geoffrey developed a large tuberculosis abscess in his chest and yet three weeks after the removal of this abscess he went to the United States to lecture and perform surgery for two weeks. He returned to Shadwell feeling rather weary: should he carry on the heart repair work? The waiting list was growing daily, so the answer was to

Geoffrey Hubert Wooler – Pioneer of Open-heart Surgery

reduce his work load by appointing a third Consultant and working on less-demanding procedures.

In 1971 he was invited to lecture and demonstrate at Cairo. Staying at the Sheraton Hotel he had the misfortune to be there when the Jordanian Prime Minister was assassinated on the steps of the hotel. Deeming his situation to be fraught with danger, he quickly moved to another hotel, performed a number of operations and then enjoyed some sight-seeing which included the new Nasser Dam. Incredibly, within months of its construction the lake formed as a result of the dam was teeming with fish. Returning to Cairo, he was arrested as a suspected spy – he was a keen photographer and had been spotted taking pictures in a sensitive area above Cairo. Fortunately, the Head of Police there knew Geoffrey, who had operated on a member of his family, so once again he extricated himself from a precarious position.

Post-operative death rates in heart operations were still unacceptably high so he worked alongside others to improve surgical techniques. It was at this time that he met Dr Christiaan Barnard who was to achieve fame by carrying out the world's first heart transplant operation. Geoffrey had a wide circle of friends; he

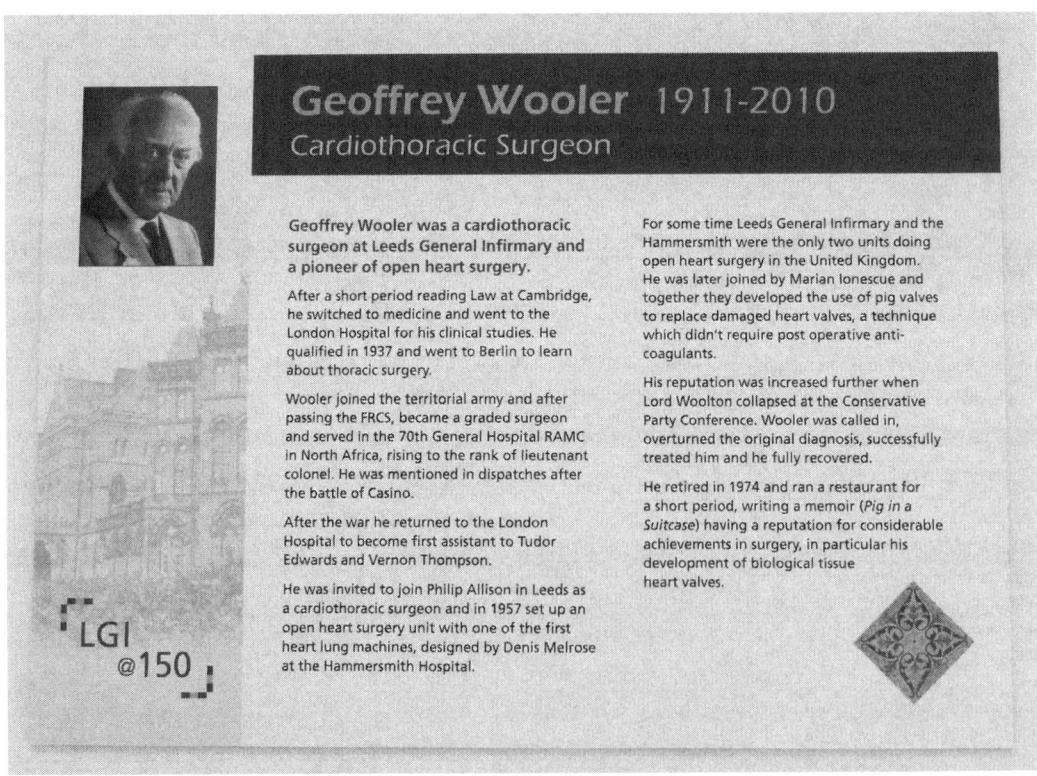

Wooler's plaque on the first floor corridor of the LGI

invited Dr William Pickles [OL02] from Aysgarth to the annual meeting of the Thoracic Surgical Society; and he met and befriended Marian Ion Ionescu, a refugee from the Ceausescu regime in Romania. This was very fortunate because Ionescu later became a Consultant in Cardio-thoracic surgery and it was he and Geoffrey Wooler who pioneered the use of pigs' aortic valves in open heart surgery.

As his eyesight deteriorated, Geoffrey operated less and less until, in 1974, he made the decision to resign from the Health Service after 25 years' dedicated service. He was presented with a cheque for £11!

Life after surgery was interesting but not quite so successful. He tried to run a restaurant in Grove Lane, Headingley, but after a year he sold it on to the chef. However, living next door, he did patronise the restaurant for many years, entertaining his wide circle of friends with his reminiscences.

Many of the colleagues and friends who had worked with him over the years wished to show their appreciation of Geoffrey both as a professional and an esteemed bon viveur so, unknown to him, they formed a group known as 'The Wooler Society' which met every year to renew friendships and catch up on the latest news. In 1989, to commemorate these annual meetings, the American members had a plaque fixed to the wall at the main entrance to the LGI. It is still there today.

He died on New Year's Day 2010 aged 98.

Bibliography:

Daily Telegraph, 17 March 2015
Royal College of Surgeons; biographical entry under Plarr's Lives of the Fellows Online; 2010
Wooler, Geoffrey, *Pig in a Suitcase*, Smith Settle, 1999
Wooler, Geoffrey, *A History of Cardiac Surgery: an Interview with Geoffrey Wooler FRCS, October 6 1997*, a DVD from the Annette and Erwin Eskind Biomedical Library, the Vanderbilt University Medical School, conducted by William S Stoney MD [interview took place on 10 June 1997 at Leeds]
Yorkshire Post; Obituary January 2010

Pilot Officer John Freeborn at the age of 18

19

John Connell Freeborn DFC & Bar 1919-2010
Wing Commander RAF: Fighter Ace in World War Two
At LGS 1928-1934

JOHN CONNELL FREEBORN, DFC and bar, was one of the RAF's leading fighter "aces" in the Battle of Britain, during which he flew more operational hours than any other pilot.

He was born on 1 December 1919 at Middleton, then on the outskirts of Leeds and an area of open farmland. His father, Harold, was a bank manager with the Yorkshire Penny Bank and the family moved to 27 Broomfield Crescent in Headingley, where they lived a comfortable middle class lifestyle as evidenced by the employment of a nurse. His mother, Jean, a somewhat dour Scot, came from agricultural stock and was to be a great influence on John's life and career. Besides John, there were two sisters and three brothers; all four boys attended Leeds Grammar School. Discipline at home was tough; retribution in the form of sound beatings was the inevitable consequence of unruly behaviour.

He attended Brudenell Road Council School and then followed his two brothers, William Archibald (at LGS 1922-1929) and Harold (at LGS 1925-1928) to Leeds Grammar School. Bob Cossey, in his biography of Freeborn, *A Tiger's Tale*, relates how John 'hated his school days and the prime reason for this was a growing aversion to authority – something which was to stay with him throughout his life and which in truth has led him into many a sticky situation with his superiors both in his military service and indeed in civvy street'. [BC, p.1] John conceded that authority did have its place in any organization, be it school, the RAF or business, but 'it is the abuse of authority by those who should know better or by those who contrive to exercise and manipulate it for their own ends that John despises'. [BC, pp.1-2] He was not very interested in the academic curriculum forced upon him by the teachers and let his feelings be known to the staff, who tended to treat him as a rebellious, impudent boor. 'On one occasion he was assaulted by a teacher who persistently knocked him over the head with the edge of a ruler. John retaliated and both ended up on the floor with fists flying.' [BC, p.2] His father, on hearing the cause of the fracas, supported John but made it clear that discipline had its proper place and that rules were there for a purpose. This incident is further elaborated upon in a letter sent by him to the author. I have made one or two judicious corrections to John's prose:

> I was persistently bullied by the masters. It started with Dr Johnson [Rev W L Johnson at LGS 1903-1931], Head of the Junior School. A clergyman and a disgusting snob. This put me onto the track of self-defence, of course. This attitude of Johnson's infected Miss Jones [at LGS 1918-55] who couldn't leave my hair alone, even on sight, until Miss Christie stopped her doing it.
>
> It is an unfortunate fact that the pacifist [sic] Headmaster Terry Thomas was a confirmed bully, and when he administered punishment he required Sgt Young to be in attendance.
>
> Sgt Young rescued a science master [who] was hitting me on the head with the edge of a ruler, one that was fitted a metal strip. The reason for inflicting this punishment was I dared to smoke and was doing it. It was a silly thing for him to do and I told him if he did it again I would hit him. So the fool did it again and made my head bleed. I knocked him down, sat on his chest, took his ears and was banging his head on the floor when Sgt Young, who was passing the room, heard the commotion, came into the room and saved the master from possible injury.

In fairness to those members of staff alluded to above, it is as well to remember that John never pulled his punches and was notorious throughout his life for his abrasive candour. However, all was not confrontation and sparring. Later in his letter John writes, 'School was not all like this. I had great friends amongst the masters – Mason Clarke, Dr Osborn, Rev Cranmer, Miss Christie and others. The friendship lasted until I went to live in Spain. But many times a year Dr Osborn visited my Masonic Lodge and I his.' [letter, ibid]

His parents encouraged him to be proud of his country and, though

An older and more experienced John Freeborn

patriotism may be the 'last refuge of a scoundrel', for John it was natural that he should think of serving his country in the face of increasing provocation from Italy and Germany.

He left the Grammar School at 16 but he was destined to return on the famous occasion when he 'borrowed' a Gloster Gauntlet aircraft and landed on the cricket pitch after an aerobatic display. John treasured the irony of seeing his teachers, many of whom had beaten him severely a short time previously, hold him up to the pupils as an example of British pluck. As Christopher Yeoman wrote in *Tiger Cub*,

> John remembers one particular occasion at home with fondness. It was the time he met up with his old Physical Training teacher, Mason Clark in a local pub. Mason was possibly the only teacher John ever liked and so when he asked John if he would fly over the school on his return to

Hornchurch, the Pilot Officer gladly obliged. On the morning of his return [to his squadron] John flew over the school and landed his aircraft down on the green grass of the cricket pitch at the front of the school and taxied around to see young boys cheering. Although he couldn't hear them over his noisy engine, the sight of those boys waving their arms at him filled him with elation as he prepared to take off again. "I hoped that nobody else had seen me land because I would have been in for some trouble, but nobody did and when I got back to Hornchurch, all was well." [*TC*, p.29]

Great friend and school master Mason Clarke

Having left school, he was, like many other boys, unsure what he wanted to do. Cossey suggests it was a stark choice between the coal mines and the armed services, but this seems odd given his father's professional status. Possibly John's exam results were so poor that he would have found entry into the professions difficult. So he joined the Reserve of Air Force Officers, in which choice he may have been influenced by his experience of the School's OTC as a drummer and bugle boy. He was interviewed at Aldwych and eventually accepted. He took an immediate liking to the RAF and, in particular, flying.

The RAF in the mid-thirties was undergoing a radical expansion and reorganization. Recognizing the increasing threat from Germany, the government proposed to establish an RAF consisting of 124 squadrons hosting 1,737 aircraft. To accommodate these, new airfields were constructed at an increasingly furious pace.

Carrying his suitcase, John left home and travelled to Leeds Central Station where, waiting for his train to Sywell, he was spotted by a group of older boys looking for trouble. They found it when they attempted to set about John. 'They chose the wrong person – John got stuck in, they fled and honour was maintained. This was one of a number of practical lessons of life that John was learning. He was now making his own way in the world and part of that involved learning to look after himself.' (BC, p.173]

John reported to the Elementary Flying Training School at Sywell on 17 January 1938 and proceeded to train on the Tiger Moth. The course lasted three months and he went solo after just four hours and twenty minutes. Typically, he relished the practical aspects of the course – flying – but was falling behind with the classroom work, so his fellow pupils dragooned him into working each evening on his paperwork. This ruse succeeded and he passed.

From Sywell he moved to No. 8 Flying School at Montrose and flew the Hawker Hart. He proved adept at air firing and dive bombing. At the end of his training, John was appointed Acting Pilot Officer. He was posted to RAF Hornchurch in October 1938 to fly with B Flight of 74 Squadron, the famous Tigers, regarded as one of the best units in the RAF. It had started life in the First World War as a fighter unit and had earned a formidable reputation. It was re-formed in 1935 and sent to Malta to deter any possible Italian aggression but returned to the UK after eleven months. Here, John joined a programme of progressive training under the watchful eye of the squadron's OC, Squadron Leader George Sampson. John swiftly transferred to A Flight under a South African, Sailor Malan and at first flew the Gloster Gauntlet. However, by February 1939 the first Spitfires arrived (74 Squadron was the second unit in the country to receive them) and John joined his fellow pilots on the conversion course. This consisted of a few words of instruction, hardly sufficient given the radically different nature of this beast compared to the Gauntlet. He recalled his first flight:

> The aircraft was nose heavy – the complete opposite to the Gauntlet. Taking off from the grass of Hornchurch I treated things very gently! Off I went between the hangars at 180 mph, faster than I had ever been in my life before!.. Once at altitude I settled down and found the Spitfire to be a lovely aeroplane. [BC, p.20]

John was lucky enough to be chosen to participate in the Fall of the Bastille celebrations in July 1939. The Spitfires proved to be of great interest to the French – and also the German observers who were present and clearly impressed by what they saw. The squadron stayed for a fortnight and made good use of the facilities and hospitality on offer in Montmartre.

The outbreak of war on 3 September was followed by a tragic case of "friendly fire" three days later. A Flight, led by Adolph 'Sailor' Malan, was scrambled at 07.00, and very quickly Malan was heard to shout 'Tally Ho!' which sent John and another pilot screaming into the attack on two planes which happened to be Hurricanes of 56 Squadron. Both were shot down and one of the pilots was killed.

John later wrote, 'It was a very misty morning but it was a beautiful day. I remember looking down and seeing we had cut a line through the haze where we had taken off. Malan was well in front… We saw these aircraft and Malan gave the order: "Number One attack – go!"

They made an attack at these aircraft and then pulled away. And so we went and attacked.' [quoted from Patrick Bishop, *Fighter Boys*, p.107] This so-called Battle of Barking Creek caused an outcry; both John and Byrne (the other 74 pilot) were briefly put under close arrest and then appeared before a court martial. Both were completely exonerated but it led to strained relations with 'Sailor' Malan who had appeared for the prosecution.

74 Squadron spent the period of the Phoney War escorting convoys from Dover to Calais and undertaking further training. In October they transferred to RAF Manston and then to RAF Rochford. The first enemy aircraft destroyed in the war was a reconnaissance HE111 on 20 November – but John was not the pilot responsible.

By May 1940 the Phoney War was over and fighter aircraft were called upon to try to achieve air superiority over the Germans while the British and French armies retreated to Dunkirk. 74 was held back along with other squadrons to ensure home defence. By 21 May all RAF units were returned to the UK (that is, away from French airfields) to concentrate on covering the retreating Allied forces. There was a persistent rumour that the RAF was nowhere to be seen at this crucial stage, but the records show that Fighter Command lost almost 100 aircraft (including 42 Spitfires) during the 2,739 sorties that had been flown in direct support of the retreat. The Tigers were prominent in patrolling the skies over Dunkirk in an effort to stop the Luftwaffe from attacking the retreating men.

Just prior to the start of the Battle of Britain, John was promoted to Flight Commander, retaining the rank of Pilot Officer. The Tigers returned to Hornchurch on 6 June 1940. Fighter Command emerged from the Battle of France (as the covering operation over Dunkirk was called) in a seriously depleted condition, having lost a total of 453 Spitfires and Hurricanes. A brief hiatus in hostilities allowed some recuperation, enabling Fighter Command to muster 644 aircraft and 1,259 pilots. Command HQ was at Bentley Priory. Morale was raised when 74 received the Spitfire IIa, John's favourite variant.

When the Germans switched tactics from airfield attacks to the Blitz on London, 74's men reacted angrily and volunteered for night flying over the capital. This was particularly dangerous, not least from friendly fire, and on one occasion he was twice almost killed by his own side. On another sortie he was nearly brought down by a goose that happened to be in the wrong place at the wrong time.

The summer weather of 1940 was in the main idyllic with long, hot days and clear nights. The popular image of pilots sunning themselves, reading newspapers and drinking coffee, only to be rudely interrupted by the warning triangle to "scramble" is accurate. Landing Spitfires were turned around within minutes, so intense was the fighting. The average time taken between "Scramble!" and take-off was around two minutes.

Frequently, the British pilots faced overwhelming odds, sometimes a handful of Spitfires taking on a huge armada of bombers and Messerschmitt fighters. John recalls, 'Once we entered the fray we were on our own. We concentrated on the German we were after and as such we were our own masters… One thing that did astound us all was the fact that despite losses, the Luftwaffe could continually send such numbers of aircraft against us.' [BC, p.51]

On one occasion the Tigers intercepted a single photo-recce Do17 and 30 escorting Bf109s over North Foreland. John shot the leading Me109 down into the sea. 'I was so close I could see everything on this Messerschmitt and could very clearly see the man in it. I fired from fifty yards and it seemed to go sideways in the sky – then he turned over on his back and dropped out of the sky.' [quoted in BC, p.52]

On July 28 John found himself in the middle of 36 Me109s at 18,000 feet and immediately shot one down but the others chased him as far as Brighton Pier, so he dived down towards it, shattering his engine's big ends in the process but fortunately at an airspeed of 360 knots was able to glide back to Manston. Unfortunately his rudder had been hit and knocked into the main fin which locked the aircraft into the left rudder position. The Spitfire tipped over on its nose and then luckily bounced back onto its wheels and John made a quick exit, covered in blood and glass splinters. He was lucky: the blood was washed away to reveal only minor abrasions and within the hour he was in the air again.

74 was losing aircraft and – more importantly but ominously – pilots at a prodigious rate. The Battle of Britain made such huge demands on pilots' stamina, endurance and courage that inevitably for some it all became too much. In July alone, 74 lost seven pilots. For John there was the consolation of being awarded his Distinguished Flying Cross on the last day of the month. The *Yorkshire Post* rather breathlessly reported, 'When older heads were perturbed about the trend of events in 1938, seeking some means of averting what we all dreaded, a Headingley boy left the Leeds Grammar School and went into the RAF... He has been awarded the DFC. Seven Nazi warplanes have fallen to his skill and daring....' [quoted in BC, p.56]

In August, the second phase of the German offensive concentrated on targeting coastal airfields and radar stations. 74 was still flying from Hornchurch and Manston, sometimes managing 70 sorties a day. On the 11th, the squadron flew into battle four times between dawn and 14.00 and destroyed 23 enemy aircraft as well as one probable and 14 damaged. This feat elicited a congratulatory telegram from the Chief of the Air Staff and a personal visit to Hornchurch by Winston Churchill.

Manston was heavily attacked on the following day but luckily 74 was recuperating at Hornchurch.

On the 13th, the Germans threw everything into a make or break attack on the South-East but all to no avail. They lost 45 aircraft against the RAF's 13 and the German High Command began to think that an invasion of Britain was a forlorn hope. But the incessant exposure to danger and death was taking its toll on the British pilots and 74 was pulled out and sent to RAF Wittering to recuperate. John is quite frank about the pilots' feelings and anxieties: they suffered from overwhelming attacks of fear, from nausea and from introspection. Courage was not measured by foolhardiness but by fighting on despite fear and if this is so then John was just such a pilot. 'There was a job to do. We didn't necessarily like it – indeed there were many times when we were frightened out of our wits and hated it. But overall all we could do was make the best of it and make the best of the people around us.' [quoted from BC, p.61]

By this time, 74 had pilots of varied nationalities.

There were two Poles, some Australians and New Zealanders and a Canadian. The Squadron moved to Kirton in Lindsay and then on to Coltishall and readied itself to face the next phase of the Battle of Britain, German attacks on inland airfields around London and the capital itself. John had been promoted to Flight Lieutenant and received his DFC at Buckingham Palace. The citation included the words, 'His high courage and exceptional abilities as a leader have materially contributed to the notable successes and high standards of efficiency maintained by his Squadron'. [quoted in BC, pp.63-64] Whilst stationed at Coltishall, 74 was not involved in the main defence of London but did intercept German aircraft over East Anglia. On one occasion, while attacking a Bf110, John was again hit by "friendly fire" and the culprit begged his CO to be posted to another station to escape John's wrath.

On 15 October, 74 was transferred to RAF Biggin Hill to join 92 Squadron. The station had been battered by a series of German attacks, the worst of which was on Sunday 30 August during which over 40 airmen and several WAAFs were killed. John and his fellow officers were billeted in the country home of Warren Smithers MP, and the local pub, The Crown, became their unofficial HQ. Frenetic reconstruction of Biggin Hill was accompanied by a constant succession of aircraft deployments. 74 was in action over Gravesend and Maidstone. Historians date the conclusion of the Battle of Britain as 30 October but the Germans did not appear to accede to this and continued to send waves of bombers with fighter escorts over South-East England. On 14 November, 74 accounted for 14 Stukas and a Bf109, one of the most successful days in its entire history.

From the beginning of 1941 the RAF concentrated more on offensive sweeps into France. The idea was to fly over the German airfields in northern France and then run down the coast in an attempt to provoke the Luftwaffe into retaliating. The whole scheme was a failure; the Germans were content to shoot the British planes down by using anti-aircraft guns rather than launch their own planes. Next, the British sent in bomber formations accompanied by fighters in the same way the Germans had during the Battle of Britain. This again failed, largely because of heavy British losses.

In February John received a bar to his DFC. The citation included the words, 'This officer has been continuously engaged on operations since the beginning of the war'. [quoted from BC, p.78] He continued flying with 74 but casualties were mounting, and he particularly felt the loss of such good friends as Peter Chesters and Wally Churches. He was still only 22 and 'the loss of close colleagues and friends had a profound effect on those left behind'. [BC, p.79] He, like many others, was just about burned out and his OC knew it. John was posted to 57 Operational Training Unit at Hawarden, near Chester. Typically, John grumbled that he was being taken away from 74 just at the time when they were being given the new Spitfire V, but for him, a change was as good as a rest.

57 OTU might have been a change but it was not much of a rest. John joined a team of instructors whose remit was to convert pilots who had completed their initial training in Canada to the Spitfire. Many trainee pilots came to grief in the mountains of Snowdonia. Many got lost through disorientation and had to land elsewhere; such minor misdemeanours were fined and the proceeds put into a kitty to pay for end-of-course celebrations at the local pub. More seriously, the OTU

Model of a Spitfire Mk IIa

training period was reduced because of the demand for replacement aircrew, but this led to corners being cut and consequently a higher accident and fatality rate.

From Hawarden, John was sent on an Instructor's Course at the Central Flying School (CFS) at RAF Upavon. He became familiar with the basic Instrument Flight Rules (still used today) which entailed flying blind using the instrument panel only. Having passed the course, he returned to Hawarden to command D Flight and found his training schedule to be as demanding as taking part in the Battle of Britain.

In December 1941, John was posted to Catterick to join 145 Squadron but almost immediately went on leave. He returned to discover that he had been posted to the United States as a Liaison Officer. Before departing, however, John pursued a new flame, Rita, who had taken a shine to him having seen his photograph in the *Yorkshire Post*. Typically, he took advantage of a task he had been given that entailed flying a Spitfire back from Ringway Airport, Manchester, by performing some audacious aerobatics over his parents' home in Headingley. On other occasions he would perform low-level passes over Rita's house and then land his Spitfire at Yeadon when on week-end leave. Inevitably, he was reported and dragged in front of AOC (Air Officer Commanding) Training Command.

Eventually, John sailed in the *SS Rangitiki* and was despatched to Alabama via New York and Washington. He had, hitherto, been favourably impressed by American hospitality but he was shocked by the racism evident in the Deep South. His duties were mostly office-bound, but there was an interesting interlude when he struck up a friendship with the actor, Tyrone Howard, who had been enlisted to star in a training film.

John was then accepted as a test pilot on the new P47 Thunderbolt, conceived first as an interceptor, but eventually adopted as a ground attack aircraft. John hated it because the ergonomics were all wrong and it was an oversized gas guzzler. John much preferred the P51 Mustang – his favourite aircraft of the war. As an escort it had the inestimable advantage of a huge range, its ergonomics were excellent and it was safe, sturdy and strong. Another role for him was testing the P38 Lightning and the B17 bomber.

After a year in the States, John received his posting back to the UK. He endured a rough passage home in the *MV Cavina* as part of a convoy subjected to appalling weather. During a three-week leave, he married Rita but barely had time to settle into married life before he was called down to London and told to join an organization under the auspices of the Ministry of Supply whose sole purpose was to go out into the country and give information talks to factory workers and the like. John quite liked the seemingly unlimited expenses allowances and generous rail warrants. This lasted for three months until he was told to report to RAF Exeter. From there he went to Bolt Head on the North Cornish coast and was appointed Station Commander, but once again he was quickly moved on to RAF Perranporth to join 602 (City of Glasgow) Squadron in March 1943.

602 was equipped with Spitfire Vs and tasked with escort duties. John flew several escort missions across the Channel to bomb German installations around Brest. Then the squadron was re-located to RAF Lasham near Andover, where facilities were primitive to say the least. Accommodation was in tents – and this was in bitterly cold April weather. A speedy transfer to Fairlop did not improve matters as that was a tented camp as well. Thankfully, he was posted as OC to 118 Squadron at RAF Coltishall on 17 June 1943 and they flew the Spitfire Vb which was not the best variant available but was good at attacking enemy shipping. The highlight here for John was very low level flying between Coltishall and Beachy Head so as to avoid enemy radar. He imposed a strict discipline on his unit and quickly inculcated a strong camaraderie within it. He flew many missions, typically escorting Allied bombing raids on targets such as French power stations and the marshalling yards at Rouen.

John returned to a training role when 118 was moved to Peterhead and he was promoted to acting Station Commander. The squadron was mostly involved in dawn and dusk patrols, in conjunction with the Army and the Royal Navy. There was very little contact with the enemy. There followed a short stint at Castletown where John and his squadron were given free rein to explore the large country estate of Sir Archibald Sinclair, the Secretary of State for Air. Shooting and fishing took up a great deal of their spare time, of which there was plenty. More seriously, their task was high-level interception and escorting American B17s and B24s en route for East Anglia from their American bases.

In January 1944 he was ordered to attend the Air Ministry, a move he initially regretted because within a week of being posted away from 118, the squadron was sent south to Detling where Spitfire IXs awaited them. John would dearly have loved to fly that very superior aircraft. 118's Intelligence Officer, referring to John, noted in the official diary, 'A man of strong personality he has wrought many changes during the period he has been our CO [and] he has succeeded by sheer determination in keeping up a maximum effort. A fine flier and a good friend, he is a man who has the outlook expected of a regular officer.' [quoted from BC, p.139]

John's next posting took him to Grottaglie, situated on the heel of Italy, to be Wing Commander Flying with 286 Wing. Its main function was the defence of ports, convoys and airfields on the Italian peninsular along with reconnaissance and offensive operations in Yugoslavia in support of Tito's partisans. John, despite his fear of ditching into the sea, loved flying over the Adriatic at 1,000 feet and pulling up sharply over the mountains to reach his target. As winter turned quickly to spring, John found the work load a heavy strain so he put in a request to the Station Medical Officer that he, John, be allowed to return to the UK.

A short period of leave was followed by a rapid succession of roles. First, he was Chief Flying Instructor at Tern Hill; then, second, at Acklington; and third at Hawarden. Morpeth, Hawarden (again) and Netheravon followed in quick succession. John was appointed Station Administration Officer at Netheravon, which was a huge support Station with over 5,000 personnel, but the canteen could only cater for 500. In other respects, too, the facilities were woefully inadequate: there was little in the way of entertainment or education. John gave this conundrum some thought and came up with a plan; he started a farm that supplied the canteen, then provided a cinema, organized dances and purchased books and learning equipment. Sporting fixtures took place between squadrons, stations and the three Services. By this time, though, the war had ended and John knew that he no longer had a place in the RAF. He had no respect for the senior ranks running the Service and so it was time to return to civilian life.

John did return to the Reserve of Air Force Officers and he did fly the Tiger Moth, but in 1954 he was diagnosed with a hearing problem and that put an end to his RAFRO flying days. He had found employment with the Ministry of Transport and then joined Tetley Walker as Regional Manager of their soft drinks division. His wife, Rita, died in 1980 and three years later he married his second wife, Margaret Ena and spent 14 happy years in the south of Spain. Margaret (or Peta as

John called her) died in 2000. John himself died at Southport and Formby Hospital on 28 August 2010.

John Freeborn was something of a loose cannon. He resolutely defended himself when necessary and was never cowed by authority or his superiors. He came to realise that there was a valid role where discipline was concerned. He had the reputation of being draconian in his use of it. But, looking back on his days at Leeds Grammar School, he was happy to note that 'I am grateful for my time at school. [My] opposition to discipline was quickly dispersed and I found out that discipline is a necessary part of our life and must be adhered to without question.' [letter to the author]

Bibliography
Bishop, Patrick, *Fighter Boys. Saving Britain 1940*, Harper Perennial (London: 2001)
Cossey, Bob, *A Tiger's Tale*, J & KH Publishing (Hailsham: 2002)
Freeborn, John Connell, Letter to the author dated 31 October 2003
Yeoman, Christopher and Freeborn, John Connell, *Tiger Cub*, Pen and Sword, 2009

Rodney Hill, courtesy of Lafayette Studios

20

Professor Rodney Hill FRS 1921-2011
Professor of Applied Mathematics
At LGS 1932-1939

RODNEY HILL WAS born on 11 June 1921 at The Grange in Stourton, to the south east of Leeds. His father, Harold Harrison Hill, had been educated at Leeds University where he read for an MA in History and then took an external London degree in Economics. Eventually he became Senior History Master at Leeds Boys' Modern School. Rodney's mother, Lena, had been a student at Leeds School of Art. Rodney was their only child and was encouraged to read widely. At some point the family moved to 11 Victoria Walk, Horsforth and from 1926-1932 he attended Featherbank Council School.

Rodney came to Leeds Grammar School having won a scholarship in 1932. He soon displayed an all-round ability in maths, art, English Literature and other arts subjects, as well as participating in the games programme, the chess club, helping to edit the School magazine, actively supporting Clarell House and eventually becoming a full prefect.

His academic record was impressive. He clearly worked hard throughout his school life and this led to success in the Northern Universities School Certificate examinations at the end of his year in the Classical Fifth Form. He gained distinctions in history, Latin and mathematics. Later, at the conclusion of his Sixth Form studies, he passed his Higher School Certificate with distinctions in pure mathematics, applied mathematics and physics. He had regularly been the recipient of Form and Special Prizes: the Fourth Form English Literature Prize and Form Prize; the Fifth Form English Literature Prize and Form Prize; the Lower Science

Prof Rodney Hill FRS – Professor of Applied Mathematics

Sixth Form Prize; and the Upper Science Special Form Prize. All this demonstrates that Rodney was a consistently committed scholar with some talent in a wide variety of subjects.

Outside the classroom, Rodney was fully engaged in extra-curricular activities. As a supporting member of Clarell House, he helped to organize junior games, played chess and squash, and took up fencing. Eventually, as a senior pupil, he was appointed Head of Clarell in September 1938 and wrote the House notes. As with Chess, he was keen to encourage his fellow pupils and enthuse them with a desire to participate in as many extra-curricular activities as possible. Characteristically, he praises others but does not mention his own successes:

> This term, we must congratulate Hutton and Nicholson, who play regularly for the 1st XV, and Clucas, who plays for the 3rd XV. Though our contributions to the School teams are characterized by their quality rather than their numbers, the keenness and willingness shown by most of the other members of the House, and especially the Juniors, atone in no small measure for what little they lack in talent. [*Leo*, Vol. LVII, No. 6, p.222]

His chief contribution to the extra-curricular programme was School chess. The report for June 1936 starts, "The chess Competition is now over and Hill has won the Championship. He thoroughly deserves his victory as his play throughout the tournament has been consistently sound." From Year Five upwards, he wrote the Chess Club reports for the *Leodiensian* and his enthusiasm for the game is evident. "Chess, like other games, should be started early, and intending beginners should bear in mind that with a little practice, they will soon become as proficient as older members…. Beginners! Hurry up and give your names to Mr Brittain." This exhortation must have worked, for in the next Chess Notes, he writes, "Since the last notes were written, there has been a marked increase of enthusiasm, and our numbers are now well-augmented". In his final year at school, he won the Chess Shield and his last report for the Club displays an unusual tendency towards purple prose: "The Club is hotly engaged in the mêlée of the annual tournament for the Chess Shield. The tense atmosphere and steely silence which surrounds the players gives promise of a hard struggle, contested with more than usual vigour owing to recent increases in our numbers. The outcome is still in the balance…."

Rodney gave up quite a lot of his time to the School magazine. In November 1936, he was asked to join the *Leodiensian*'s team as a reporter; a year later he became a sub-editor with responsibility for Art; and by November 1938 he became joint editor with Kenneth Gore [OL39], who sadly was killed in action in the Second World War. His experience as report writer and editor proved very useful later in his career, particularly in the development of a taut and precise prose style. Apart from Chess Notes, Rodney contributed much else to the magazine. He was fairly proficient at drawing with depictions of Kirkstall Abbey, Cookridge, and Horsforth Church. He also contributed some poems, starting with "The Stream of Life", an allegory on the ageing process, whilst in Classical Fifth Form. From an ebullition of spontaneous joyful spirit, the evolving life enters a darker phase:

> *But suddenly*
> *As in the twinkling of an eye, the plain*
> *And all around it vanished, and sheering cliffs*
> *Looked down upon the swollen spate which foamed*
> *And frothed about the ragged crags of rock,*
> *That tried to stay the impulse of the flood.*
>
> [*Leo*, Vol LV, No. 1, p.20]

The poem ends on a calmer note, with the explicit suggestion of passing into a "land of wondrous beauty" before gliding "gently to an eternal home". There is a spiritual message here of some sort, though whether Rodney was imbued with any religious sentiment is not clear.

There is a similar spiritual element to a prose piece he submitted to the February 1937 *Leodiensian*. Titled "On the glimpse of a vessel on the horizon", Rodney imagines resting on a cliff top looking out to sea, experiencing a calm, serene moment of reflection. He catches for a brief moment what appears to be a ship on the horizon, but it is an unsubstantial mirage for a second glance reveals only "far above the horizon, a stately ship, draped in white vapours, [that] sailed towards the heavens and was caught up in everlasting light". [*Leo*, Vol. LVI, No. 1, p.18]

More sombre in tone, his next offering, "Growth", is a transparent message that human endeavour pales into insignificance in the context of mortality. Man might embrace knowledge and, with it power,

> *But, as the sap of youth his very self did fire,*
> *He thrusts abroad, and realms of learning did embrace,*
> *So came he to manly strength, and new experience.*
> *Yet even when it seemed his sun was soaring high,*
> *Life's Evenstar burst forth, and waned into eternal night.*
>
> [*Leo*, Vol. LVI, No. 3, p.104]

This is not to claim that Rodney was imbued with any exceptional poetic skill, but his poems do have some merit and surely offer some insight into the mind of a young man whose thoughts and ambition reflected a broader view of life than might be expected of one so gifted in mathematics. Not a polymath, but someone perhaps heading towards being a savant. As Professor Michael Sewell says in his article on Rodney, published in 2015 under the auspices of the Royal Society: "Thus were developing the powers of accurate observation and analysis that were brought to bear on the mathematics and physics that became his specialisms from the age of 15 years".

At around this same time, Rodney taught himself to play the piano and quickly became proficient, and he continued to play for most of his life. Again, Professor Sewell draws on his fond memories of a cherished colleague: "The long fingers of a pianist could later be recognized politely tapping on his desk while waiting for an answer to his question during a research supervision". [*MJS*, p.164]

Rodney had clearly demonstrated that he was fully committed to playing a full role in the life of the School. He showed a surprising all-round ability, excelling in both arts and sciences. He engaged with his fellow pupils, encouraged where necessary and showed by example the benefits of positive behaviour. It therefore came as no surprise that, following his excellent Higher Certificate examination results, he was awarded a West Riding County Major Scholarship in Mathematics at Pembroke College, Cambridge, and a State Scholarship.

In December 1938 he was awarded an Open Major Scholarship of £100 at Pembroke College, Cambridge and, together with his other scholarships, this enabled him to be financially independent as an undergraduate. He went up to Cambridge in October 1939 against a backdrop of conflict in Europe. War-time rationing led to inconveniencies such as no hot water in rooms and very little coal for heating. Despite these discomforts, Hill won a first-class prize for maths in his first year and became a Wrangler, having been awarded a first-class honours degree in Part II of the Mathematical Tripos in June 1941. He graduated with a BA in 1942, subsequently awarded an MA in 1945 and then a PhD in 1948. To round off this series of academic honours he graduated with an ScD in 1959.

Eschewing advanced training for Part III of the Mathematical Tripos, Hill volunteered himself for war work. He joined the Cambridge Mathematical Laboratory to work on external and internal ballistics, later working on plasticity in the Cavendish Laboratory. This vital contribution to the war effort delayed his PhD until 1948.

The Cambridge Mathematical Laboratory worked closely with the External Ballistics Department of the Ordnance Board which was under the control of the Ministry of Supply. Hill worked on the task of calculating the trajectories of shells for the compilation of range tables. After a while he progressed to helping with the operation of the Bush differential analyser for solving the internal ballistic equations with reference to shells travelling down the gun barrel. This work led to his first research paper.

An Old Boys register

In May 1943 Hill joined Professor Lennard-Jones, Chief Superintendent of Armament Research at Fort Halstead, who had set up new research groups headed by distinguished scientists, including Professor Nevill (later Sir Nevill) Mott FRS. Working alongside other brilliant scientists at the Theoretical Research Branch, Hill contributed to vital advances in the field of armaments, especially the performance of a range of artillery weaponry. Working conditions were testing to say the least: Fort Halstead lay directly in the preferred flight path of V1 and V2 flying rockets, one of which exploded in the Establishment, fortunately at night so there were no human casualties.

Hill worked on the problem of deep penetration of very thick armour by so-called Munroe jets and by high-velocity shells with tungsten carbide cores. This required a mechanics of plastic deformation with unrestricted magnitude. It was this work that set Hill on the course of a specialist field of the mathematical theory of plasticity. A practical application of this theory was Hill's work on the penetration performance of a shell with a tungsten-carbide core and with a pure ogival head whose performance was adversely affected if too much of the tip was ground in a conical shape, which was the manufacturing practice at that time.

There was a lighter side to life at Fort Halstead, despite the pressure of work and the threat of aerial bombardment. One pleasant distraction was ballroom dancing, at which Hill proved to be adept. His chosen partner, Jeanne Kathlyn Wickens, was soon to become his wife.

After the war, Hill returned to the Cavendish Laboratory at Cambridge. By this time, he had become a leading adviser in the country on continuum plasticity with special reference to the new theories of metal-working processes relevant to the steel industry. In 1948 he was awarded his Cambridge PhD for a thesis entitled "Theoretical studies of the plastic deformation of metals".

In February 1949 he moved to Sheffield to be head of the new Solid Mechanics Section in the Metal Flow Research Laboratory of the British Iron and Steel Research Association. He found himself working in a run-down, polluted area of the city and for a while he and his team were forced to work in a hut while new accommodation was built. He did some part-time lecturing at Sheffield University and, when time allowed, he and Jeanne went walking in the countryside around Sheffield.

By this time Hill was acknowledged as the leading figure in mathematical plasticity. Based on his PhD thesis, he wrote a book, *The Mathematical Theory of Plasticity*, published by OUP in 1950 and still in print in paperback form. This cemented his reputation as a world-class scientist in his subject.

In September 1950 he moved to Bristol University for a three-year Research Fellowship, during the course of which he combined physics and engineering. After a while he was promoted to Reader in Plasticity at the university.

He contributed many articles to the *Journal of the Mechanics and Physics of Solids* which was launched in 1952. Very soon after it started, he became Editor-in-Chief and remained so until 1968. He not only contributed his own articles, always written in an economical, succinct style, but was happy to accept contributions from other specialists in the field. In addition, he regularly reviewed books submitted to the Journal.

In October 1953 Hill was appointed to the post of Chair of Applied Mathematics at Nottingham University at the age of 32. He immediately set about modernising the teaching of undergraduate applied mathematics. His courses included the dynamics of particles and rigid bodies as well as elasticity. His lectures were delivered in a concise, clear manner, often not taking the full 50 minutes allocated by the time table.

In 1959 J E Adkins was appointed Reader in Theoretical Mathematics working within the Faculty of Engineering. Hill was approached by the Mining Engineering Department at the university to look into the problem of mining subsidence in the area around Nottingham. In 1962 he resigned his Chair, and the title of Professorial Research fellow was conferred on him for the year 1962-63.

Hill was awarded the degree of ScD by Cambridge University in 1959. This was followed by the highest honour granted to any British scientist when he was elected a Fellow of the Royal Society.

Hill taught undergraduate courses at Nottingham for nine years, concentrating on classical dynamics and elasticity. The dynamics courses led to a second book entitled *Principles of Dynamics*, published by Pergamon Press in 1964. His chief concern in the book was, "to present classical dynamics primarily as an exemplar of scientific theory and method". A little later, he became joint editor (with Professor Ian Sneddon) of a sequence of volumes, *Progress in Solid Mechanics*, that contained articles contributed by some of the leading figures in the field.

In 1963, Hill returned to Cambridge to Gonville and Caius College on a Fellowship. He received a grant from the Science Research Council for work on elastic and plastic macro-properties of varied materials including fibre composites. After working on this project for six years, he then became Reader in the Mechanics of Solids within the Department of Applied Mathematics and Theoretical Physics. In 1972 he was awarded a Personal Professorship which he held until he retired in 1979.

In 1969 his mother was killed in a car accident and this meant that Hill had to spend time caring for his father until Harold's death in 1977. His mother-in-law died in 1971 and Jeanne's father needed support until his death in 1976. In 1979 he resigned his chair at Cambridge but continued his research work for another 20 years, working at home to the accompaniment of classical music. At this time he had established new working contacts with eminent scientists from abroad, many of whom came to Cambridge to visit him.

In 1993 Hill received a Royal Medal, one of three given annually on the recommendation of the Royal Society. The citation included the wording, "...for his outstanding contribution to the theoretical mechanics of solids, and especially the plasticity of solids".

In his leisure time Hill was a keen gardener, botanist and mycologist. He supported important projects like the creation of Heartwood Forest, the largest native woodland to be planted in England. In his will he left a generous legacy to the Woodland Trust. He and Jeanne enjoyed long walks in the English countryside.

The Rodney Hill Prize in Solid Mechanics was established in 2008 by Elsevier Limited. It is an award given every four years and consists of a plaque and a cheque for US$25000. In return, the recipient is required to deliver a Prize Lecture at the meeting of the International Congress of Theoretical and Applied Mechanics.

Jeanne died in 2003 and Hill became less mobile. He was supported by his many friends. In 2007 he moved into a nursing home at Cottenham Court and it was here that he spent his last four years. He died on 2 February 2011.

This chapter is closely based on the Royal Society Biographical Memoir on Rodney Hill, *written by Professor Michael J Sewell and published by the Royal Society on 26 August 2015. My thanks to Professor Sewell for giving permission to use his material.*

John Townsend

21

John Rowe Townsend 1922-2014
Author and Literary Critic
At LGS 1933-1939

JOHN ROWE TOWNSEND was born on 10 May 1922. His father, George Edmund, was the chief clerk in a copper mill. Unfortunately, George suffered from Parkinson's Disease and this was to have a deleterious effect on his earning capacity. The family were far from affluent, so it was fortunate that John won a West Riding County Council scholarship (they lived on Station Road in Scholes, a village outside Leeds) to Leeds Grammar School at the age of 11. He admitted later that, although he received a good education, his school years taught him very little other than the importance of passing examinations. He passed his Northern Universities Joint Matriculation Board School Certificate in 1937 and went on to be successful in his Higher School Certificate in 1939. Given the delicate state of the family's finances, he immediately took a job in the Leeds tax office and remained there briefly until the outbreak of war.

His war-time service saw him trained in the deciphering of codes and ciphers, a somewhat disappointing role as he had volunteered to become a navigator in the RAF. If excitement was what he was after, there was some consolation in the fact that he was sent out to Italy as a front-line operator, ending up at Monte Cassino with an Anglo-American unit by the name of Number One Field Intelligence. In this capacity, he was part of a team searching material left behind as the Germans and Italians retreated northwards. Prior to this, with the stiffening of German resistance at Monte Cassino, he found time on his hands so he visited Florence and stayed there for some months enjoying the cultural delights of the city.

After the war, he was demobbed close to Cambridge and decided he would like to study at the university. By all accounts he took a bus into town, alighted at the first college, Emmanuel, and simply walked up to the porter's lodge and announced he would like to enrol as a student. The Senior Tutor of the college happened to be passing and promptly gave him an extended interview, at the end of which Townsend was accepted into the School of English.

He married Vera Lancaster, a girl he had met in the Leeds tax office, settled down to his studies and edited the magazine *Varsity*, the university's independent student publication. It was first published in 1947 and was devoted to the encouragement of student journalism. As editor, he was responsible for commissioning articles and keeping a check on the enthusiasm of would-be contributors. It was this experience that made him determined to pursue journalism as a career. He completed his undergraduate course in two years.

After graduating, Townsend worked as a reporter for the *Yorkshire Evening Post* and then the *Evening Standard*. In 1949 he applied in writing to various national newspapers requesting a job but the response was emphatically negative. The *Guardian* distinguished itself by not replying at all and at this Townsend took offence, withdrew his application and wrote back lambasting the management for their discourtesy. By a supreme irony, the then editor, Alistair Hetherington, immediately responded with the offer of an interview and, subsequently, a position with the paper. He stayed there for over 30 years, as a sub-editor, an art editor and later editor of *Guardian Weekly* from 1955.

In 1960 he proposed to write a feature article on the work of the National Society for the Prevention of Cruelty to Children with special reference to the Manchester area. To gain first-hand experience of the conditions in which some of the more impecunious families lived, he accompanied an officer of the NSPCC to see for himself the extent of deprivation, neglect and suffering endured by the children. He was shocked. It struck him that there was a yawning gap between the comfortable, secure middle class lives of children depicted in junior fiction at that time (a lot of which he reviewed as part of his journalism) and the harsh reality on the streets. This was the immediate and direct stimulus that led to his desire to write his own children's novel in which a startling and disturbing realism would prevail over the current widespread, sanitised depiction of happy families enjoying the comforts of modern consumer-oriented existence.

The result was *Gumble's Yard* (1961), what was for then a hard-hitting portrayal of indigent working-class mores, in which the adults desert the children who then must fend for themselves, sometimes coming close to breaking the law, but desperate not to be separated and hunted down by the authorities who would almost certainly put them into care. *Gumble's Yard* earned the distinction of being the first post-war children's book that dealt candidly with such harrowing realities.

Emmanuel College, source: Wikimedia Commons

It might be said that Townsend was carrying on the tradition of Dickens by awakening the public conscience by bringing to its attention the glaring inequalities in society. As he himself put it in his *Writing for Children*, he 'wrote about city streets similar to those he knew as a child. [*WfC*, Third Edition, Penguin Books 1987, pp.261-2] The book was a publishing success.

It is worth digressing for a moment from his biography to examine *Gumble's Yard* in a little more detail. Reading the book today, the reader might be forgiven for thinking what the fuss concerning its focus on "realism" is all about. Essentially, it is a stirring story of teen and pre-teen bravery overcoming the machinations of some dastardly villains. Cobchester (the fictional Manchester) is described almost exclusively in terms of its poor housing, run-down industry and a sluggish, polluted canal. 'It's [the Jungle, a collection of terraced streets] a dirty old place and

John Rowe Townsend – Author and Literary Critic

Jill Paton Walsh

one of these days the Corporation are going to pull it all down – if it doesn't fall down of its own accord first.' [*GY* p.7] There is also the threat of homelessness and institutional care, thanks to the fecklessness of the dysfunctional Uncle Harold and his partner, Doris, who simply clear off; as the narrator, Kevin, puts it, '"If they're not back tonight," I said, "we'll have to go the police, or the Cruelty"'. [*GY* p.17] As an anti-romantic story it does deal honestly with the diminished lives of the poor. Sandra, the twelve-year-old daughter of Harold, 'will never be a romantic girl, but after all there isn't much romance in the Jungle. She'll know which shop to buy her potatoes at, and that's more important.' [*GY*, p.52] And Townsend does not allow happiness ever after at the conclusion of the novel: 'He [Townsend] was commended for not giving the book the usual 'happy ending' but allowing his child characters simply to return to the unpleasant household from which they came at the beginning'. [Carpenter and Pritchard, *The Oxford Companion to Children's Literature*, OUP 1984 (1987)] The problem is that Kevin and the other children keep lapsing into middle-class expressions such as 'I'm quite healthy myself as a matter of fact' and 'He's a really good sort' and 'I was doing splendidly'. But these criticisms may have the advantage of hind-sight; children's fiction today can be much more challenging and disturbing. When it was published, *Gumble's Yard* certainly represented a discernible shift away from mainstream literature aimed at children.

As there was another writer by the name of John Townsend being published at the time, the editor of Hutchinson's asked if he had a second name, to which Townsend admitted his middle name was Rowe. This proved later to be an embarrassment because he was perceived by some fervent critics to have had an affluent middle class upbringing which was not the case. Additionally, he was accused of dishonestly claiming to write from his own experience as a deprived child and having an outsider's condescending view of the working class. John Rowe Townsend simply did not sound sufficiently proletarian. It might even be suggested that Station Road, Scholes, was not quite the 'city streets he knew as a child'.

Other critics disagreed and firmly came down on the side of Townsend's genuine concern for the realistic portrayal of working-class mores. As Kaye Webb, the reviewer in the *Illustrated London News* of 27 November 1965 put it,

> Adolescents need to start exploring the grown-up world without being too involved in its emotions or weighed down by its problems. But they have a sure instinct for condescension or manufactured situations. Many writers take refuge in the past, for ruffles and periwigs somehow take the curse off mistresses and murders. However, during the last few years a number of modern books have been published and many have considerable quality. *Widdershins Crescent*, by John Rowe Townsend (Hutchinson 15s.): Here is one author who avoids self-consciousness when he writes about working-class children. He is also skilled at extracting excitement from the problems of moving house, failing to keep up the H.P. payments, and the suspicion of arson in the warehouse. And if this hero is slightly too good to be true, well that's inspiring for everyone. [Kaye Webb, *ILN*, 27 November 1965, p.34]

Peter Hollindale and Zena Sutherland, in their chapter entitled 'Internationalism, Fantasy, and Realism', in the book *Children's Literature. An Illustrated History* edited by Peter Hunt, observed that the growing trend towards writing fiction for a specific teenage audience naturally tended to deal with more contentious issues than the sheltered experiences of the middle and upper classes. They give Townsend a crucial role in spearheading this movement with the publication of *Gumble's Yard* and his later novels.

> 'There are representative prophetic texts which achieved great popularity at the time and also set precedents for a far greater output of such writing in the quarter-century that followed. John Rowe Townsend's *Gumble's Yard* (1961) is set in derelict areas of Manchester and concerns the resourcefulness of urban children abandoned by their feckless parents. Not only the topographical, economic, and social setting but also the systematic demythologizing of parental adequacy, the ruptured cliché of familial harmony, point the way to a more

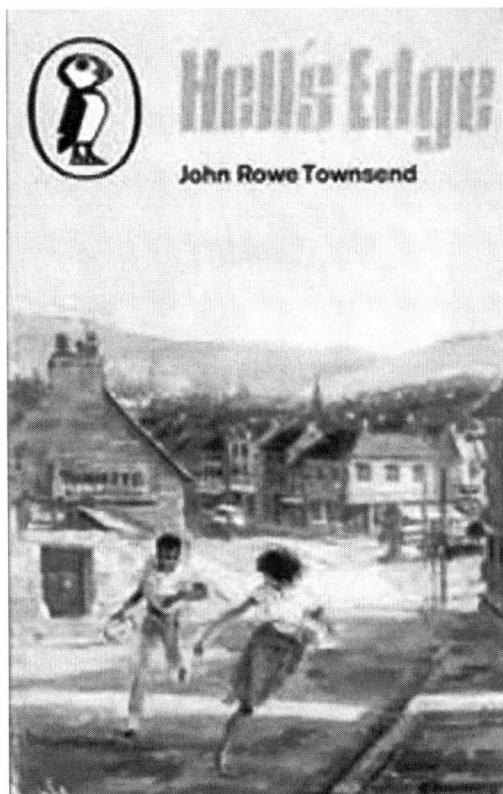

Townsend's novel Hell's Edge has been called Dickensian

observant, sceptical, and candid social fiction for young children.'
[*CL.AIH*, pp. 279-280]

He wrote more than 20 children's books as well as the authoritative *Written for Children* (1965), an analysis of the best British and American children's literature from 1840. As his interest in children's fiction grew, so did the size and scope of his book. In all, there were nine editions. Another book, *A Sense of Story*, first published in 1971 and later revised and re-titled *A Sounding of Storytellers* (1979), offered essays on contemporary writers that exhibited both an extensive knowledge and a critical astuteness. Regarding his fiction output, further hard-hitting or even provocative novels had followed *Gumble's Yard*, including *Hell's Edge* (1963), *Widdershins Crescent* (1965), *The Intruder* (1969), *Goodnight ,Prof, Love* (1970) and *Noah's Castle* (1978). By 1969 he found it difficult to combine his journalistic career at the *Guardian* with his literary ambitions so he left his full-time post with the paper but continued to edit the children's book pages until 1978, and to write columns until 1981. He also founded the Guardian Book Prize for children's fiction, an award that excelled at identifying new writers in the field. Winners included Leon Garfield (1967), Alan Garner (1968), K M Peyton (1970), Richard Adams (1973), Nina Bawden (1976) and Anita Desai (1983).

Townsend's *The Intruder* won the Edgar Allan Poe Award by the Mystery Writers of America in 1971.

In 1978 he was approached by a group of American literary enthusiasts who were campaigning to establish a Master of Arts Course in Children's Literature at Boston University, in which the genre was to be studied on exactly the same terms as adult literature. This was a bold and innovative departure from established critical orthodoxy and when the course was established, it placed junior fiction on a par with its senior cousin. Townsend was invited to lecture in Contemporary British Children's Literature as part of an annual summer school attached to the MA. He became Permanent Visiting Faculty Member of the Center for the Study of Children's Literature at Simmons College in Boston as well as a Board Member of Children's Literature New England which is still offering courses today. Thanks to his efforts, junior fiction had become a legitimate area for serious study, something that could not have been imagined back in 1965.

On the death of his first wife, Townsend moved to Cambridge. He began a long and mutually rewarding relationship with the novelist Jill Paton Walsh and they were married in 2004. They founded Green Bay Publications, later producing Paton Walsh's Booker shortlisted *Knowledge of Angels* (1994) and in 1989 were the British organizers of the international conference of Children's Literature New England, publishing its papers, "Travellers in Time", in 1990.

Townsend died on 24 March 2014 aged 91. His legacy is formidable: that children's literature is unquestionably a discipline worthy of serious analysis.

Bibliography

Carpenter, Humphrey and Pritchard, Mari, *The Oxford Companion to Children's Literature*, OUP (Oxford: 1987)

Chevalier, Tracey (ed), *Twentieth-Century Children's Writers*, St James Press (London:1989), entry by Leonard R Mendelsohn, pp.970-972

Green Bay Publications, Obituary on John Rowe Townsend (n.d.)

Hollindale, Peter and Sutherland, Zena, 'Internationalism, Fantasy, and Realism 1945-1970', in Hunt, Peter (ed.), *Children's Literature. An Illustrated History*, Oxford University Press, (Oxford: 1995), pp. 279-280)

Nettell, Stephanie, Obituary on John Rowe Townsend, in the *Guardian*, 2 April 2014,

Illustrated London News, 27 November 1965, article by Kaye Webb

Townsend, John Rowe, *Gumble's Yard*, OUP (Oxford: 2001)

Townsend, John Rowe, *A Sense of Story. Essays on Contemporary Writers for Children*, Longman (London: 1971)

Townsend, John Rowe, *Written for Children: An Outline of English Language Children's Literature*, 3rd edition, Penguin Books (Harmondsworth: 1987)

Gerald Kaufman as a student at Queen's

22

Sir Gerald Bernard Kaufman PC, MP 1930-2017
Politician and member of the Shadow Cabinet and Junior Minister
At LGS 1941-1949

SIR GERALD KAUFMAN was a Labour Member of Parliament from 1970 to his death in 2017, a government minister and a member of the Shadow Cabinet in the 1980s. Knighted in 2004, he became Father of the House of Commons in 2015. He was a fierce critic of Labour's extreme Left and successive later Israeli governments, advocating a two-nation peace policy.

He was born on 21 June 1930 in Leeds, the youngest of seven children of Louis, a tailor with Montague Burton, and Jane Kaufman, Polish Jews who had moved to Britain prior to the First World War. The family home was originally at 31 Roundhay Road but they moved to 81 Grange Avenue, Chapeltown, then a reasonably prosperous suburb of Leeds. Gerald attended Cowper Street Council School before gaining a Governors' Free Place at Leeds Grammar School, which he entered in 1941. One abiding memory of his pre-teen years was being taken to the Rialto Cinema on Briggate (later demolished to make way for a new Marks and Spencer store) to see the Walt Disney cartoon *The Three Little Pigs*, an experience that triggered his life-long love of the silver screen. Writing much later, in 1985, he was happy to recall,

> 'To this day I can see those plump, self-important creatures up on that huge screen bustling about and singing their feckless ditty, 'Who's afraid of the big bad wolf?' I looked up at the singing and dancing animals, an inexplicable phenomenon far beyond anything I had ever

experienced before. I had no idea how they worked, but I was enchanted; I was hooked. I wanted more.' [*My Life in the Silver Screen*, p. 15]

He was not alone in his growing addiction to the cinema; his older sisters, Dora, Martha, Anne, Gertie and Hilda, all scoured the local paper to identify the new release films on offer in the many cinemas then operating in Leeds. One of the cinemas frequented by the whole family was the Forum which showed some Yiddish films. For a special treat, his mother would occasionally take him to the Clock cinema at the junction of Roundhay Road and Easterly Road, though sometimes the more adult Gothic and horror films would cause him to close his eyes or duck beneath the seat. However, with 55 cinemas to choose from in the city he was never at a loss to select movies he really wanted to see. When not glued to the screen, he would frequently be taken to Roundhay Park to feed the ducks.

On entering Leeds Grammar School, he found it hard to adjust to new demands and new discipline. As he admits, 'I found the Grammar School hard going, since there I was only one of many bright boys instead of being, as I was at Cowper Street, just about the brightest boy in the school and spoiled by always being told so.' [*MLITSS*, p. 28] It is possible to see, from his participation in extra-curricular activities at the School, early evidence of his personal enthusiasms and passions that were to stay with him for the rest of his life, especially theatre, film, music, debating and, naturally, politics. He quickly learned that the value of his pocket money was granted in direct proportion to his performance at school. After one appalling report when aged 13, he was temporarily banned from attending cinemas, but a subsequent improvement reversed the diktat. He took an active part in several school Societies, including those devoted to Literature and Debating, Politics, Drama and Classical Culture, as well as being a pupil-librarian and sub-editor of the school magazine, the *Leodiensian*.

He was elected to the committee of the Literary & Debating Society whilst in the Fifth Form and he quickly earned a reputation for outspoken views. Opposing the motion, "That this House considers that the centre of culture in England lies to the South of the River Trent", the magazine report reveals that, 'He had, by dint of careful research, found another Trent – in Dorset, and from this he progressed, by easy stages, to a proof that almost all culture lay north of this'. [*Leo*, March 1947, p.62] He is described as 'Liberal in everything he does: the number and length of his speeches; the abuse with which he greets members of the Committee. Something *of* an institution; according to certain members of the Society he ought to be something *in* an institution.' [*Leo*, July 1947, p.104] On another occasion, a fellow member of the Society, J N Wright, wrote of him, 'If amusement derives from insensitivity, wit from rudeness, brilliance from egotism, sanity from insanity, the

Queens College hall at the University of Oxford

Hon. Member is amusing, witty, brilliant and sane'. [*Leo*, July 1948, p. 94] The following year he was elected Honorary Secretary of the Society.

He took part in a number of dramatic productions, starting with *Twelfth Night*. In this he played the part of Maria, a gentlewoman attending on Olivia. He appears to have contributed some mirth to the performances since the anonymous reviewer commented that, 'Of Maria I can say little. If I could put on paper the chuckles which came from me when I saw the play they would be a fitting tribute'. [*Leo* July 1946, p. 532] His next appearance was in *Macbeth*, in which he played the First Witch and, according to the writer of the review in the school magazine, 'If the witches in Act I seemed to achieve the grotesque rather than the numinous, that was partly because we knew them too well; and they made ample amends in Act IV'. [*Leo* July 1947, p.101] The following year he took the part of the Nurse in *Romeo and Juliet* and he 'had obviously put a lot of hard work into his characterization of the Nurse; he had studied the part carefully, made up his mind how it should be played and then carried out his intention; and his portrayal was certainly comic and extracted

Sir Gerald Bernard Kaufman MP – Politician and member of Shadow Cabinet

full value from the Nurse's stupidity and garrulity'. [*Leo*, July 1948, p.91] His next appearance on stage was in Sheridan's *The Critic*, in which he played the part of Sneer, but sadly there is no review to give an insight into his interpretation. Again, writing much later, and dwelling on the fact that he had never had the slightest inclination to appear in any film as an actor, he recalled

> True, during my long-ago Leeds Grammar School days I had taken part in the ventures of the school dramatic society, graduating from playing a highly realistic First Witch in Macbeth [sic], via Nurse in *Romeo and Juliet*, to the plum role of Sneer in Sheridan's *The Critic*. I achieved a massive success as Nurse, principally because I transformed it into a broad comedy role, with the line 'Ay, ay, the cords', as the show-stopper of the evening. Not only was this not what Shakespeare had intended, but it was not what the producer (an enthusiastic master reduced to chronic despair by his performers' taking control of the play) instructed. Indeed, at one performance the laughter of the audience – highly relieved that all those lines of blank verse were unexpectedly being turned into entertainment - during the scene intended movingly to depict the discovery of Juliet's body became so great that the curtain was hastily rung down. In the brief unscheduled interval that followed, my remaining lines were removed from the script. After this, Sneer came as an anti-climax, since all I could think up to enliven this languid character's part was to keep falling off my chair, an approach to the role which did not exactly match the sophistication of Sheridan's social comedy. I indulged in these antics because I did not really enjoy acting, which appealed to me even less than driving a fire-engine as a possible calling in life. (*MLITSS*, p.104]

His interest in Classicism was, perhaps, tinged with a touch of pedantry. During a meeting in November 1947 he proposed to members of the Classical Society 'that a complaint be lodged on the mispronunciation of certain Greek names during broadcasts [and he] was duly entrusted with the task of writing to the B.B.C.'. [*Leo*, March 1948, p.54]. The following month he contributed to a debate on the merits of studying Ancient History, saying 'that the deep thought necessitated by the great gaps in our knowledge of the ancient world developed the mind. An age that produced such men as Aeschylus and Pericles must surely be ranked among the greatest.' [*Leo*, ibid] One master in particular, E D Scott (Head of Classics from 1944-67), seems to have engaged Gerald's imagination and enthusiasm and he wrote for the magazine an amusing observation of one of Scott's lessons as interpreted by a "Romantic Novelist", a "Reporter on a Well-known "Red" Newspaper", an

"Advocate of Modern Educational Methods" and "One of the Pupils". A little later he rendered the part of the "Chorus" in a reading of Sophocles' *Oedipus Tyrannus*.

A nascent interest in politics may be deduced from his involvement in the Political Society. Meetings started in 1947 and from the beginning he seems to have been a leading figure. At the second meeting, he presented a paper entitled "The Tories" and it 'was a vigorous denunciation of this party and was warmly applauded'. At a later meeting, there was a debate on the motion, "That this house approves of the Liberal Party". 'G.B. Kaufman, proposing, said that the papers given at previous meetings showed that the Tories and Socialists were no good, so we must have Liberals.' [*Leo*, March 1947, p.79] In another article written for the *Leo*, he considers the 'decision made by the Board of Trade to set up a Leeds Grammar School Working Party'. His prescient analysis is entertaining: 'As this is a Government Working Party, it will naturally have a strong Left-wing bias, though appearing evenly balanced. This means that P.A. Burnstone, G.B. Kaufman, H.T. Read and J.C. Scott will have to be co-opted, and J.M.H. Wright brought in for ballast.' [*Leo* December 1948, p.33] His capacity for satirical observation is further illustrated by an article he wrote in April 1949 concerning the spoof proposal that the School's 'Pound', wherein lost property was stored under the control of a single master and pupils could redeem errant items on payment of one penny, be nationalized with all the attendant bureaucracy. He wrote

> 'To put it on a par with other nationalised industries, provision will be made for converting its present regular profit into a comfortable loss... .New premises will be taken over, since the present Pound is regarded as too small for the much larger scope of the new organisation. The Junior Library will be requisitioned, and refurbished and redecorated at enormous expense.' [*Leo*, April 1949, p.72]

As for his famous erudite wit in the debating chamber of the Commons, he claimed that he was influenced most by a very unlikely hero. 'When I became active in politics Groucho Marx, far more than Aneurin Bevan or Demosthenes, was to have, for better or worse, a fundamental influence over my speaking style.' [*MLITSS*, p.81]

He had already developed a love of classical music, something spurred on when he first saw *The Marriage of Figaro* and became a devotee of Mozart's oeuvre, and he joined the Gramophone Social Club, which met at lunchtimes and in which masters would bring along a favourite recording. The 1948 season of meetings elicited this response from a young Kaufman, who clearly had his tongue firmly in his cheek: 'An ambitious programme has had amazing results. Huge crowds turned up in their fives and sixes to the Mozart Festival which included well-known works, such as Symphonies 36 and 40 and *Eine Kleine Nachtmusik*.' [*Leo*, December 1948, p.18]

During this period at the School, he befriended a fellow pupil by the name of Wood (almost certainly John Ewbank Wood, who was an exact contemporary of Gerald's) and together they frequently visited cinemas – like Gerald he was not especially discerning in his choice of film. This same Wood, eschewing the staple diet of games and the Junior Training Corps, 'tried to learn the violin under the tuition of an earnest but despairing instructor by the name of Walter Jorytz' [*MLITSS*, p. 37] Like many others, Gerald failed to spell Walter's surname correctly - it was Jorysz.

Despite a heavy involvement in these and other societies, he was able to produce excellent academic results and was awarded a number of prizes. He achieved a Distinction in Latin in the Higher School Certificate in 1948, was elected to the Hirst Exhibition, worth £50 for boys going up to Queen's College, Oxford, and was awarded the Hook Classical Prize (founded by the Very Rev. W F Hook in 1859) in the same year. (Barry Cryer was awarded the Third Form General Knowledge Prize at the same time.) He did cause some embarrassment and attracted a great deal of opprobrium when he chose as his Speech Day Prize a copy of Marx's *Das Kapital*. [*Guardian* obituary, 27 February 2017]

From the Grammar School, he went to Queen's College Oxford, something he really did not expect to achieve. He later recalled his interview there and felt it

Labour leaders – Michael Foot and Harold Wilson

did not go well at all. However, all's well that ends well and, 'I returned to Leeds deeply depressed at what I considered a brief and cruelly finite taste of life at Oxford. Arriving home from school one day not long afterwards, I found almost hysterical excitement. A telegram had arrived with the news that I had won the exhibition.' (*MLITSS*, p. 78] Whilst at Queen's he went through a very Left-wing phase in his political views, verging almost on Communism. He eventually became Secretary of the University Labour Club. During one Oxford Union debate in which he argued against the establishment of the Common Market, he impressed Denis Healey, then a prominent Labour back-bencher.

He graduated in 1952 and returned to Leeds where he applied for several positions, all unsuccessfully, including a vacancy on the editorial side of the *Eagle* comic, then a must-read for countless boys. Two years later he became the Assistant General Secretary of the Fabian Society (1954-55) and was frequently in the company of Harold Wilson, Richard Crossman and Anthony Crosland. As a frequent visitor to the House of Commons, he developed a passion for the place second only to his abiding love of cinema. Sadly, the pay was exiguous (£9 per week) and he could only just afford a tiny bed-sit in Stamford Hill miles away from his place of work. Now, above all, he yearned to become an MP but was unsuccessful in contesting the Conservative seat of Bromley in 1955, and four years later failed to take Gillingham.

He then became a leader writer for the *Daily Mirror*, at that time edited by Hugh Cudlipp (1955-64). His primary role was that of research assistant to Richard Crossman, a demanding task since Crossman was ever careless with facts while Kaufman was meticulous in his attention to detail, something that Cudlipp demanded with editorial severity. The work load was onerous and he still yearned to write film reviews for any organ that would have him. Salvation, albeit temporary, came when he was offered the position of cinema critic for an obscure publication called *Forward*. He was happy to employ his trademark sarcasm in his critiques. When *Forward* ceased publication, he concentrated on writing leader articles for the *Daily Mirror*.

Following this he was appointed a political correspondent on the *New Statesman* for one year. At that time, the paper was edited by John Freeman and it was a highly regarded publication. Whilst there, he moonlighted as film reviewer for the *Listener*.

Briefly eschewing politics, he became a writer and contributed many sketches to the satirical programme *That Was The Week That Was*. He had been invited to do so by the producer of the programme, Ned Sherrin, and as a consequence almost certainly came into contact with Barry Cryer [q.v.], who was by then beginning to make a name for himself as a successful comedy script writer. Like Cryer, he also contributed material for the successor series, *Not So Much a Programme, More a Way* of Life. Sherrin also asked Kaufman to write an entire programme named *ABC of Britain*, starring Gordon Jackson (who later shot to fame in the series *Upstairs, Downstairs*).

He became Political Correspondent for the *New Statesman* and in 1965 interviewed Harold Wilson at 10 Downing Street. During the course of their meeting, Wilson invited him to become his political press adviser and there began a long association between the two men. Later, Kaufman was to hail Wilson as the most successful Labour Prime Minister up to that time and wrote of him in glowing terms.

In the 1970 General Election, which brought in the Heath government, Kaufman successfully contested the Manchester Ardwick seat, a very safe Labour stronghold. He was to serve as its MP until 1983, when boundary changes forced him to stand for Manchester Gorton, a seat he represented until his death.

During the Labour government of 1974 to 1979, he was a junior minister, first in the Department of the Environment under Anthony Crosland, and then in the Department of Industry under Eric Varley, first as Parliamentary Under-Secretary and then as Minister of State. He was a member of the so-called Wilson "Kitchen Cabinet". He managed to secure landing rights in the United States for Concorde, despite severe American opposition and this achievement should not be underestimated. The *Daily Mirror* reported on 24 September 1977

> The US Government will allow Concorde flights to Anchorage in Alaska, Boston, Dallas, Honolulu, Los Angeles, Miami, Houston, Chicago, Seattle, San Francisco and Philadelphia as well as Washington. Industry Minister Gerald Kaufman said in Bristol last night that he was a "passionate advocate of Concorde but refused to guarantee the jobs of aircraft workers". [*Daily Mirror*, 24 September 1977]

He joined the Privy Council in 1978. He was then destined to serve only as a member of the Shadow Cabinet while Margaret Thatcher and John Major held the office of Prime Minister between 1979 and 1997. Under Harold Wilson and Jim Callaghan he was Shadow Environment Secretary from 1980 to 1983, then Shadow Home Secretary from 1983 to 1987, and finally Shadow Foreign Secretary from 1987 to 1992. He was appalled by the Labour Party's left-wing 1983 election manifesto, calling it 'the longest suicide note in history'. He was virulently opposed to both Anthony Wedgwood Benn (plain Tony Benn from 1972) and Michael Foot. On the other hand, he was a vociferous critic of Margaret Thatcher, dubbing her the female Mussolini and accusing her of behaving like a 'fishwife' during heated exchanges in the Commons.

He was an influential back-bencher, for a time chairing the Select Committee for Culture, Media and Sport (1992-2005) and was a member of the Parliamentary

Committee of the Parliamentary Labour Party (1980-1982), and of the Labour Party National Executive Committee. At a time when Radio 3 was undergoing clear changes in policy and presentation, Kaufman was appalled by what he perceived to be a process of dumbing-down:

> Radio 3 is employing more and more celebrity presenters but that is not what it should be about. This is all a way of trying to popularise Radio 3 but it is not there to be popular. It is there to offer music of a high intellectual standard and if it keeps dumbing down there is no point in having it. [Kaufman speaking to *The Stage* magazine, 25 September 2003]

He was a loyal supporter of Tony Blair, despite disagreeing with some of his policies. He reluctantly supported Blair over the invasion of Iraq, notwithstanding serious misgivings. He served on the Royal Commission on the House of Lords Reform in 1999.

He had the courage on occasions to vote against the Labour whip when urged by his conscience, in particular regarding the Welfare Reform Bill of 2015, when official Labour policy was to abstain and he chose, along with many other Labour MPs, to vote *against* the Bill.

He was knighted in 2004 for his services to Parliament.

He had strong views concerning the direction in which the House of Commons was going, and in particular its tendency to become self-absorbed. When Damian Green, the Tory MP, was arrested in 2008, Kaufman wrote in the *Guardian* of 12 December of that year,

> I am getting increasingly worried about the mental condition of the House of Commons. I do not refer to individual MPs. Most of them are sensible and hard-working. I am talking about the Commons as a collective, which seems these days to be carrying self-absorption into the realm of solipsism.

> This week we have had two ministerial statements about welfare reform. Attendances in the chamber were respectable, but no more. On Monday there was a debate about the rights of MPs, and the chamber was crammed. The welfare statements affected the lives of millions. The debate about the arrest of a Tory MP and the police search of his parliamentary office was of scant relevance to anyone outside Westminster.

Sir Gerald Bernard Kaufman MP – Politician and member of Shadow Cabinet

In the same year he wrote scathingly of the BBC's craven response to the infamous Jonathan Ross/Russell Brand phone call, whilst broadcasting on Radio 2, to Andrew Sachs in which they made obscene suggestions. Kaufman wrote, in the *Daily Mail* of 28 October, an article castigating the BBC's lack of a coherent editorial policy:

> But apart from being deeply unpleasant in itself it [the Radio 2 broadcast] demonstrates conclusively that an effective editorial chain of command, control and correction within the BBC does not exist, ought to have been created long ago, and very much needs to be implemented without any further delay whatever…The [BBC] Trust also needs to have a deep think about the huge financial rewards for broadcasters such as Brand and Ross. Ross, it is reported, receives a grotesque £6 million a year for his BBC television and radio appearances. And Brand is said to be in the six-figure bracket. This is the kind of money that, these days, the Government frowns on being paid to bank executives. Yet every penny that Ross receives from the BBC is taxpayers' money, funded by the licence.

In 2009 he was found to have made excessive expenses claims, including £8,865 for a television and £225 for a pen. In addition he claimed over £328,000 for home improvements, and when called before the Parliamentary Fees Office enquiry, was required to reduce his claims by almost half. He blamed a faulty memory for these misdemeanours.

He was the author of several books, including *How to be a Minister*, a somewhat tongue-in-cheek observation of the difficulties faced by ministers attempting to control the civil service, and a study of the 1944 Judy Garland film, *Meet Me in St Louis*.

He considered Barack Obama to be a very poor President of the USA.

Perhaps most surprisingly, Kaufman was a severe critic of Israeli foreign policy, in particular the treatment of Palestinians in the West Bank. He vented his wrath on the Sharon government over its military operation codenamed "Defensive Shield". He gave a speech in Parliament, one that attracted much opprobrium from, among others, his fellow Jewish MPs, saying, 'The Jewish people, whose gifts to civilised discourse include Einstein and Epstein, Mendelssohn and Mahler, Sergei Eisenstein and Billy Wilder, are now symbolised throughout the world by the blustering bully Ariel Sharon, a war criminal implicated in the murder of Palestinians at the Sabra and Shatila camps and now involved in killing Palestinians once again'. [Stuart Littlewood, Middle East online, 14 January 2009, quoted from Wikipedia] Some political commentators have praised him for his principled stand against terror of all kinds and have defended his stance on the Palestinians. 'Kaufman was Jewish, Leeds Jewish, Polish immigrant Jewish, even a Zionist, of a civilised and deeply troubled sort. He spoke as a proud Jew, but not proud of Israel under Sharon.' [*Independent* newspaper, Obituary, 27 February 2017]

He went on to demand economic and military sanctions against Israel, and called for the extradition of those Israeli soldiers responsible for the deaths of two British citizens, Tom Hurndall and James Miller, in 2006. For these forceful denunciations of Israel, he was himself severely criticised by a number of MPs. He made other, equally contentious assertions, including the suggestion that Tory MPs were seduced by Jewish pressure groups, and as late as 2015 he was soundly denounced by Jeremy Corbyn for remarks made in Parliament regarding a spate of knife attacks by Palestinians on Jews.

Gerald Kaufman died on 26 February 2017, aged 86, after a prolonged illness. He was succeeded as Father of the House by Kenneth Clark.

Kaufman was a complex character, not easily categorised and certainly not universally admired and liked. He could be abrasive, pugnacious and offensive, and quite clearly lacked any self-doubt. Yet he was intelligent, painstaking in his research, admirably fluent in argument and lucid in delivery. Too often he allowed an habitual sarcasm to vitiate the effect of his gift for witty repartee. He was courageous in his views and opinions and was able to face up to strong personalities like Michael Foot and Tony Benn. He remained throughout his political career a loyal supporter of core Labour policies and only became exasperated when they veered to the Left, an aberration he felt was anathema to the majority of party supporters. It might be seen to be ironic that the most Left-wing Labour leader in decades, Jeremy Corbyn, felt obliged to hail Kaufman as a man who could be 'iconic and irascible' who sported 'dandy clothes' and 'loved life and politics'.

Bibliography

Daily Mail, "An apology from the BBC for these two isn't enough, says the former chairman of the Commons' media watchdog", 28 October 2008
Daily Mirror, 24 September 1977
Guardian newspaper, Obituary, 27 February 2017 and "House of solipsism", 12 December 2008
Kaufman, Gerald, *How to be a Minister*, Faber & Faber, (London: 1997)
Kaufman, Gerald, *To Build the Promised Land*, Weidenfeld and Nicolson, (London: 1973)
Kaufman, Gerald, *Inside the Promised Land – A personal view of today's Israel*, Wildwood House, (London: 1986)
Kaufman, Gerald, *Meet Me in St Louis*, BFI, (London: 1994)
Kaufman, Gerald, *My Life in the Silver Screen*, Faber & Faber, (London: 1985)
Independent newspaper, Obituary, 27 February 2017
The Stage, 25 September 2003

Comedy giant – Barry Cryer

23

Barry Cryer OBE 1935-2022
Comedy Script Writer, Entertainer and After-Dinner Speaker
At LGS 1946-1953

YOU MAY BE forgiven for not instantly recognising the name of Barry Cryer, but his wit and repartee will be familiar to all who enjoy the very best of British humour. He, in collaboration with others, wrote scripts for the most famous names in comedy and undoubtedly brought happiness to untold millions. For over 30 years he contributed jokes, sketches and sitcoms for radio and television, and only when a new generation of comedians preferred to write their own material did his output begin to falter. Characteristically, he always had a high regard for those new comedy acts that some find edgy or even unpalatable. This even-handed attitude was expressed lucidly in his book, *Butterfly Brain*:

> Personally, I have no problem with profanity as such, if used sparingly and well placed, but it takes style. I once asked Billy Connolly, the patron saint of the well-chosen expletive, why he swore so much and he said that it was part of his 'street rhythm', which is a fair point. However, Frank Skinner, a similarly brilliant exponent of the cuss, decided to leave out all of the swearing in his act one night and said it went just as well…. Lesser lights should beware of using an excess of expletives just for the sake of them. It often ruins a good set. I have a theory that if young stand-ups do swear more than their predecessors, it's because they have come through a tougher school of heckling

audiences. They feel that they have to fight back in some way. Then, when they progress and begin to face kinder audiences, it becomes difficult to change this now ingrained approach. [BC, *BB*, pp. 27-28]

He was quite happy to defend those younger comedians who face a barrage of criticism from their elders. 'They [the critics] would find that the scene out there is funny, refreshing and challenging'. [BC, *BB*, p. 28]

Barry Charles Cryer was born at 12 Mount Pleasant Avenue, Roundhay, on 23 March 1935, the son of John Carl, an accountant, and Jean. Barry hardly knew his father, who died in 1940, but he was given the impression of a 'friendly, well-liked man'. [BC, p.26] Carl had served in the First World War in the artillery, was a keen golfer, and was a Worshipful Member of his Masonic Lodge. Barry's mother worked hard to keep him and his elder brother, John, in the family home; but with John leaving to join the merchant navy and then the Ministry of Agriculture and Fisheries, in effect Barry was raised as an only child.

He had vivid memories of his time at Talbot Road County Primary School, where Mrs Gannon put the fear of God into him – and presumably the other children. If he played a wrong note whilst learning the piano, she would strike him hard across the knuckles by way of 'encouragement'. Among his closest school friends at this time, John Andrews and Anthony Dean Tasker were later to join him at Leeds Grammar School. When not attending to his school prep, he would watch the local football team, the Yorkshire Amateurs, or chase the local girls or, interestingly, watch the speedway races at Odsal Stadium, an activity he emulated on a smaller, more amateurish scale, in the dell behind his house.

The war affected him only in that his neighbours, the Patemans, had an Anderson Shelter in the garden, and in the event of the warning siren being sounded, he would be carried into this shelter. Leeds got off lightly as far as bombing was concerned, though he did mention a tenuous connection with Sir John Hawkshaw [q.v.] when he wrote, 'The only direct hits, as I remember, were on the gallery [and Town Hall] and a pub, the Golden Cock [the public house where Hawkshaw was born]'. [BC, p.30] He did, rather tongue in cheek, claim that he was so upset by the war that he could not concentrate on his undergraduate studies at Leeds and so made an early retreat from there.

He remembered Winston Churchill visiting Leeds after the war.

Perhaps his first prompt in the direction of entertainment came when he met an unnamed gentleman who had worked at the old Leeds theatres, the Hippodrome and the City Varieties. He entertained Barry with amusing tales of the visit to Leeds by Fred Karno, the impresario, who was at that time cultivating the talents of Charlie Chaplin and his understudy, Stan Laurel. Surely such stimulating stories engendered in the young and impressionable Barry a feeling for the theatre and comedy.

In 1947, he won a scholarship to Leeds Grammar School. His career started infelicitously when, on attempting to cross the road close to the school, he was knocked down by a car on his very first day. Even he would not have claimed to have been a model pupil. He became involved in the selling of black-market dinner tickets, which earned him a sound caning in the Headmaster's study. Next he sold a short-cut for that infamous ordeal, the cross-country run, a 'sporting' activity held in even the most inclement weather. Sadly, this came to an end, not by being punished but by being undercut by an equally devious pupil. He wrote:

> Always a cutter by instinct, I would write essays culled from reference books with deft application of cross reference. Once it went awry. One teacher, H K Black [later sadly killed in a motoring accident], known to his intimates as Hugh, sadistically read out to the class an essay I had 'written' on Henry IV: "The narrative grips," he said, "but turn the page and lo! we have changed kings! behold – Henry V." My last form master, P H Kelsey, who laboured under the soubriquet 'Pip', wrote on my report: "He must learn that glibness is no substitute for knowledge." Have I ever learnt!

Barry had some notable friends and acquaintances at school: Tony Harrison, later to become a distinguished poet and playwright; Harry Ognall became a judge; and Richard Price became the head of a company selling television programmes worldwide. Brian Walsh QC was another of his contemporaries.

Barry was a leading light in the School's Literary and Debating Society and he ultimately became the Hon. President, Hon. Treasurer and Hon. Senior Member. He, with other members, was responsible for the spoof proposal of a Coat of Arms:

> After prolonged deliberations, the committee has decided upon a motto and coat of arms for the Society. The motto is "Ludi supplementaris nobis sunt faciendi" ["Supplementary games must be done by us", or, more colloquially, "We must engage in extra-curricular activities"] and the coat of arms consists of Crossed Bananas and Sandwich Rampant on no grounds whatsoever. [*Leodiensian*, December 1952, p.53]

Whether or not Barry was universally acclaimed by his fellow debaters may be gauged from the following comment on him by the then Hon. Secretary, R D Morrish: 'Falstaffian irrelevance has been his main object in life. His manner of speaking has been of more interest than his subject-matter.' [*Leodiensian*, July 1953, p.124]

He took part in a number of dramatic productions whilst at school. On one occasion he played the part of Abel Merryweather in Stanley Houghton's *The Dear Departed*, and the reviewer noted that, 'It was delightfully funny and enabled B C Cryer to give another of those impressions of low-life at which he excels. He was, as usual, superbly at ease...and was most ably aided and abetted by the others who appeared with him.' [*Leodiensian*, April 1953, p.72] On another occasion, he performed in the annual Shakespeare play: 'Talking of *Henry IV*, I played Falstaff and shared the acting cup with my friend John Gledhill. This fell apart when presented to us by the then Princess Royal....I took the cup and gave the base to John, getting my first laugh from an audience. The seeds were sown.' [BC, p.33]

He won an Exhibition to Leeds University to read English and met, among others, Wole Soyinka (who later won the Nobel Peace Prize) and became reacquainted with Tony Harrison with whom he struck up a long-lasting friendship. He recalled singing with the university jazz band busking outside the town hall and quite by chance meeting Humphrey Lyttleton who happened to be performing there that night. [BC, *BB*, p. 97]

He spurned the midnight oil and indulged in a hedonistic lifestyle that was not compatible with academic honours. However, he did gain invaluable experience in the varied arts programme on offer at the university. He produced a Rag Revue and took part in a bewildering variety of shows. The result was inevitable: his first-year exam results necessitated leaving the university and taking a series of mundane jobs and spending too many evenings in the Fforde Greene pub in Harehills, later closed down by the authorities. At around this time, he applied to The *Yorkshire Post* with a view to becoming a trainee journalist but the interview with the editor, Linton Andrews, did not go particularly well. Apparently, Barry was neither suited to a novice's post nor was he experienced enough to enter the cut and thrust of investigative journalism. From this nadir he was saved by being asked back to the university, not as a student, but as the producer of the then-current Rag Revue. A London agent appeared to watch the show, liked what Barry did, and offered him work at the Leeds City Varieties. For five days in April 1956 he performed in front of a small audience of slightly shady characters in raincoats (it was sunny outside), whose main interest was confined to the strip shows, and elicited absolutely no response or applause from them. Following this, he went on the road, appearing in third-rate theatres (so called "Number Threes") that seemed to specialise in titillating flirtatiousness. After a series of flops, he left the circuit and returned to the student shows at the Empire Theatre, not as a performer but as a stagehand, in which capacity he studied the acts and began to analyse what constituted success. So he carefully assessed the likes of Jimmy James and Petula Clark and started to plan the way ahead. Thus prepared, he returned to Leeds.

His lucky break came when he was called in at short notice to assist the magician David Nixon, who had come to Leeds to star as Buttons in *Cinderella*. A

Television producer and interviewer Sir David Frost

friendship developed between the two and it was Nixon who encouraged Barry to head to London, which he duly did to join the Windmill Theatre, famous for launching the careers of comedians like Harry Secombe, Peter Sellers and Jimmy Edwards, where he remained for the following seven months as a supporting comedian, drawing a few laughs and a lot of audience ennui. This might be partly explained by the fact that Barry was competing with the theatre's famous strip shows. It was a demanding schedule, six shows a day, six days a week. It was here that he met Bruce Forsyth who happened to be top of the bill. Eventually he was fired and for a time signed on for the dole but was then offered an interview to join the musical *Expresso Bongo* at the Saville Theatre in 1958. This was a pretty savage attack on the contemporary pop music scene and was later made into a film starring Cliff Richard and the Shadows. He was taken on by Wolf Mankowitz and Monty Norman and stayed with the show for its ten months' duration. Rather unexpectedly, the lead role was taken by no other than Paul Scofield, the famous Shakespearian actor. Other members of the cast included Millicent Martin and Susan Hampshire. The show went on tour and was well received.

There followed another short hiatus in his meteoric career during which he met and teamed up with Doug Camfield, later to become a successful television

Barry Cryer OBE – Comedy Script Writer, Entertainer, After-Dinner Speaker

director. They collaborated on scripts produced for Jimmy Logan, the Scottish comedian then attracting a degree of fame. Four sketches were accepted and these represent his very first successes in his writing career. A little later, along with Ted Dicks, he wrote a revue for the show, *And Another Thing*, starring Bernard Cribbins and Joyce and Lionel Blair. By good fortune, Danny La Rue was in the audience and he asked to meet the two co-writers, whereupon he invited them to write a script for him for a nightclub act at Winston's Club in the West End. For Barry, it was a revelation to see Danny perform his drag act with a remarkable number of costume changes. This mutually advantageous collaboration was to endure for many years, but at the start it was a bit of a culture shock for Barry to start writing what was, in effect, somewhat crude, bawdy, innuendo-fuelled comedy.

Ronnie Corbett

In time, Danny La Rue acquired his own eponymously named nightclub in Hanover Square and Barry was his writer-in-residence. Ronnie Corbett had joined the show. On one famous occasion, Dame Margot Fonteyn and Rudolph Nureyev were in the audience and she was so taken with Danny's depiction of her (using Barry's script) as a randy ballerina, and Ronnie's take on Nureyev, that she requested a private show to which she invited the entire Australian Ballet Company. It was, perhaps surprisingly, given the nature of the show, an unmitigated success.

Another distinguished visitor to the club was Noel Coward, who was treated to an adapted version of a number of his most famous songs. Again, despite Barry's jitters, the show was a huge success. He was at this time to meet other famous celebrities: the Beatle, John Lennon, and John Osborne, the playwright, to name just two.

At this time, he met Roger Hancock, brother of Tony the famous comedian. Roger became Barry's agent, an association that lasted decades. In his capacity as agent, Roger was famed for driving hard bargains yet despite this he was popular in an industry that could engender unhealthy enmity. He was so good, rising stars like Graeme Garden and John Cleese used him to promote their careers.

Yet another break came when he was offered the role of MC at the Players'

Theatre in London. In this, he followed the excellent example of Leonard Sachs, who had perfected the use of polysyllabic language and an auctioneer-like use of the gavel, and anyone who has seen him in action at the BBC's *The Good Old Days* will know exactly what I mean. In the three years he worked there, Barry learned how to handle an audience and steel his nerves against audience apathy. He regularly appeared on *The Good Old Days*, both solo and with Bernard Cribbins. Meanwhile, he was still working at Danny's Club and it was here that his really big break came when David Frost asked him, along with David Nobbs (of *Reggie Perrin* fame) and the Monty Python team, to write for *The Frost Report* and other shows, including *Frost on Sunday*. Barry recalls

> In comparison to 'That Was The Week That Was', 'The Frost Report' was more thematic than satirical. We'd have a full writers' meeting at the start of the week, in a church hall in Crawford Street, Marylebone to discuss that week's topic. Anthony Jay would outline the thesis for the show and we would respond with what he called the 'Continuing Development Monologue', or CDM, which would knit that week's theme together. Then, after a game of football, we'd clear off to each other's houses to start work. [BC, *BB*, p. 46]

This career break allowed Barry to escape from the nightly grind of treading the boards in a cabaret nightclub. He found himself working on the pilot show for *That Was The Week That Was* which Frost co-hosted with Brian Redhead and which during its run of two seasons, counted among its crew Gerald Kaufman [q.v.]. It was a show that broke the mould of political satire, bringing with it an irreverence that many found distasteful. Along with the other scriptwriters, Barry found Frost to be engaging and encouraging, always ready to praise but occasionally gently suggesting that a proposed script might be improved.

With Graham Chapman he worked on the *Doctor in the House* series and co-wrote (along with Eric Idle) sketches for Ronnie Corbett. Later, he wrote scripts for *The Two Ronnies*. With Nobbs, he wrote 68 editions of *Sez Les* for Les Dawson, and more for *Jokers Wild*, the ITV comedy show which Barry presented, featuring Ted Ray and Arthur Askey. Nobbs granted Barry the accolade, 'His fertility of ideas and knowledge of show biz was more than matched by his feeling for, and love of, words. He is an immaculate writer.' [BC, p.127]

Barry was taken on to the Python team, a group of comedians he had first met when writing for Frost, and was asked to do the warm-up act, which entailed welcoming the audience, telling a few choice jokes and say a little about the show's content and then introduce the cast. There is an engaging story concerning one of the early shows. The BBC had not quite perfected the art of matching the invited audience to the content material of the show and in its naivety had bussed in a large number of old age pensioners, who no doubt believed they were to be entertained by a real circus, to enjoy the Pythons' wacky humour. It is not on record how they reacted to sketches featuring dead bodies in bin bags or the subsequent scene at the undertakers.

By way of variety, in 1972 he was asked by Humphrey Lyttleton to join the cast of Radio 4's *I'm Sorry, I Haven't a Clue*.

His career in comedy now took off with a vengeance. Through his appearances on *I'm Sorry, I Haven't a Clue*, he met Willie Rushton, who was to become a life-long friend and fellow comedian. Their first collaboration was *Two Old Farts in the Night*, which they took to the Edinburgh Fringe in 1990 and then toured the country. It was, as Barry wrote, 'a haphazard melange of jokes, songs and Will's spiralling imagination'. [BC, p.103] Each offered his own contribution but did not appear together on stage apart from at the very beginning and end. It was a measure of Barry's affection for him that, when Rushton died in 1996, he was devastated by the loss of a dear friend. Barry was equally fond of Humphrey Lyttleton, another chairman of *I'm Sorry*, a show that had been running for 37 years.

He wrote, in partnership with Roy Cameron, scripts for the Kenny Everett show over a period of eight years, first for Thames Television and then for the BBC. As he ruefully admitted, he was writing innuendo-laden smutty material guaranteed to offend Mrs Whitehouse.

He worked with Jack Benny and Victor Borge. The show, *Frost Over England*, won the Golden Rose at the Montreux Festival of that year (1967). He teamed up with John Junkin and others to produce material for Morecambe and Wise, when their main contributor, Eddie Braben, was unavailable. On one occasion, Vera Lynn was the guest on the *Morecambe and Wise Show* and Eric suggested to the two script writers that it would be a laugh if Vera pretended that she did not know she was expected to sing and to keep this a secret from Ernie. The wheeze worked perfectly, with Ernie suffering a near-panic attack and whispering to Eric how on earth they were going to entice her to perform. Thanks to Barry and Junkin, Eric spoke the immortal line, 'Short of starting another war, I've no idea!' [The *Yorkshire Post* magazine, 29 September 2018, p. 19] [BC, *BB*, p. 167]

The list of those stellar comic geniuses for whom he provided material, always in collaboration with others, reads like a roll-call of British humour; in addition to those already mentioned, he worked with Bruce Forsyth, Tommy Cooper, Stanley Baxter, Dick Emery, Dave Allen, Frankie Howerd (whom he famously described as 'a series of comebacks'), Mike Yarwood, Billy Connolly, Russ Abbot, Kenny Everett and Jasper Carrot. Among American comedians for whom he wrote may be counted Bob Hope and Phil Silvers of *Bilko* fame. He wrote and performed alongside Dick Vosburgh, a man for whom Barry had the greatest respect and fondness, regarding him as one of the most underrated comic geniuses of the period.

Barry was happy to admit that he found it more conducive to inspirational thinking when working in partnership with other script writers. 'If there was any continuity in those partnerships, it was that I tended to work with people who were good at construction. I was good at punchlines, gags, stories, retorts, but not so good at what happens next. In terms of comedy writing, I became what the Americans describe as a 'line-man'. [BC, *BB*, p. 34]

Barry, over the years, featured in a large number of television panel games, including *That's Show Business*, *Blankety Blank*, *What's My Line?*, *Punch Lines* and *Give Us a Clue*. He was for a time chairman of the panel game, *Jokers Wild*, a show that was born in the Kirkstall Road studios of ITV and ran from 1969 to 1973 and featured such comic stalwarts as Ted Ray, Les Dawson and Arthur Askey as well as newer up-and-coming comics. He appeared in a number of pantomime roles including playing the Dame in *Sleeping Beauty* at the Shaw Theatre, King's Cross, London (1984), the King in *Jack and the Beanstalk* in Leicester (1988), and Dame Daisy in *Jack and the Beanstalk* at the Hackney Empire (1994).

He was the 'victim' of *This Is Your Life* in 1995, being set up by his friend, Willie Rushton, and was awarded the OBE in 2001. He recalled that Her Majesty asked if he was still writing and encouraged him to 'Keep it up'. For once in his life he refrained from picking up on the obvious innuendo.

In 2008 he went on tour with Colin Sell (the pianist in *I'm Sorry, I Haven't a Clue*) in a comedy review, *Strictly Come Joking*, kicking off at Taunton, and repeated the show annually, but in November 2018 he was forced to cancel his appearance at the Capitol Theatre, Horsham, after falling and breaking his hip. He underwent an operation in which a pin was fixed in place to mend the fracture.

In 1999, Barry was invited to return to LGS to be guest speaker at a formal function. He took the opportunity to compose a witty ode in which he made reference to both William Sheafield and John Harrison. Of the School he knew, he wrote:

> In 1859, they raised the final rafter
> It sometime seems I arrived soon after.
> Ah, the memories! Classes, games
> But most of all, those masters' names:
> Pip Kelsey, H K Black, Sam Hill
> Beefy Hoggett – oh, the thrill
> As I remember Doc Wilson, who
> Oft spoke in riddles, I swear 'tis true;
> You may not believe it, but I beg

Barry Cryer OBE – Comedy Script Writer, Entertainer, After-Dinner Speaker

> You to accept that Danny Robinson hit us with a chair leg,
> Ben Osborne, the incredibly tall Joe Lee
> Chips Chippindale – an aesthete, or so it seemed to me
> Carp Whitmore, with the profile of a fish
> R J M Evans and oh, I wish
> I could meet again Horace Bradbrook
> Who taught me love of Shakespeare and does this lad brook
> No argument on that – and H M Wells
> Monty Montagnon – but how this list tells
> Of my memories….

Displaying astonishing vigour and vitality as he grew older, he continued to fill his time with a wide variety of entertainment activities. From the late 1960s he became a popular after-dinner speaker, a sought-after corporate events entertainer, and presided over countless award ceremonies. One long-standing commitment was to the Edinburgh Fringe festival, having performed there from 2002 to 2018 with only one break in 2013. For some years he partnered Ronnie Golden, song-writer and musician, late of The Fabulous Poodles band; two appearances in 2017 in their two-man, all-song show entitled *Just the Two of Us at Six* and a further two appearances in 2018, *Historical Objects*, the latter title a wry description of themselves, were a great success.

Meanwhile, in September 2018, Barry received the British Music Hall

The original line-up of BBC Radio 4's 'I'm Sorry, I Haven't A Clue', Willie Rushton front left

Society's Life-time Achievement Award at the Brick Lane Music Hall, London, in recognition of his contribution to British comedy over the previous 50 years. The award consisted of an engraved Chairman's Gavel and Block in a presentation box. Typically, Barry 'complained' that he had been invited to the occasion under false pretences, in that Roy Hudd had told him the meeting had been arranged to pay tribute to West End and film actress, Julie Sutton, before being surprised with the award. Even Barry would have agreed that this was an improvement on his earlier ambition to win the Job Centre lifetime achievement award. [BC, *BB*, p. 5]

In 2018, Barry was also commissioned by Sky Arts to pay tribute to some of those he had worked with for the programme, *Comedy Legends*, featuring in the first series Tommy Cooper, Frankie Howerd, Joan Rivers, Ronnie Barker, Bob Hope, Jack Benny, George Burns and Morecambe and Wise.

Barry was for many years a Lord's Taverner, taking to the cricket field with the likes of Denis Compton, Bill Edrich, Freddy Trueman and Brian Close. By his own admission he was not a competent cricketer, but he enjoyed some memorable moments such as the occasion when he bent down to field the ball and his flannels split, to the delight of the crowd. Ever the crowd-pleaser and showman.

From 1967 he lived at Hatch End, near Pinner, and was for a long time a close neighbour and friend of the late Ronnie Corbett. The house was perfect for entertaining Barry's many showbiz friends and the local pub, the Moon & Sixpence, was warm and welcoming. Hatch End was very convenient as Barry did not drive and the commute on the train to Euston Station was short. He married Terry (Theresa) Donovan and the couple had four children, Tony, a university professor, David, a computer wizard, Bob, who co-authored two books with Barry, and Jackie, a choirmaster and singer

Barry possessed an endearing modesty. I wrote at the beginning of this article that some readers may not immediately recognize the name Barry Cryer and, to some extent, this was what he preferred. In *Butterfly Brain*, he wrote that he never wanted to become a star because he believed he did not have the 'X Factor' or possibly even the ego to become one. Rather, he always remained thankful that, throughout his professional career, he enjoyed many good breaks, rode his fortune and made a great many friends whose company he cherished. Barry died on 25 January, 2022.

Bibliography
Cryer, Barry, *Butterfly Brain*, Weidenfeld & Nicolson (London: 2009)
Cryer, Barry, *The Chronicles of Hernia*, Virgin Books (London: 2009)
Cryer, Barry, speaking on *Titter Ye Not. The Frankie Howerd Story* on BBC Radio 2, 15 September 2009
Cryer, Barry, unpublished poem dated February 1999
The *Leodiensian*, the magazine of Leeds Grammar School, various issues
The *Yorkshire Post* magazine, 29 September 2018, p. 19

The Right Honourable Lord John Dyson PC

24

The Right Honourable
Lord John Anthony Dyson PC 1943-
Eminent Lawyer and retired Master of the Rolls
At LGS 1951-61

LORD DYSON IS one of the most eminent legal figures in Britain today. He was awarded a Harmsworth Scholarship when he took silk in 1968 and then appointed QC in 1982. Four years later he became Head of Chambers at 39 Essex Chambers, a position he held until 1993. His next appointment was to the High Court and in 2001 he became Lord Justice of the Court of Appeal in England and Wales. By 2010 he was a Justice of the Supreme Court of the United Kingdom. His crowning achievement was to be appointed Master of the Rolls, a position he held from 2012 to 2016, when he retired to become an Arbitrator and Mediator in both domestic and international arbitrations. He continues in this role today.

In his autobiography, *A Judge's Journey*, published in 2019, he first dwells upon his Jewish roots, giving details of his grandparents and parents. His mother, Gisella, was highly intelligent and an accomplished pianist as well as a keen hiker, both of which interests John still shares. She went to Paris from her home in Bulgaria to learn about the fashion industry and this came in very useful later when she moved to Leeds. At Chamonix, she met Richard Dytch (later anglicised to Dyson) and they were soon married.

Richard Dytch was born in 1909 at Kenealy Street in Leeds, close to Clay Pit Lane where many recent Jewish immigrants had settled. He was the son of a bespoke tailor who eventually worked from rented premises at Grafton Street. As a young man he was keen on cinema and followed Yorkshire cricket; the latter John emulated during his school days. On leaving school, Richard trained as a chartered accountant, though he never qualified, so he practised as what is now called a certified accountant with Dytch, Sayers & Co. at Albion Street. However, the lure of retail proved very strong and he went into partnership with close family members, eventually running a number of shops dealing in women's clothing in Leeds city centre.

In time Richard and Gisella traded from a shop called 'Chanal' which specialized in haute couture. In this they were very successful. It was Gisella who persuaded Richard to change the name Dytch (a corruption of Deutsch) to the more English-sounding Dyson.

John was born around midnight on 31 July 1943, accompanied by a terrific thunderstorm. The family home at this time was at Broomhill Drive, Moortown; and it was there that his brother Robert, not to be outdone, was born on 5 November 1945, accompanied by the usual pyrotechnics and explosions. A little later, in 1947 they moved to Belvedere Road. One of John's earliest memories was hearing the thriller series *Dick Barton, Special Agent*, on the Light Programme, thanks to the 'home help', Elsie, who was an avid fan.

John, and a little later, Robert, were sent to the local prep school, Ingledew College, which boasted sections for boys and girls, the two strictly segregated. He recalls wearing his school uniform away from the confines of the school – even on the beach during family holidays at Scarborough. The teaching was traditional and based on Victorian virtues, though there was some relief. As John recalls, in the assembly hall

> ...we listened to Music and Movement. This was a BBC programme which was broadcast each morning for young children. We had to float about to the accompaniment of wafting music, taking on various guises, such as clouds or trees by raising our arms towards the ceiling. It was a gentle way to start the day which called for no input from the teachers. [*A Judges' Journey*, p.23]

Astonishingly, Latin was taught from the age of five or six alongside French. Few details of his lessons are recalled, but the memory of excessive discipline remains. Punishments ranged from the slipper to chalk and board rubber missiles. Such signs of displeasure would not be tolerated today. Away from the classroom, conkers, marbles, and various sports occupied the pupils' time. Whilst there, John enjoyed Ingledew College because he performed well academically, but in retrospect he found the place to be just a little too old-fashioned.

In September 1951 John entered the Junior Section of Leeds Grammar School.

The Headmaster at the time was Dr Terry Thomas (at LGS 1923-53), a strict disciplinarian, who had taken the School out of the Direct Grant system in 1945. (It was T G C Woodford, Headmaster from 1954-62, who took the School back into the DG system whereby a quarter of each intake was from local primary schools, their fees being paid by central government.) John joined J1; he recalls his first day:

> The journey from our house to the school involved two buses and a walk. The first bus journey took rather less than 30 minutes and was from the main road at the top of Belvedere Road to the Central Bus Station in town. The second took about 10 minutes and was from the bus station to a stop opposite the Main School. The final leg of the journey was a 10-minute walk down Clarendon Road. [*AJJ*, p.26]

No eight-year-old pupil would be expected to make such a journey today.

His form teacher in J1 was Miss Hilda Jones whom John remembers as a kind person. Miss Christie, in charge of J2, was not so affable. He joined Nicholson House and tried to engage fully in the ambitious games programme, though with limited success. His love of cricket was not matched by his team performances. He recalls his early cricketing practice at home:

> We [John and Robert] spent hours playing what passed for a version of conventional cricket (but with each team comprising one player). The wicket was drawn in chalk on the wooden garage door. I assumed the role of my hero Len Hutton and Robert the role of his hero Willie Watson. [*AJJ*, p.27]

He remembers attending the Roses matches at Headingley and the febrile atmosphere they engendered. Both he and Robert supported Leeds United at Elland Road, standing in the schoolboys' enclosure for the princely sum of 6d, and they would go to the Soldiers' Field at Roundhay Park for a game with friends. Again, with Robert, weather permitting, he played games like hide and seek and 'tig' or constructing dens for hours in the garden, eschewing any indoor entertainment. Dark, wet evenings were devoted to popular board games like *Monopoly* and *Cluedo*.

He was promoted to J5 at the end of his first year. To celebrate the coronation of Queen Elizabeth II the entire Junior School hiked from Otley to Ilkley with a picnic on Ilkley Moor. His piano playing was improving and towards the end of Summer Term 1953 he performed Bach's *Minuet in G* at the Junior School Music Festival. The more formal curriculum was not ignored, and he made such good progress that he was entered into the highest of the three first year classes in Senior

School. He joined Sheafield House, later to be joined by Robert, whose sons and grandchildren have done likewise.

According to John, his first form master was Rex Farebrother, who taught geography, but I can only find a J R Fairbrother, ARIBA, who taught Art and Workshops and who left LGS in 1953. His Latin master, 'Doc' Wilson (at LGS 1933-67), enforced discipline with a thin wooden pole named Eustacia which he employed liberally and methodically. Rather contentiously, if one of the boys caught out the 'Doc' in an error, he (the pupil) was required to administer the same punishment on the master. John freely acknowledges that Wilson was an exceptionally gifted Classicist, but a rather sad and lonely man whose whole existence seemed to be centred upon the School.

The Grammar School at that time did not generally invite intellectual curiosity and like many if not most similar schools relied simply on imparting unquestioned knowledge supported by over-zealous discipline. Among the teachers, there were a few exceptions, including Tom ('Froggy') Beckett (at LGS 1944-66), another Classics master who treated his pupils almost as friends and engaged them with enthusiastic and inspirational teaching. Under his guidance and encouragement, John and some friends entered a Latin reading competition which they won. Other teachers failed to inspire, including Larry Moore (at LGS 1920-58), whose classroom control left much to be desired.

On the sporting front, John did not excel. Like many others he was forced to endure the ordeal of the cross-country run, usually in foul weather. Also, like many others, he found that sporting prowess was the key to fame, glory and popularity, while those preferring scholastic achievement were unkindly dubbed 'swots'. However, when he was awarded an LGS Foundation Scholarship, along with another boy, John Templeton [*OL*56], the greater part of the School was awarded an extra half-day holiday, and this attracted much favourable comment and a degree of popularity.

John practised his cricket with determination and fervour, encouraged by Frank 'Beefy' Hoggett (at LGS 1922-63) and undertook some training at Johnny Lawrence's cricket academy at Rothwell. Sadly, his first outing with the U15 squad, against Drax, resulted in an ignominious duck; thereafter he restricted himself to House matches.

From the age of 13, John was fortunate to have piano lessons with Fanny Waterman. Another of her pupils at that time was Allan Schiller, with whom he would play cricket in Fanny's garden. Michael Roll, another pupil, won the first Leeds International Piano Competition in 1963 when aged just 17. John continued his lessons with her until he took his 'A' levels.

He contributed a great deal to the LGS House Music competitions. John was praised on several occasions for his organization and training of Sheafield's House

l-r: Robert, Richard (father) and John at home. Photo courtesy of Robert Dyson

Choir which regularly was awarded the top marks. In the end-of-term Summer Concert he was afforded the opportunity to play the piano accompanied by an orchestra, albeit one of indifferent standard:

> But I did play at these competitions pieces such a Schubert's *Impromptu in A flat Op 90 No 4* and some Chopin Nocturnes. On two occasions, I also played fairly easy piano concertos with the school orchestra. One was the little concerto in C major by Haydn; the other was a rather attractive concerto by the seventeenth-century English composer, John Stanley. I had never played with an orchestra before nor have I done so since. [*AJJ*, p.40]

Success at 'O' level was followed by entry into the Classical Sixth in which he studied Latin, ancient Greek, and Greek and Roman history, developing analytical skills that would come in very useful in a later existence as a lawyer. His teachers were 'Doc' Wilson, Tom Beckett, Eddie Scott (at LGS 1929-67) and Frank Chippindale (at LGS 1940-73). He became very active in the Classical Society. In October 1958, he gave a lecture on Verona and Ravenna 'with the help of graphic colour slides and a short-sighted projector'. [*Leo*, LXIII, No. 1, p.15] As a Sixth-Former, he was elected Treasurer of the Society and gave a talk on 'The Miracle of

Pompeii'. At the following meeting, he spoke ardently in favour of a Classical education as opposed to a Mathematical one. At around this time, he won the Henderson Ancient History Prize.

During Michaelmas Term 1958 he joined the editorial team of the School magazine. In time he was made a school prefect, a student body which then had disciplinary powers. Some prefects interpreted this rather too liberally, John less so.

John joined the Literary and Debating Society whilst in Middle School. He was one of two principal speakers for the motion, 'That this House deplores Horse-racing and all that it entails', and particularly enjoyed 'balloon' debates. On another occasion, he opposed the motion, 'That this House thinks that Britain should get to the moon first'. [*Leo*, ibid, p.18] He admits that, being innately shy, he was not a natural public speaker, but the Society afforded him opportunity to hone his skills. On joining the Senior Lit. & Deb. Society, he 'spoke on a variety of topics ranging from Murder and dachshunds called Max, to Alsatians in the New Inn'. [*Leo*, Vol LXIII, No. 1, p.14] He also remembers a visit to the School by a high court judge:

> I recall the visit to the school by Mr Justice Ashworth, a high court judge who was sitting at the Leeds Assize Court (now the Crown Court). I cannot recall a word of what he said. But I do recall being inspired and excited by him. [*AJJ*, p.42]

By Michaelmas Term 1958, John had been appointed Hon. Treasurer of Chess, and it was in this game that he truly excelled. He moved up from the Junior Team to the Senior one and soon made his mark in inter-school competitions as well as in the LGS Club competitions. In Lent Term 1959 both Dyson boys were making excellent progress and the *Leo* magazine for March 1959 reported that, 'R A Dyson (III.A), must be congratulated on reaching this stage of the competition where he will meet his brother'. [*Leo*, Vol LXXIII, No. 2, p.81]. Next term, a further report made clear that, 'The main strength of the team lay on the lower boards where both Dyson and Friedman [M J Friedman *OL61*] played well. Dyson, particularly, had a good record…' [*Leo*, Vol LXXIII, No. 3, p.136].

Taking his 'A' levels in the summer of 1960 he performed well, gaining distinctions in two of his subjects, and earned a state scholarship to fund a university course to read Law. This brought John another claim to popularity because the half-term holiday on Wednesday 22 February 1961 was extended 'to celebrate the Classical Scholarships gained by J A Dyson…and D[avid] Godfrey [*OL61*] and a Scholarship in Modern History gained by D N Waite [*OL61*]'. [*Leo*, Vol. LXXV, No. 2, p.79] His teachers recommended Oxford rather than Cambridge and Wadham College in particular. Careful preparation and extra tuition from his masters combined to ensure he was ready for the four-day programme of interviews and examinations at Wadham, whose Warden at the time was Sir Maurice Bowra. On being accepted, John took his advice and read Classics.

John reflected on the nature of his Grammar School education:

> Overall, I was very happy at LGS. I received a solid rather than an inspiring education there. The school had not shaken off the rigid stays of the Victorian era. It is easy enough to be critical of some of the things that were done there, such as corporal punishment. But there was nothing unusual about that in those days. [*AJJ*, p.44]

Going up to Wadham in October, John joined the rowing club briefly but found the training regime too arduous, preferring instead to go punting on the Cherwell. As for his studies, his tutor was Tom Stinton, a brilliant classicist specializing in Greek tragedy. For the first five terms he studied Classical Moderations, both literature and language. His special subject was ancient Greek sculpture and he spent many happy hours in the Ashmolean and the British Museum. He became particularly interested in Euripides' *Hippolytus*. Translation work improved his skills in fluency and accuracy of thought, all useful attributes in his later career. At the end of Hilary term, 1962, he took his examinations and obtained a First.

John made a few close friendships while at Wadham. One was with Brian Rosen, brother of Michael, the famous author of children's books. Another was Mark Sharpe, another law undergraduate, who introduced John to the delights of youth hostelling. There was evidence of some antagonism between those undergraduates who had been to public schools and those from grammar schools, but this did not unduly affect him. (It should be noted here that LGS was one of three Direct Grant grammar schools to be recognized as 'public' schools.)

In the Hilary term of 1963, John studied Greats, a course comprising ancient Greek history and ancient Roman history. His tutor was George Forrest, a Marxist with a particular interest in the history of Sparta. The course also included study of the great philosophers, including Plato's *Republic* and Aristotle's *Nicomachean Ethics*. Again, having to read the texts in the original Greek refined his skills in recall and interpretation. More modern philosophers were also studied, and John took a particular liking to moral philosophy:

> I was more interested in trying to understand the ethical principles that underpin human behaviour than the meaning of existence and theories of knowledge. In view of the course that my life was to take, it is perhaps of some significance that I enjoyed the philosophy of law (or jurisprudence as it was called). [*AJJ*, p.57]

The preoccupation existing at that time with language, the study of Latin and Greek, and close linguistic analysis was fundamental in shaping his need to express himself with care and precision.

Away from the tutorials and occasional lectures, John took up a number of sports. Squash and tennis were his favourites, with the rather less exhausting bouts of 'shove ha'penny' in the bar. Very briefly he tried horse riding and dinghy sailing. Rather more successfully, he joined the Wadham and Lady Margaret Hall choir and took part in concerts, performing Brahms' *German Requiem*, Carl Orff's *Carmina Burana* and Beethoven's *Mass in C*. In the meantime, his brother, Robert (*OL64*), joined the LGS school choir and the first work he sang in was Haydn's *Nelson Mass*, this despite his parents' initial objections. To their credit, they attended the performance in St Michael's Church, Headingley and enjoyed it so much they bought a recording of the work. Robert also played for the First XV, under the tutelage of Jim Collard, and was appointed Deputy Head of School.

John's fourth year at Wadham brought with it complications. Due to take the examinations in May 1965, he returned home for some weeks' much-needed respite but just before his planned return to Oxford, he was rushed to the LGI hospital in Leeds with Crohn's disease. As a result, he missed his examinations. He decided to remain at home with a view to returning to Wadham in the summer of 1966 to take his Finals. It was time to decide the course of his future career: possibly the Civil Service?; academia?; or take articles with a firm of solicitors? The latter was chosen so he undertook a correspondence conversion course. Sadly, the year off meant that when he did eventually take his Finals, he missed out on a First by a whisker and took a Second instead.

In the summer, he joined the Middle Temple and read for the Bar. This took two years, completing his conversion studies and eating his dinners in Middle Temple Hall. He successfully applied for a Middle Temple Harmsworth Scholarship and started upon his career in the law.

John entered into a six-month pupillage with Patrick Garland whose chambers were at 11 King's Bench Walk in the Temple. One of the barristers there was Donald Keating who had published a book, *Building Contracts*, and specialized in construction law. A second London pupillage was offered and accepted, though this meant that John would see a lot less of his family and Yorkshire. He was offered a seat in chambers and readily accepted. He entered a world of restrictive practices and – more ominous – anti-women prejudice. His first brief was concerned with matrimonial issues. At the same time, he lectured on company law at the Regent Street Polytechnic, now Westminster University. His county court work consisted largely of landlord and tenant disputes. But it was not all work and no play; leisurely lunches were taken at a Fleet Street restaurant or 'The Feathers' pub in Tudor Street; and afternoon tea was enjoyed at the 'Golden Egg' in Fleet Street.

It was at this time that he became acquainted with his future wife, Jacqueline Levy. They first met at a party; then, in early August he bumped into her in the Middle Temple library, where she was working in preparation for her Bar Finals. His opening gambit was to ask where he might find *The Times* law reports, followed by an invitation to lunch. She must have been impressed because there followed a brief, successful courtship. They were married on 5 July 1970.

Meanwhile, John's practice developed apace. For two years he was chiefly concerned with family law cases, including divorce cases in the county court. On one occasion, he was required to attend a divorce hearing at Southend County Court and, instead of taking the train and preparing his notes, he elected to be driven there by his legal executive, Mrs Bull, with the result that

> I rushed into the robing room and skimmed over the papers. Fortunately, they revealed no problems and all was well. But I don't believe that I was ever again so cavalier in my preparation for a case or indeed anything else. [*AJJ*, p.75]

Disputes over custody and access to children upset John to the extent that he decided to change course. He began to concentrate on construction law, re-joining Donald Keating and Patrick Garland. During the 1970s his practice grew substantially, and Douglas advised John to apply for silk. John was unsure. He had been in practice for only 12 years and considered himself, at 37, to be too young. Wiser counsels prevailed and eventually, two years later in 1982, he was successful.

John was invited to apply to become an Assistant Recorder, a temporary post that no longer exists. In effect he was a probationer, subject to a process of assessment. His duties were essentially the same as a Recorder, that is a part-time judge with the powers of a circuit judge. He was required to shadow one as part of his training. By 1986 he was promoted to Recorder. He remembers the drama of hearing evidence, listening to witnesses, and then hearing the jury's verdict:

> There was an element of drama even in the less serious cases. The unfolding of the story through the mouths of the witnesses was often unpredictable and fascinating. The return of the jury after they had reached a verdict was always a moment of tension. When the foreman of the jury rose to announce their verdict, the silence in the court was almost tangible. Once the verdict was given, the atmosphere in court changed immediately. [*AJJ*, p.86]

Back in 1984, chambers removed to 10 Essex Street and John was tasked with organizing the logistics, including refurbishment. However, construction law had

RT Hon Lord John Anthony Dyson – Eminent Lawyer and Master of the Rolls

John, Robert, Richard and Gisella dining out. Photo courtesy of Robert Dyson

by now lost some of its appeal and he was surprised and pleased that Edwin Glasgow invited him to become the Head of his chambers. He moved to 2 Garden Court in September 1986 and at first things did not go too well, with little work coming his way, though things improved soon after. One of his first cases was representing the Football Association in the Inquiry into the Hillsborough disaster. John's key role was in persuading a committee of the chairmen of five football clubs to put forward an agreed set of recommendations to avoid any possibility of such a catastrophe ever being repeated. They were, after some compromises were reached, accepted by Lord Justice Peter Taylor who presided over the Inquiry. Major soccer grounds became all-seater stadia with a greater emphasis on health and safety.

In another case, John appeared on behalf of the FA to defend the proceedings brought by the Football League which declared the proposed setting up of a Premier League in order to maximise commercial and financial gain to be unlawful. There can be no question that the success that John and his team enjoyed changed English and Welsh football for ever, thanks to lucrative television deals. The more than generous salaries that Premier League footballers enjoy today are evidence of this momentous decision, though whether that is something of which to be proud is debatable.

In 1990, John was elected to the Bench of the Middle Temple, making him one of its senior members. Then, after a few years, he was appointed as a Deputy High Court Judge and this entailed giving judgements rather than summing up criminal trials to assist juries to give their verdicts. It was early in 1993 that he was called in for an interview with the Lord Chancellor of the day, Lord Mackay of Clashfern, whereupon he was offered the position as a judge in the Queen's Bench Division of the High Court. After a very brief period of indecision, John accepted, and so he left the Bar after 24 years and became a judge.

John was sworn in as a High Court Judge on 30 March 1993. At the ceremony in the House of Lords he was accompanied by his wife, his two children, his mother, his parents-in-law, his brother-in-law, and his brother, Robert. A knighthood followed a few months later. First, he sat for three weeks each term for the duration of his tenure of office, in the Court of Appeal Criminal Division (CACD) and in this capacity he was helped to some extent by his previous experience as a Recorder. He learned a great deal by sitting with eminent Lord Chief Justices like Tom Bingham (Lord Bingham of Cornhill).

Following his first session with the CACD, he went on circuit to Leeds and Sheffield. Whilst in Leeds he stayed at Carr Manor, down Stonegate Road in Meanwood. Whilst in lodgings, High Court Judges, who were looked after by the local high sheriff, were able to invite guests to formal dinner parties, and during his first stay in Leeds John invited Fanny Waterman and members of his family to join him. On his second stay, he shared lodgings with two LGS Old Boys, Sir Harry Ognall [OL52] and Sir Christopher Holland [OL56], while Brian Walsh [OL54] arranged a dinner at Moorland Road in their honour on 27 July 1995, two years before the School moved to Alwoodley. John remembers that

> The three of us sang the school song in Latin and more or less in tune. I doubt whether many of those present knew a single word of it. It was quite a nostalgic affair. [AJJ, pp.94-5]

Between 1993 and 2000, John went on circuit many times, preferring to go to the larger cities like Leeds, Birmingham, Manchester, Newcastle, Nottingham and Cardiff. A measure of his competence is that very few appeals against his judgements were upheld. Moreover, in coming to his decisions, he always strove to be fair, balancing what were, in many cases, complex and competing arguments.

In 1997, John was invited to become the first High Court Judge to take the post of head of the Official Referees. He was almost certainly appointed with the aim to improve the performance of the court and so he worked closely with Peter Bowsher on the top floors of St Dunstan's House in Fetter Lane. He did implement some changes: he altered the name 'Official Referee' to 'Judge'; and the name of the court to the Technology and Construction Court (abbreviated to TCC). These, along with other changes, boosted the morale of the judges and raised the profile of the court. His tenure of office was considered wholly successful.

In 2000, he was invited by Tony Blair to become a Lord Justice of Appeal and he was sworn in by Lord Irvine the following year. Since all Lord Justices of Appeal become members of Her Majesty's Honourable Privy Council by virtue of position, John now added PC to his post nominals and as such he was sworn in at Buckingham Palace on 14 March 2001. He sat in the Court of Appeal from January 2001 to March 2010. He found his fellow judges to be friendly and supportive, for which he was very grateful as they had to cover all areas of law – civil, criminal, and family. Every judge was required to cover all these areas whatever their speciality might be. Generally speaking, most appeals raised difficult issues of law. Appeals were only heard if there was a good prospect of success and it was up to the Appeal Judges to decide which to allow and which to reject. So great was the workload because of the number of lodged appeals that, when John became Master of the Rolls, he limited the right to renewal if an appeal was rejected.

The work of the Court of Appeal was shaped first by the passing of the Human Rights Act of 1998, which incorporated the European Convention on Human Rights into our domestic law; and second Lord Woolf's civil procedure reforms which improved the efficiency of the conduct of civil litigation among other changes. On the downside, these reforms substantially boosted the cost of litigation.

In 2003, John was appointed as Deputy Head of Civil Justice and as such became de facto chairman of the Civil Procedure Rule Committee. Lord Phillips, then Master of the Rolls, left the running of this committee to John, who brought about many changes, including the introduction of hearings by telephone conference.

As Deputy Head of Civil Justice, John became an unofficial member of the inner group of the most senior judges, including the Master of the Rolls. In this capacity, he frequently attended meetings with the Lord Chancellor when discussing senior judicial appointments. He retired as Deputy Head of Civil Justice in December 2006 and concentrated on what he liked best, hearing appeals and writing judgements. Interestingly, John was the first English judge to serve on a jury, something brought about by reforms in 2004. Having served as a juror at one trial, he was called in to a second, only to be rejected by the Resident Judge with the words, 'This man is well known to me', words taken by one of the other potential jurors to mean that John had at some time been before the judge in an altogether different role! This salutary experience made him even more aware that jurors needed to be treated with tact and consideration (though he no longer was required to deal with them).

In 2009, the position of Master of the Rolls became vacant and John was invited to apply for the post, alongside Lord Neuberger of Abbotsbury. John recognized Neuberger to be the favourite and this turned out to be the case. However, a few months later, a vacancy occurred in the Supreme Court and John, who was suffering badly from the effects of ME at the time, decided to apply. He was successful and took up his new position in April 2010.

John's appointment as Justice of the Supreme Court took effect from 12 April 2010. At first, there was the small problem of his title:

> At the outset, I was 'Sir John Dyson SCJ'. Since all my colleagues were known as 'Lord X' or 'Lady Y', this made me feel uncomfortable. It was as if I was a second tier Justice. After an unconscionably long time, it was agreed that I would be given the courtesy title of 'Lord Dyson'. [AJJ, p.129]

The Supreme Court consisted of 12 members rather than the 38 who constituted the Court of Appeal. Another difference was the arrangement by which Supreme Court Justices lunched together in the dining-room in the court buildings in Parliament Square, whereas Appeal Court judges tended to eat at their own Inns and this meant that John now found he spent far more time in the company of his fellow Justices. He was given a friendly welcome by them, especially Lord Alan Rodger, who sadly died in the year following John's appointment. Lord Rodger was known for his clarity, intellectual sharpness and rigour, qualities that were not lost on John.

The work consisted mainly of a relatively small number of appeals each year. These tended to raise interesting questions of law. The Supreme Court dealt only with the most important cases. Justices were encouraged to write their own judgements whereas judges of the Court of Appeal were discouraged from doing the same. For over a year, John was the junior judge and he found that this placed him in a delicate situation, as he explains:

> Immediately after the conclusion of a hearing, we retired to the conference room to discuss the case. Each judge was asked in turn to express his or her views. The most junior member of the court invariably went first. This placed a considerable burden on that judge [i.e. the most junior Judge] because they were expected not only to say immediately how they would decide the appeal, but also to give cogent reasons for their view. This meant marshalling their thoughts within a short time. [AJJ, p.132]

John uses a cricketing analogy that it is more comfortable to bat lower down the order than to bat first.

Some of John's judgements involved interpretation of the European Convention on Human Rights. Two cases dealt with individuals who faced the threat of persecution in home countries if their claims for asylum were dismissed. One involved sexual orientation; the other political oppression. Another case was that of Julian Assange, who contested the request that Britain surrender him to the Swedish authorities under the European Arrest Warrant. John, despite pressure from Lord Phillips' judgement in the Court of Appeal, supported Assange.

During his two years at the Supreme Court, John wrote many leading judgements and earned the reputation as a fearless advocate for what he believed to be the truth based on close analysis of the issues involved. He made excellent use of his powers of rigorous interpretation, recognizing that his classical education played an important contributory part in this.

John gave many lectures throughout the country, on occasion voicing his unqualified support for the European Convention on Human Rights. He is always happy to point out that his embrace of all things European owes much to his family's history.

In November 2011, he presented prizes at the GSAL Speech Day. He was delighted to return to Leeds Town Hall:

> It was a moving experience for me to present the school prizes in the magnificent Town Hall where I had received school prizes myself more than 50 years earlier. Earlier in the day, I had visited the school in its large new site in the green belt on the Harrogate side of Leeds. I was shown round the school by senior students who seemed far more mature and confident than I was at their age. I was particularly impressed by the music facilities, which included several practice rooms and many pianos. I spoke to some of the students about the Law. They were bright and asked searching questions. It was an exciting experience for me. I hope it was for them too. [AJJ, p.137]

The full version of John's speech at the Town Hall may be found in his book *Justice: Continuity and Change*, Chapter 28, pp.417-420.

After two years in the Supreme Court, John felt that now might be the time to retire and possibly work as an independent arbitrator. However, enjoying good health and ever more confident that he was making a significant contribution to the development of the law, when he was offered the opportunity to put himself forward for the position of Master of the Rolls he rose to the challenge. Against stiff opposition, he was appointed by an interview panel at the Royal Courts of Justice. He had reached the pinnacle of his illustrious career.

The Master of the Rolls, first named in 1286, was originally responsible for the safe keeping of charters, patents and records of important court judgments written on parchment rolls. In effect he was the keeper of the public records. Later, the holder was a Judge in the Court of Chancery and assistant to the Lord Chancellor, with his own court, the Rolls Court. Since 1881 he has been a judge of the Court of Appeal only but retains important duties in relation to public records. Until recently, he also admitted all solicitors to practice. He is Chairman of the Advisory Council on Public Records and Chairman of the Royal Commission on Historical Manuscripts. The MR is, ex officio, chairman of the Magna Carta Trust. By virtue of his office, the Master of the Rolls is President of the Civil Division of the Court of Appeal. Traditionally, the most complex cases come before him.

John was sworn in on 1 October 2012, at the same time that Chris Grayling was sworn in as Lord Chancellor and Secretary of State for Justice. In his new capacity, John had weekly meetings with the Lord Chief Justice (LCJ), Igor Judge, besides hearing appeals. As Head of Civil Justice and Chairman of the Executive of the Civil Justice Council (CJC), he had meetings with its Executive Council. Other meetings took place with the Judicial Executive Board and were a forum for discussion of a wide range of legal issues. In fact, meetings were to become something of a bane, far too frequent and many frustratingly ineffectual in their outcomes. They required a great deal of preparation. Life was hectic enough without them.

Although it was mostly incredibly hard work, there was also a little play. Each December, John

> ...entertained [his] staff as well as the Vice-President of the Court of Appeal (Civil) and the DHCJ [Deputy Head of Civil Justice] to a Christmas lunch in the George, a nearby pub. I did this in each of my four years. These were happy occasions which, I think, were much enjoyed by my hard-working staff. [*AJJ*, p.152]

During his four years as MR, John worked hard to establish the principle of fixed recoverable costs, in an attempt to overcome the scandal of the excessive costs of litigation. Eventually, in consultation with Michael Gove, then Lord Chancellor, there was something of a breakthrough. Another of his laudable desires was to improve the status of civil law as opposed to Crime and Family law. He got nowhere with Chris Grayling, who was under pressure from the Treasury to cut costs.

In February 2013, he chaired a meeting of the National Archive Advisory Council (NAAC) at Kew, where discussions revolved around the restricted release of documents deemed sensitive by various government departments. One such discussion involved evidence given at the Inquiry into the 'Profumo Affair' and as a result, the period of non-disclosure was shortened. He felt strongly that the courts were being unfairly blamed for encouraging the 'compensation culture' that appeared to be gripping the country, especially whiplash claims. The media had stirred up some antipathy towards what they perceived to be a soft approach towards manifestly unmeritorious claims. John firmly countered this by pointing out that the courts were aware of the problem and took it into account when hearing such cases.

John promoted the idea that all appeals, with a few exceptions, should be televised. He also supported the view that an online court be established. In quite another area, he refused a request to increase solicitors' hourly rate of remuneration. In a bid to speed up the appeals in family cases, he managed to divert some classes of appeal to the High Court rather than the Court of Appeal and this helped to some extent.

2015 marked the 800th anniversary of the sealing of Magna Carta and John was at the heart of preparations for the momentous occasion. On 15 June, John, in the company of other judges, journeyed to Runnymede. The VIPs included Her Majesty the Queen, Prince William, David Cameron in his capacity as Prime Minister, Justin Welby and Loretta Lynch the US Attorney-General. John spoke for about three minutes – his allotted time – and concluded by saying

> Lord Denning had gone so far as to describe Magna Carta as 'the greatest constitutional document of all time, the foundation of the freedom of the individual against the arbitrary authority of the despot'. I concluded: 'With those words ringing in our ears, it now gives me great pleasure to invite the Prime Minister to speak'. I had not intended to imply that the Prime Minister was a despot even in jest. But that is how my words must have been interpreted because there was much laughter around the meadow. Many told me that it was the only joke of the day. [AJJ, p.176]

Towards the end of his tenure of office, John and Jacqueline visited Poland, first to an event marking the seventieth anniversary of the Nuremberg War Crimes Trials. On the second day of the visit they were taken to Auschwitz-Birkenau to take part in the March of the Living in which they joined over 10,000 young Jewish people who were there to demonstrate emphatically that the Nazis had failed in their bid to commit genocide. John thought the exuberance of the youngsters, while understandable, made it difficult to reflect upon the enormity of the crimes committed there.

Officially, John retired as Master of the Rolls at the beginning of October, but July was effectively the last month of his judicial career. One of his last formal engagements was to attend the Mansion House Dinner hosted by the Lord Mayor for the judges.

At his Valedictory in the Lord Chief Justice's Court, John spoke of his affection for his country and its firm adherence to the rule of law. Just as important, he stressed the part his family, and especially his wife Jacqueline, had played in his life and career. He was deeply moved by the tributes paid to him by many of the 200 senior judges and lawyers present. He was freely acknowledged as one of the most successful judges of his day, a man dedicated to fairness to all.

During his time as Master of the Rolls, John heard and gave judgements on many important legal cases brought before him. This is not the place to give details; interested readers can find excellent summaries of them in his autobiography, *A Judge's Journey* (2019), Chapter 12, pp.186-195.

On retirement he was approached by 39 Essex Chambers to join them to undertake some arbitration and mediation work which he gladly accepted. He was not at first overwhelmed by offers of work, so he attended and spoke at conferences and networked with some zeal. He chose wherever possible to work in London and concentrated on construction, commercial and sports arbitrations. One project involved the redevelopment of a site in Lewisham which included Millwall's ground known as The Den. John exonerated all the Lewisham council members and officials of any wrongdoing. He also applied himself to reforming and modernizing the civil procedure rules of the Republic of Cyprus (the South). He is now very much in demand as an arbitrator.

Apart from engaging once again in a series of lectures in many different countries, John became the Treasurer of Middle Temple based at Elizabeth Hall. The Inn possesses a portfolio of expensive premises, awards degrees, calls student barristers to the Bar and provides legal education. As Treasurer, he was able to invite many important guests and arrange visits from the highest echelons of Society, including Prince William, Duke of Cambridge.

In 2018 he retired as Treasurer and was able to concentrate more on his enthusiasms: travel, walking, music, and family. If he has one regret, it is that he was not offered a life peerage. He would have welcomed it; Jacqueline was not so sure.

Bibliography

Dyson, Lord John Anthony, *A Judge's Journey*, Hart Publishing (Oxford and Portland, Oregon: 2019)
Dyson, Lord John Anthony, Justice: *Continuity and Change*, Hart Publishing (Oxford and Portland, Oregon: 2018)
Leodiensian magazine, various volumes

Kaiser Chiefs
Yours Truly, Angry Mob

25

Charles Richard (Ricky) Wilson 1978 - Musician and Media Celebrity At LGS 1986-96

RICKY WILSON WAS born at Keighley on 17 January 1978. His father, Geoff, was a noted TV Producer and his mother, Glynne, was known to many as the scorecard girl on the popular BBC show *It's a Knockout*. At some point, the family moved to Middleton, near Ilkley. Both James Edward Francis, Ricky's elder brother, and Ricky attended Ghyll Royd School at Burley in Wharfedale before moving on to Leeds Grammar School, James in 1984 and Ricky in 1986. Both boys joined Nevile House.

James was active in the theatre productions at LGS and joined the editorial team of the School magazine, the *Leodiensian*, contributing a number of articles as well as photographs and art work. He worked behind the scenes as sound engineer in the School performances of Peter Shaffer's *Black Comedy* and R C Sherriff's *Journey's End*. His photograph of a basketball match was chosen as the front cover of the 1992-93 *Leodiensian* magazine. (In the same issue, brother Ricky provided a line drawing of Leeds Town Hall and the School Speech Day on page 4.) He co-wrote the Bands' Night report for 1992-93 and was sole author of the Insight into Management report of the same year. However, it was as conductor of the House Choir that he really set a precedent for Ricky when he won the Best Conductor award; following Thoresby's brave effort in the competition, their leading man 'didn't manage to beat the style and panache of James "Ringer" Wilson's conducting of Nevile's version of 'Help' (way better than Tina Turner's version) and 'Music of the Night' from 'The Phantom of the Opera', which earned him the Best Conductor Prize. [*Leo*, Volume 108, p. 18] As Ilan Sherman put it in his House

Report for Nevile, what might have been a disaster brought about by lack of practice was rescued 'mainly due to the astounding commitment and imagination of conductor [Wilson], who managed to produce one of the best performances ever from a Nevile choir'. [ibid, p.95]

Ricky, not to be outdone by his brother, played a key role in Nevile's House Play of the same year, a version of *Absolutely Fabulous*, and Sherman was equally fulsome in his praise: 'Special mention must also go to Tom Drife, Harry Campbell-Rickets, Charles du Pre and Ricky Wilson for outstanding acting and all the backstage crew for their unsung heroics'. [ibid, p.94]

The following year brought further accolades. In his House Music Competition report, Andrew Losowsky was happy to acknowledge that, 'Overall, the winner of the choir contest was adjudged to be Nevile, a popular choice, and this result, coupled with their position of joint first after the afternoon competition, easily won them the House music competition of 1994, with Ricky Wilson and a tearful Mr. Day gratefully accepting the trophy for the first time in many years for Nevile'. [*Leo*, Volume 109, p.25] That afternoon, Ricky had conducted the choir in a rendition of 'Leaving on a Jet Plane' and 'I dreamed a Dream' and he was the only conductor to be awarded the full five marks out of five and Best Conductor title, a success he repeated the following year. Mr Day, Nevile's Housemaster, must have been doubly grateful to Ricky because his performance in the House Play of that year was very well received. 'Ricky Wilson may not have quite perfected Cilla Black's accent but whatever accent he provided in its place was still very funny,' wrote Chris Armitage. [*Leo*, ibid, p.37] Mr Day, in his House Report was happy to heap further praise on Ricky, who had co-written the House Play, "Channel Surfers", which 'overcame a disastrous rehearsal period to brilliant effect on the night. I'm not quite sure how they managed to pull it together at the last moment, but the results were both slick and very funny, and thanks are due to Ricky and Andrew [Andrew Smith] for pulling it off at the last!' [*Leo*, ibid, p.83]

It is a fair assumption that Ricky was a member of a music group whilst at LGS, but sadly there is no report in the magazine on any performances he or they might have given whilst competing in Bands Night. Thanks to Andrew Smith, a close friend of Ricky's and fellow music enthusiast, there is a little light shed on the music scene at that time:

> In terms of music and bands night, Ricky and I were in different bands – and I think we only did one bands night. Probably in lower sixth which would have been 1994/5 school year. I can't remember the name of his band, but he did early rock n roll numbers with a guy called Joe Spencer [OL96] on lead guitar, Craig Rose [OL96] on drums and someone else (non LGS person) on bass. Their opening number was

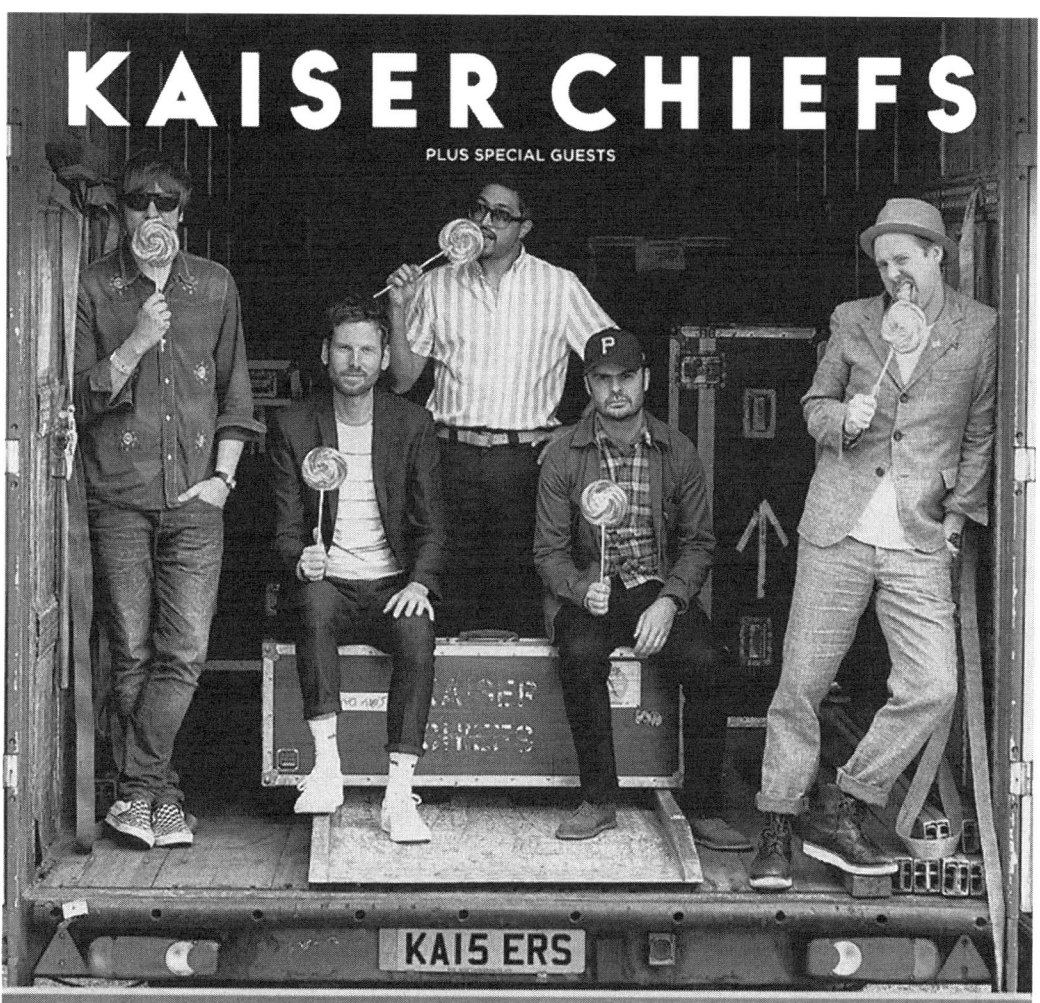

Johnny Be Good. I can still remember it today. Ricky was fantastic even then as a front man, prowling round the stage and getting the audience going. [email to the author dated 3 February 2019]

However, he did contribute artwork to Chris Walbank's occasional publication of *Scattered Verse*, some of it demonstrating a talent for matching image with words, and he contributed at least one poem which might be considered evidence of his juvenilia. Titled 'Playgrounds, Parks and question Marks' he wrote:

> *Maybe I'm not used to the system,*
> *maybe the system's not used to me,*
> *maybe I'm the only one who's bothered by seeing this,*
> *maybe I'm the only one who's bothered to see.*

Both brothers did well at GCSE O-level and at A-Level. James and Ricky passed 10 O-Levels, including five A grades; and at A-Level, James managed three As and one B and Ricky managed two As and 2 Cs.

From LGS he moved to Leeds Metropolitan University where he undertook a course in Graphic Arts and Design. He was awarded BA (Hons.) in 2000 and went on to achieve an MA in the same subject. He must have impressed his tutors because he was appointed a part-time lecturer at the university, teaching two days a week, and only resigning from this post after a year when his musical career took off in earnest.

Meanwhile, some time earlier.... Tracing the fortunes of other soon-to-be band members, Nick Hodgson, Simon Rix and Nick Baines had met up on their first day at St Mary's Catholic School at Menston, finding themselves in the same class and sharing a love of pop music. Nick Baines was already nick-named 'Peanut' after drawing a self-portrait in which his head very closely resembled a peanut. This led to his obsession with wearing hats both on stage and off. The three of them formed a band called Strawberry Jam with Simon being the most accomplished musician, coming as he did from a musical family. Into their teens, the boys formed a succession of new bands with Peanut playing keyboard and guitar and Nick Hodgson taking on the role of songwriter. Nick soon came to realise that some of the best songs ever produced were written by two people working in collaboration with one another so it was a lucky break when, during his visits to the Leeds night scene – clubs, discos and pubs – he met one Ricky Wilson.

It was whilst taking his course at Leeds Met. that Ricky, along with Nick Hodgson, Nick 'Peanut' Baines and Simon Rix, now formed a band named Runston Parva, a deliberate misspelling of the East Yorkshire village Ruston Parva. Sadly, they were unable to clinch a record deal and this problem was compounded by the fact that two members of the group had dispersed away from Leeds to higher education; Simon went to Glasgow where he joined a number of different bands. The rump of Runston Parva struggled on, playing their first gig the following summer at the Duchess Pub in Leeds in summer 1997. It was at this time that they were joined by guitarist Andrew White who had previously performed with various groups. For two-and-a-half-years, Runston Parva struggled on playing Britpop to near-empty halls in and around Leeds and trying to fit in college courses and dead-end jobs. By February 2000, they realised they were going nowhere so they brought in Simon (bass) and Peanut (keyboard) who were down from their respective universities that summer and re-formed as Parva with a debut gig at The Fenton, playing to a full house and later performing at Joseph's Well. Parva had reinvented themselves with a new sound, new songs and significant change of dress - grungier and less dapper and owing allegiance to Detroit garage rock influences.

By this time, those band members who had entered tertiary education had graduated and joined the others doing menial jobs to pay the rent while they kept up a hectic schedule of small-time gigs. Careers were put on hold in the hope that they would make it big in the music world.

Nick Hodgson and Ricky opened their own Leeds nightclub, Pigs, chiefly because they wanted a cheerful venue where they could relax and enjoy the sort of music they preferred. They did not anticipate that the club would become a huge success; held once a month, it became Leeds' in-place to be, hosting some notorious acts including Black Wire.

On 22 June 2001, Parva signed a record deal with Mantra Recordings and recorded (though never released) a debut album, "22", in 2002 and three singles, 'Heavy' in October 2001, 'Good Bad Right Wrong' (May 2002) and 'Hessles' in October 2002). These enjoyed some limited success, especially 'Hessles', a slice of New Wave Gothic Punk, that depicted the grim Leeds streets of the same name, close to Hyde Park, where Ricky was then living. However, things began to fall apart when Mantra Recordings closed down in 2003 and the group was left stranded with neither a contract nor hits. It was time to move away from punk with its limited following and embrace a wider, pop-fuelled audience. As a result, things were soon to take off with a vengeance.

In the same year that "22" was recorded, and while Ricky was still part-time lecturing, the band was re-named Kaiser Chiefs, the name owing some allegiance to the South African football team the Kaizer Chiefs for whom Lucas Radebe, the Leeds United captain, had once played. The band was managed by James Sandon, who must have seen their potential because he was willing to take on a group that had achieved little previous success. In a later interview with *HitQuarters*, some time after becoming their manager, Sandon revealed, 'No one would touch them

Ricky Wilson – Musician and Media Celebrity

[Parva] because they had a history [of unoriginality]. A lot of people used their history against them.' [*HitQuarters*, 28 May 2007] This must have been the primary reason for changing the name and starting out again with a new image and fresh songs. As Eamon Carr wrote in the *Dublin Evening Herald*, Parva didn't work so 'the grammar school boy turned college lecturer had another idea. Parva decided to reinvent themselves as a smart, relevant, modern band. They ticked all the boxes for what they believed the public wanted to see and hear in an exciting new band.' [*Dublin Evening Herald*, 22 February 2007] Sean Adams, boss of Drowned in Sound, had heard the Kaiser Chiefs perform and he contacted Sandon and recommended he hear them for himself. Sandon duly obliged: 'I went to see a couple of shows and you were just bombarded by a series of potential hit singles'. [ibid] Shortly after, the band was signed up to a recording deal with B-Unique Records. At the same time they performed many gigs at which they attracted a modest but loyal following, and these included a tour with The Ordinary Boys in June 2004. Samuel Preston, lead vocal and guitarist with that group, commented, 'I can remember some gigs that we did together in really weird places and tiny venues. No one would really show up and these gigs would be non-events. Yet every night they [Kaiser Chiefs] would have so much energy.' [*A Record of Employment*, no pagination] It was Preston who spoke forcefully to Mark Lewis of B-Unique Records urging him to sign up the Kaisers.

In July 2004, when still relatively unknown in the UK, the band were invited to perform at the Moscow Rock Festival by an impresario called Sacha who had

Ricky Wilson, centre, with Kaiser Chiefs

read about them in *Time Out* magazine. In their naivety they thought they would have to pay their own expenses but happily they were generously catered for and treated like rock royalty into the bargain. For the first time, they enjoyed all the trappings of fame: crowd surfing, screaming girls and prime-time television interviews. On returning to the UK they appeared at the Reading and Leeds Festivals in August and while they were politely received at Reading, they enjoyed greater success at their home town. Ricky did suffer from pre-show nerves and admitted to being sick before and after their performances.

But it was early in 2005 that the big breakthrough in the UK happened. They were involved in the NME *[New Musical Express]* Awards Tour and enjoyed the benefit of being the opening act and this attracted a lot of positive media attention. In March their debut album *Employment* was released to critical acclaim, inspired by new wave and the punk rock music of the late 1970s and early 1980s. Dorian Lynskey in the *Guardian* wrote enthusiastically, 'That Employment is derivative is both undeniable and irrelevant. It is so confident, so smart, so full of life, that a more enjoyable 45 minutes is hard to imagine.' [*Guardian*, 4 March 2005] Ricky admitted to Roy Webb in an interview for BBC South Yorkshire that, 'There are some serious bits on the album…but generally we like to have a lot of fun and just try and amuse ourselves'. [Interview, April 2005] It achieved the No. 2 slot in both the UK Albums Top 75 and the Ireland Albums Top 100 and enjoyed limited success in Holland and Belgium. It was nominated for the Mercury Music Prize in 2005 and in the following year it won the Ivor Novello Album category award, the Meteor Music Award for the Best International Album and the NME Best Album award. Ricky was awarded the NME Best Dressed Musician award in the same year, a fitting tribute to his undoubted penchant for snappy dressing and sartorial elegance.

Perhaps the most obvious secret of the album's success was that it offered good, catchy tunes and was released at a time when the pop-buying public appreciated what British bands did best, with their lyrics portraying everyday modern life with wry self-effacing humour and a little bit of swagger thrown in for good measure. [Maximum Kaiser Chiefs CD, Track 1]

In July 2005 they were chosen to open Bob Geldof's Live 8 festival in Philadelphia, a performance that was broadcast live by satellite to every Live 8 venue in the world and this represented a huge media boost for the band. Live 8's benefit concerts were timed to precede the G8 summit held at the Gleneagles Hotel in Scotland from 6 to 8 July, during the course of which the London bombers struck.

'Oh My God' was the first single to be released from the album and reached No. 6 in the UK singles chart. 'I Predict a Riot' also reached No. 6 and was ranked 36th in the NME's Greatest Indie Albums Ever countdown. The song's introduction owed something to the punk style of The Damned, and The Jam. It was nominated for Best Contemporary Song category of the Ivor Novello Awards. There was some speculation concerning the inspiration behind this song, but Nick Hodgson was certain that it came from driving home through Leeds city centre after a DJ session at The Cockpit club on Swingate. Driving past Majestyk's night club, he witnessed scenes of chaos as the revellers were leaving at closing time; drunken disorder in which the police were put under severe pressure and missiles thrown. The lyrics say it all:

> *Watching the people get lairy*
> *It's not very pretty I tell thee*
> *Walking through town is quite scary*
> *It's not very sensible either*
> *A friend of a friend he got beaten*
> *He looked the wrong way at a policeman*
> *Would never have happened to Smeaton*
> *An Old Leodiensian.*

Majestyk's nightclub had previously featured in a shocking incident in January 2000 involving a number of Leeds United players, in particular Lee Bowyer and Jonathan Woodgate who, following a drunken evening at the club, assaulted a 19-year-old student in a racially-motivated attack and were later put on trial.

On Sunday 21 May 2006, Ricky was involved in an accident in Leeds when he was hit by a car and thrown onto the bonnet, hitting the windscreen with some force. He suffered a broken toe and severe bruising.

The group's second album, *Yours Truly Angry Mob*, was recorded at the Oxfordshire studios of Hook End over the period September and October 2006, with 22 tracks to choose from. 18 made the final compilation. The songs were in part inspired by Led Zeppelin and American rock bands. It became the group's second million-selling album and the song 'Ruby' was a number one singles hit and won the 2007 Q Awards Best Track Video. The second singles release from the album, 'Everything is Average Nowadays' made it to No. 19 in the UK singles chart while 'The Angry Mob', the third release, made it to No. 22. There is an interesting biographical allusion in the track 'Highroyds'. Three members of the band attended St Mary's Catholic Primary School at Menston, and the local asylum – adjacent to the school across the Guiseley-Otley road - was then a daunting Victorian Gothic-revival edifice surrounded by wooded and lawned grounds but later closed to make way for housing. Clearly, memories of adolescent bravado are dredged up in the lyrics:

> *I remember nights out when we were young*

They weren't very good they were rubbish
Running round Highroyds isn't fun
Just teenagers testing their courage.

Got news from Uncle Hugh
Through a second cousin once removed
Too late there's a housing estate
It's called Highroyds.

The band was now experiencing a great deal of adulation from a huge following. In December 2007 they played two sold-out shows at Earls Court, London, to capacity crowds of 30,000. On 24 May 2008 they gave a concert at Elland Road to a packed audience of 40,000 and released a DVD of the full programme plus highlights from their live appearance at the earlier BBC Electric Proms. There followed a succession of tours which were intended to promote the new album, *Off with Their Heads*, produced between 2008 and 2009. The first single to be released from it was 'Never Miss a Beat'. In October 2008 the band went on tour with another group, Late of the Pier, and their first venue was the Leeds Academy. Between February and March, 2009, they undertook an Arena tour, starting at Nottingham and finishing at London. In July they played at the Mares Vivas in Vila Nova de Gaia, Portugal, and nine days later they were at Croke Park in Dublin opening the concert there for U2.

After a break of around two years, the Kaiser Chiefs announced that a new album, recorded over a period of 18 months at various locations, was to be released called *The Future is Medieval*. When it first became available to the public in June 2011, it was issued in a unique format in that fans could choose ten tracks from the 20 on offer in order to create a personalised compilation – and all for a fee of £7.50. This marketing initiative attracted the attention of pop celebrities like Chris Moyles as well as the *Guardian* newspaper. The idea was that £1 from each purchase was given to the Alzheimer's Society and this created some very positive media coverage. Jeremy Hughes, Chief Executive of the Society at the time, wrote on its website, 'We're thrilled that the Kaiser Chiefs have chosen to support us in this exciting way. We'd like to call on music fans to download a unique celebrity version of the album, and raise funds for people with dementia at the same time.' [Alzheimer's Society website dated 3 June 2011] Three weeks later, the official version of the album was released with 12 of the original 20 tracks plus an extra song titled 'Kinda Girl You Are'.

If there had been a perceived decline in the group's popularity over the previous two years this was not only halted but a resurgence of adulation was evident from the hectic tour schedule undertaken in the following months. There were two sell-out gigs at the Falmouth Princess Pavilion followed by a tour on the Continent to take in Germany, Switzerland, Holland, Belgium, Portugal and Luxembourg. An appearance on the Isle of Wight was a huge success and in September they played a further two sell-out concerts at Kirkstall Abbey.

In an attempt to break into the lucrative US market, the album was re-released with the title *Start the Revolution Without Me*, though this contained many different tracks including 'On the Run'.

2012 was a hectic year for the band, with a twenty date tour of the UK and a thirteen date tour of the US and Canada, playing at a number of prestigious venues including Boston, New York, Washington, Vancouver and Toronto. Once again, the group was working hard to make it big in the North American scene.

In June a new album, *Souvenir*, was released, a compilation of all their previous singles from 2004 to 2012 and including a new track, 'Listen to Your Head'.

Nick Hodgson, one of the founder members of Runston Parva, announced he was leaving the band to concentrate on other projects and in his place, Vijay Mistry joined the Kaiser Chiefs in a move away from his previous band, Club Smith, who had appeared at the 2010 Reading and Leeds Festivals and who had been selected by the Kaiser Chiefs to be their support act at seven of their tour venues in early 2012. Hodgson sold his drum kit to David Letterman, host of the US *Late Show*, having announced that he was leaving the Kaiser Chiefs after their performance at Chicago's House of Blues in April 2012.

There followed another UK tour of thirteen gigs culminating in a triumphant night at the London O2 Academy. A little later they appeared as headline act at one of the Eden Sessions held at Tim Smit's Eden Project in Cornwall. Then on 12 August they featured in the closing ceremony of the 2012 London Olympics, playing 'Pinball Wizard' by The Who. In September, they returned to Leeds to appear at the First Direct Arena, being one of the very first acts to perform there. They were given a rapturous reception.

Education, Education, Education & War, the band's fifth studio album, was released as a standard CD, an LP and a digital download on 31 March 2014. It had been recorded at the Maze studio in Atlanta and mixed at the Electric Lady studios in New York. Throughout 2014-2015, the album was promoted on tours across Europe and the Americas. Later the group toured South Africa, South America and Ireland in support of US rock band Foo Fighters. The album received mixed reviews from the buying public, but it pleased many music journalists as well as fans and it reached the No. 1 slot in the UK Albums chart. Robert Ham, writing for the *Alternative Press* magazine, based at Cleveland, Ohio, gave the album an above-average rating, commenting that, 'Not everything hits the mark, but there is enough to delight in and offer plenty of hope for the Chiefs' future'. There were many who praised the album, a lot of them drawing favourable comparisons with "The Future is Medieval", which many considered a bit of a flop. As for "Education", Chris D opined, 'It's moody, angry, and more than a bit cynical…. It's a return to form from one of my favourite bands, with catchy songs, storming drums and rocking guitars.' [Amazon's Kaiser Chiefs Store] 'Anon.' agreed that the album displayed a welcome return to form. 'I must admit I was astounded. This is a return to the Kaiser Chiefs' roots. In my opinion it's on a par with Employment which is something I never expected. The fabulous tongue-in-cheek lyrics are still there, Vijay's drumming is alive'n'kicking.' [ibid]

Stay Together, the sixth studio album, was released on 7 October 2016, being co-written and produced by Brian Higgins of Xenomania, whose artists included Girls Aloud and Pet Shop Boys. The title of the album was taken from one of the featured songs, 'We Stay Together' (issued as a single) and therein lies a clue as to the contents. This album could not be a greater contrast to "Education"; it deals with relationships and emotions. Another single release was 'Hole in My Soul'. The music on this album was a more dance-oriented sound and the lyrics explored love and relationships rather than politics and the horrors of war. Neil McCormick, writing in the *Telegraph*, was not particularly impressed: 'Charismatic frontman Wilson has become a television favourite as a judge on BBC singing competition The Voice and you have to wonder how much this has shaped the band's musical direction'. [*Daily Telegraph* dated 7 October 2016] Cai Trefor, writing for the British on-line news site, *Gigwise*, argued that 'Stay Together is a hook-laden dance album stacked with anthems… The guitars are cleaner and the synths are more prominent. It's like no Kaiser Chiefs' album you've heard before… Thematically, there's been a complete transition away from the protest music of their previous album "Education, Education, Education War". They've now turned their heads to that classic pop go-to: love.' [*Gigwise*, 3 October 2016) In the same article, Ricky Wilson added that, 'The thing about writing a protest album is it's straightforward. Only an idiot would disagree with you… You're just saying war is bad.' [ibid]

In early 2017 the group toured across Europe promoting "Stay Together".

Then in April 2018, they signed a new contract with their original label, Polydor, and started preparing a new album to be released in early 2019. As Robin Murray, writing for *Clash* magazine, put it:

> Kaiser Chiefs have announced plans for a new album, due out in 2019.
>
> One of British music's truly great survival stories, Kaiser Chiefs have outlasted the indie landfall to essentially carve out their own universe.
>
> With a huge new UK tour set to kick off in January – highlights include Glasgow Borrowlands and London's Brixton Academy – the band have outlined plans for new material. [*Clash* dated 17 September 2018]

In June, Ricky and Freddie Flintoff released an unofficial World Cup song, a new version of Boney M's 1978 hit, 'Rasputin'. Sadly, this was not well received by many England fans and it came in for a fair amount of ridicule. Praising the merits of the England captain, the lyrics included the memorable lines, 'Ra Ra Rasputin England's got a goal machine/ He's Harry Kane and he's gonna score.'

Fans of the Harry Potter movies may remember Ricky acting the part of Dirk Cresswell in *Harry Potter and the Deathly Hallows Part 1* (2010). Not unexpectedly, he featured as the Rockstar in the film *St Trinian's 2, the Legend of Fritton's Gold* (2009). Earlier, in the TV movie *Britain's Got the Pop Factor…and Possibly a New Celebrity Jesus Christ Soapstar Superstar Strictly on Ice* (2008) he appeared as himself and was in good company with the likes of Paul McCartney and Rick Astley. For a full listing of all his media appearances, the reader may wish to consult the exhaustive listing on the IMDb website.

In a move to extend and enhance his media presence, Ricky joined Tom Jones, will.i.am and Rita Ora as a coach on the third series of the BBC's music show, *The Voice*. He replaced Danny O'Donoghue. It was a role he slipped into with consummate ease and quickly became the viewers' favourite. His coaching talents soon bore fruit; he was the winning coach on the fourth series, when Steve McCrorie won the popular vote broadcast live in April 2015. Following this, in the next series, Kevin Simm, another of Ricky's choices, was declared the winner. As a consequence of these back-to back successes, Ricky is the only coach to win two consecutive series – a feat all the more remarkable as the runner-up to Simm was another of Ricky's acts, Jolan. However, as Simm later pointed out, winning the show was no guarantee of future success. McCrorie did have a hit single with his song 'Lost Stars' but his album "Big World" failed and he was subsequently dropped by the Decca record label. As a result, he returned to his job as a fireman and has since played clubs around the country. Simm, who had enjoyed previous success with the band Liberty X, released his winning song, 'All You Good Friends' after the show and this reached No. 24 in the UK Singles chart.

Ricky from the start demonstrated a natural talent for audience engagement, relishing quick-fire repartee and a dynamic stage presence. He was able to elicit emotional involvement when inviting those he chose to join him in his coaching set, even being called a 'charmer' and a 'smoothie'. Rita Ora joked that his 'dreamy blue eyes' were captivating. He was asked, in an interview with the BBC Media Centre, what surprised him most about the show as a newcomer and he responded, 'How emotionally attached you get to the people. I thought it was just TV. But it's real. You do care about them, you care about everybody else's team and you care about all the coaches.' During the course of the show he did reveal that he never drank tea, having some sort of allergic reaction to milk, and even managed to get in a slightly amended quotation from Shakespeare, 'Methinks she doth protest too much'.

Ricky left *The Voice* with no regrets, though he did claim on ITV's *Good Morning Show* that he was angry at being dropped when the show moved to that channel, being replaced by Gavin Rossdale. It was time to concentrate once again on the greatest priority, the Kaiser Chiefs.

Bibliography
Carr, Eamon, *Dublin Evening Herald*, 22 February 2007
Chrome Dreams, CD "Maximum Kaiser Chiefs". The Unauthorised Biography of the Kaiser Chiefs (2005)
Ham, Robert, article in *Alternative Press*
Hughes, Jeremy, article in *Alzheimer's Society* magazine
Kaiser Chiefs, *A Record of Employment*, Weidenfeld & Nicolson (London: 2006)
Leodiensian magazine Volumes 108 and 109
Lynskey, Dorian, *Guardian* dated 4 March 2005
McCormick, Neil, article in the *Daily Telegraph*
Murray, Robin, article in *Clash* magazine
Sandon, James, interview with *HitQuarters* magazine dated 28 May 2007
Smith, Andrew, email communication dated 3 February 2019
Trefor, Cai, article in *Gigwise* magazine

Afterword

I NOTE FROM my diaries that it was during an Old Leodiensian Association Leeds Lunch, held in a restaurant on Vicar Lane on 29th November 2013, that I first heard Neill Hargreaves tell me of his Grand Plan to log the names of every OL from 1820 to 1901 with a separate listing of pupils at the School up to 1820. Given the School's lengthy history, taken usually to date back to 1552, and according to some accounts even to precede this, it seemed to me to be an impossibly ambitious undertaking. Neill remained calm and confident in the face of my incredulity, and assured me that he had indeed already made a start on this monumental task. I should have had more faith.

It was during Neill's voyage through the considerable volume of material in the LGS archive that the idea was born to write a book to celebrate the remarkable achievements of some of those pupils. The numbers involved would make necessary a fairly ruthless selection process: for each of the names that would feature in the book, there would be many others that could equally well have been chosen. However, true to character, Neill did not shrink from the challenge, and succeeded in picking out twenty-five Old Boys, each of whom in a variety of different ways has achieved conspicuous success in their chosen field of endeavour. He has done an excellent job.

My time at Leeds Grammar School started in 1971, at which time the Junior School was housed in a large former mansion on Clarendon Road, with the name 'Sheafield' engraved on the gatepost. Art was taught in the white-tiled basement,

Afterword

and the caretaker lived in the attic. The two floors in between housed three first and three second year classrooms, the Headmaster's study, and a large glass tank full of stick insects. Subjects were straightforward enough; Mathematics, English, Music, Science, History, Divinity, Sports (once a week) and French. The School comprised two markedly competitive houses; Nicholson whose colours were in plum, and Smeaton, whose colours were in green. It would only be later on that the penny would drop as to the significance of those names.

Discipline was firm but fair, and foundations were laid, to a greater or lesser extent, for pupils to progress onward after two years to the 'Main School' on Moorland Road next to Woodhouse Moor. Not all Main School boys would have attended Junior School - a cohort of 'Eleven Plus' boys would join from other Leeds schools in the First or Second Form - so a remarkable feature of the School was the eclectic mix of boys who attended it. They came from all over Leeds and from all sorts of backgrounds that ranged from market traders to academics, from lawyers to builders, from surgeons to restaurateurs. Family ties were frequent, and links with the City of Leeds were strongly evident. LGS was very much a School of Leeds and a School for Leeds, and it will become apparent to the reader of this anthology of success stories that the inter-relationship goes back a long, long way.

Leeds Grammar School ceased to exist as a legal entity in 2005, at which time it merged with Leeds Girls' High School, its sister school within the Grammar School Foundation, to form The Grammar School at Leeds. Though no longer based centrally within the City, the new school boasts spectacular facilities and teaching standards, and continues to build upon the formidable reputation and achievements of its two predecessors, delivering unsurpassed levels of excellence in all fields, thereby continuing to create a new generation of Illustrious Leodiensians. William Sheafield and those who followed him would have been proud.

Prof. Tristram E J Hope
MEng, CEng, FIStructE, MICE
President, Old Leodiensian Association

References

John Harrison

Page 2....................Hornsea, *TS* Vol 33 p.116 but also in RT [DL]; *TS* Vol 33 pp.123-4
Page 3 ....Stocks, *TS* Vol 24 p.190; page 4 p429
Page 4 ....Thornton, *Story of Leeds*, p.57 [quoting from Survey of Leeds]
Page 6 ....Stocks & Thompson, *TS* Vol 24, p.220
Page 7 ....Burt & Grady, *IHOL*, p.33; *War, Plague & Trade*, p.13
Page 9..Hornsea; *TS* Vol 33, p.145
Page 11 ....Hornsea; *TS* Vol 33, p.104

John Smeaton

Page 13..........................Samuel Smiles, *Vol. 2 Lives of the Engineers*; p.106; + various
Page 14..C A Lupton, *TS* Vol 15, Part 3, p.217
Pages 14 & 15 ....Dedication service at Westminster Abbey, p.9
Page 17 ....R F Lawrence, *Smeaton of Austhorpe*, p.20 [from SS, p.28]
Page 18..R F Lawrence p.27
Page 20..*YEP*, 11/10/1934; 30/05/1938
Page 22 ....Petticrew & Austin, *The Grand Junction Canal*, online

References

Sir Charles West Cope
Page 25+ ....Cope, *Reminiscences*; various
Page 32............................Maurice Bond (ed.), *Works of Art in the House of Lords*, p.93
Page 33 ....William Cosmo Monkhouse, *Dictionary of National Biography*, [1901]

Sir John Hawkshaw
Page 36 ....+John Hawkshaw; *Reminiscences of SA*, p.83 [1838]
Pages 39-40..Martin Beaumont, *Sir John Hawkshaw*, p.123
Page 42...Petticrew & Austin, online
Page 43..*Engineering News*, Vol. 25, Issue 595 [1891]
ICE Minutes, Vol. 106, Issue 1891

George Dixon MP
Page 49 ....JHM [?], p.52
Page 50...James Dixon, *Out of Birmingham*, p.68
Page 54 ....James Marshall, *FPS*, p.37
Page 56 ....*Birmingham Post*, 17/01/1898;
London Evening Standard, 29/01/1898

Colonel Edmund Wilson
Page 60.............................+James Singleton, *TS* Vol. 24, [1919], pp.25-30; p.26; p.27
Page 63+ ....E Kitson Clark, *History of the Leeds Phil. & Lit. Soc.*, [1924], p.112
Pages 65-66..Edmund Wilson, *TS* Vol. 9, p.2;
TS Vol. 11, pp.284-5
Page 67 ....*Huddersfield Chronicle*, dated 26/01/1889
Page 68...Hope & Bilson, in *TS* Vol. 16 [1907], p.7

Field Marshal William Gustavus Nicholson
Page 76 ....J Terraine, Douglas Haig, *The Educated Soldier*, pp.43-44 [1963]

Colonel George Francis Robert Henderson
Page 81+ ....Lord Roberts, "Memoir" to *The Science of War*,
Longman Green, [1905]
Page 83 ....Sir William Topaz McGonagall, poem updated (extract)
Page 85 ....C I Archer, chapter in *World History of Warfare*, p.432 [2002]
Page 87 .....Field Marshal Wolseley, Introduction to *Stonewall Jackson*, pp.7-8 [1898]
Page 90 ....Andre Wessells, *Oxford DoNB*;
GFR Henderson, Preface to *Stonewall Jackson*, p.xxii

John Ireland

Page 93+ .... Hugh Ottaway, *Grove Dictionary of Music*, Vol. 12, p.568; p.569
Pages 97-98 .... Masefield, "Sea Fever" poem quoted in full
Page 99 .... Norah Kirby, in *Lewis Foreman* (ed.), *The John Ireland Companion*, p.355

Ernest Bristow Farrar

Page 102 .... Trevor Bray, *Frank Bridge, A Life in Brief*, [internet]
Page 103 .... Walt Whitman, "The Open Road" extract; from *Leaves of Grass*
Page 104 .... Robert Weedon, *A Biography of EBF*, in *The Music of WWI*
Page 105 .... *Musical Times*, Vol. 160, 01/11/1919, p.621
Page 106 .... John G Davies, LGS Roll of Honour
Page 107 .... *YEP*, 29/07/1953
Page 110 .... Michael S Potts, *Potts of Leeds*, pp.19-20; Mayfield Books (2006)
Page 113 .... James Marshall, *FPS*, p.35
Page 114 .... Michael S Potts email to *Yorkshire Post* 13/04/2018

Geoffrey Anketell Studert Kennedy

Page 120 .... J K Mozley, *G A Studdert Kennedy By His Friends*, pp.13,14,15, 22-23, 26;
William Purcell, *Woodbine Willie*, pp.32-33; p.47; p.57; p.115; [1962]
Page 121 .... JKM, p.17
Pages 121-2 .... JKM, p.22
Page 124 .... WP, p.47; p.57; p.118; p.107; p.115
Page 125 .... Bob Holman, *Woodbine Willie* [2013], p.31; p.116; p.141,
Lion Hudson publishers
Page 126 .... WP, p.115; GASK, *The Hardest Part*, [1918]; WP, p.118
Page 127 .... BH, p.63; GASK, excerpt from *"A Sermon in a Billet"*
Page 129 .... BH, p.116 & 141

Bishop Michael Hollis

Page 131 .... Christopher Hollis, *The Seven Ages*, p.1
Page 135 .... Constance M Millington, *Led By the Spirit*, pp.57-58 [1996]
Page 136 .... Lesslie Newbigin, Foreword to *CMM*, p.vii

Christopher Hollis

Page 139+ .... Christopher Hollis, *The Seven Ages*, p.6; p.140, pp.10-11
Page 142 .... Christopher Hollis, *Along the Road to Frome*, p.16
Page 148 .... CH, ATRTF, p.210

References

Sir Roger Henry Hollis
Page 151 ....CMM, *Led By the Spirit*, p.1;
Chapman Pincher, *Their Trade is Treachery*, p.38
Page 153..*Journal of the Royal Central Asian Society*, p.24
Pages 156-7 ....Prof. Christopher Andrew, *The Defence of the Realm*,
pp.434-5; p.432

Geoffrey Crowther
Page 160 ....Roland Bird, Geoffrey Crowther, in *ODoNB*,
Page 162 ....HMSO, Ministry of Education, 15-18, Foreword by Geoffrey Lloyd
Page 163 ......Open University Digital Archive, Lord Crowther's Opening Address
Pages 164-5 ....*Illustrated London News*, 03/09/1966

Godfrey Talbot
Page 168+ ....Godfrey Talbot, *Permission to Speak*, p.44 [1976],
p.58;91;122-23; 129,169
Page 170..*The Guardian*, Obituary, 05/09/2000

Geoffrey Wooler
Page 183 ....*Daily Telegraph*, 17/03/2015

John Connell Freeborn
Pages 187-88+ ....Bob Cossey, *A Tiger's Tale*, pp.1-2; p.173; p.20;
p.51, 52; 56; 61; 63-4; 78; 79; 139
Pages 189-90 ....Christopher Yeoman & JCF, *Tiger Cub*, p.29
Page 192 ....Patrick Bishop, *Fighter Boys*, p.107

John Rowe Townsend
Page 203 ....John Rowe Townsend, *Writing for Children*, pp.261-2
Page 204 ....JRT, *Gumble's Yard*, various; Carpenter & Pritchard,
Oxford Companion to Children's Literature, [1984, 1987]
Page 205............................Kaye Webb, in *Illustrated London News*, 27/11/1965, p.34
Pages 205-6 ....Hollindale & Sutherland, in Peter Hunt,
Children's Literature, An Illustrated History, pp.279-80

Sir Gerald Bernard Kaufman MP

Pages 209-10......................Gerald Kaufman, *My Life in the Silver Screen*, p.15 [1985]; p.28; p.104; p.37; p.78
Page 214..*The Guardian*, Obituary dated 27/02/2017
Page 216...*Daily Mirror* dated 24/09/1977
Page 217...*The Stage* magazine dated 25/09/2003; *The Guardian* dated 12/12/2008
Page 218..*Daily Mail* 28/10/2008
Page 219..*Independent* newspaper 27/02/2017

Barry Cryer OBE

Pages 221-22..Barry Cryer, *Butterfly Brain* pp.27-28, p.30; p.97; p.46; p.127; p.103; p.167; p.34; p.5;

Ricky Wilson

Page 260...................Hit Quarters, 28/05/2007; Eamon Carr, *Dublin Evening Herald* dated 22/02/2007; *A Record of Employment* [Kaiser Chiefs]
Page 261.....................Dorian Lynskey, in *The Guardian*, dated 04/03/2005; "Maximum Kaiser Chiefs", CD Track1
Page 262..Quote from the song "I Predict a Riot"
Page 263...Quote from the song "Highroyds"; Alzheimer's Society website dated 03/06/2011
Page 265.....................*Daily Telegraph* dated 07/10/2016, Neil McCormick; *Gigwise* dated 03/10/2016
Page 266...*Clash* magazine Robin Murray dated 17/09/2018

Sources

John Harrison
photo of painting of Harrison taken by JNH
Image of Harrison's school is LGS
Harrison blue plaque photo taken by JNH
(page 10): photo of OS map taken from original in Leeds Library

John Smeaton
(page 12): photo of plaque taken by JNH/PAH
(page 16): image of Austhorpe Lodge taken from out of print book
(page 21): image of Westminster Abbey Dedication service taken by JNH
(page 21): picture of Eddystone Lighthouse taken from book by AW Skempton but it an image used by many other authors

Sir Charles West Cope
(page 24): self-portrait taken from National Portrait Gallery (we could use the photo from Wilson's book (LGS)
(page 29): all three paintings taken from the internet (no identifiable source)

Sir John Hawkshaw
(page 34): portrait of Hawkshaw by G J Stodart but no known source (we could use the portrait from the Wilson book (LGS)
(page 38): Middleton Railway (supplied by Robert) no known source
(page 40): diagram of Severn Tunnel attributed to British Rail
(page 41): photo of wall plaque taken by JNH

George Dixon MP
(page 44): photo of Dixon taken from Wilson book (LGS)
(page 48): photo of Gladstone from National Gallery of Scotland
(page 53): drawing of Forster taken from Project Gutenberg

Colonel Edmund Wilson
(page 58): portrait of Wilson taken from Thoresby Society Vol XXIV, p.24
(page 62): photo of title page of Wilson's book taken by JNH (LGS)
(page 63): photo of sample page from Wilson's book taken by JNH
(page 66): drawing of Red Hall taken from John Davies book From Bridge to Moor

Field Marshal William Gustavus Nicholson
(page 70): portrait of Nicholson supplied by John Davies
(page 72): image of the Mansion at Roundhay Park supplied by John Davies
(page 77): portrait of Nicholson supplied by John Davies
In all of the above John did not know the origin, though the Mansion photo is an old postcard

Colonel George Francis Robert Henderson
(page 80): photo of wall plaque taken by JNH
(page 84): photo of Victoria College Jersey taken from Wikipedia but presumably owned by Victoria College
(page 87): Portrait of Henderson taken from Wilson book (LGS)
(page 88): portrait of Hildyard taken from The Boer War

John Ireland
(page 92): portrait of Ireland outside Rock Mill taken from Lewis Foreman, The John Ireland Companion
(page 95): image of St Luke's Church – origin unknown (internet)
(page 96): portrait of John Masefield – origin unknown (internet)
(page 98): portrait of Stanford – origin unknown (internet)

Sources

Ernest Bristow Farrar
(page 100): portrait of Farrar – origin unknown (internet)
(page 103): image of Christ Church Harrogate taken from Christ Church website
(page 104): portrait of Vaughan Williams in uniform – internet
(page 106): photo of EV Lucas book taken from the Internet – origin unknown

Potts:
(page 108): Potts with one of his clocks – probably taken from Michael S "Potts book Potts of Leeds"
(page 112): photo of LGI plaque taken by JNH
(page 113): photo of Oakwood clock taken by JNH
(page 116): photo of Thornton's Arcade Potts clock taken by JNH

Geoffrey Anketell Studert Kennedy
(page 118): portrait of Kennedy in uniform taken from Mozley book "Studdert Kennedy by his friends" out of print book (Mozley is an OL)
(page 120): image of western front – origin unknown
(Page 123): photo of Trinity College Dublin from Arcadia Study Abroad (internet)
(page 128): photo of MC from Government website

Bishop Michael Hollis
(page 130): photo of book cover (book out of print)
(page 133): photo of Bangalore College taken from Bangalore website
(page 134): photo of St Andrew's Church taken from Geograph [sic] website
(page 135): photo of Armley church taken from Wikipedia
(page 137): photo of Admission Book entry taken by JNH

Christopher Hollis
(page 138): portrait of Hollis origin unknown
(page 141): photo of Admission Book entry taken by JNH
(page 142): portrait of Evelyn Waugh from Leicester University website
(page 145): photo of Summer Fields School from their website
(page 146): photo of St Michael's Church from St Michael's website

Sir Roger Henry Hollis
(page 150): portrait of Hollis origin unknown (internet)
(page 153): portraits of Blunt and Philby; Blunt from Wikipedia; Philby from You Tube
(page 154): Worcester College attributed to Andrew Shiva
(page 156): photo of Christopher Andrew's book – internet

Geoffrey Crowther

(page 158): portrait of Crowther attributed to Alchetron
(page 161): photo of OU ceremony attributed to OU website
(page 162): photo of title page of ROSLA Report taken by JNH
(page 164): photo of OU lecture supplied by Phil Caplan (possibly OU)

Godfrey Talbot

(page 165): portrait of Talbot taken from out of print book
(page 169): portrait of Talbot in plane – permission from Second World War Experience
(page 170): reporting vehicle photo – permission given from SWWE
(page 173): portrait of Dimbleby from "Blue Plaque Guides"

Geoffrey Wooler

(page 176): photo supplied by Peter Wooler – permission granted
(page 178): photo of Wooler as student – provided by Peter Wooler
(page 181): photo of operating table provided by Peter Wooler
(page 182): photo of book cover provided by Peter Wooler (out of print book)
(page 184): photo of LGI plaque taken by JNH

John Connell Freeborn

(page 185): portrait of young Freeborn – origin not known but probably from one of the two books on Freeborn
(page 189): again, probably from one of the two books on Freeborn
(page 190): portrait of Mason Clarke (LGS)
(page 196): photo of Spitfire from model company

John Rowe Townsend

(page 200): portrait of Townsend from Green Bay Publications
(page 203): photo of Emmanuel College from Wikimedia Commons
(page 204): portrait of Jill Paton Walsh from Green Bay Publications
(page 206): photo of cover of "Hell's Edge" presumably Puffin Books

Sir Gerald Bernard Kaufman MP

(page 208): portrait of young Kaufman from Queen's College Oxford website
(page 211): photo of QCO Hall from QCO website
(page 214): portraits of Wilson and Foot: Wilson from Wikipedia and Foot from ConservativeHome [sic]

Sources

Barry Cryer OBE
(page 220): portrait of Cryer taken from Internet
(page 225): portrait of David Frost from the *Daily Star*
(page 226): portrait of Corbett from IMDb website

Ricky Wilson
Kaiser Chiefs promotional material

Every effort has been made to contact all copyright holders of material and images used in this book, but it has not been possible to identify some of them. The author apologises for any omissions in this respect.

Distinguished Old Boys of Leeds Grammar School in Chronological Order of Attendance

John Harrison	c.1589-c.1595
John Smeaton	1734-1740
Sir Charles West Cope	1821-1827
Sir John Hawkshaw	1823-1824
George Dixon MP	1829-1837
Colonel Edmund Wilson	1853-1856
Field Marshal Sir William Gustavus Nicholson	1857-1862
Colonel George Francis Robert Henderson	1862-1874
John Nicholson Ireland	1893
Ernest Bristow Farrar	1895-1903

Chronological Order of Attendance

The Potts Family at LGS	various
Geoffrey Anketell Studdert Kennedy	1898-1901
Bishop Arthur Michael Hollis	1910-1917
Maurice Christopher Hollis	1910-1911
Sir Roger Henry Hollis	1915-1918
Geoffrey Crowther (Baron Crowther of Headingley)	1915-1919
Godfrey Walker Talbot	1919-1924
Geoffrey Hubert Wooler	1920-1924
Wing Commander John Connell Freeborn	1928-1934
Professor Rodney Hill FRS	1932-1939
John Rowe Townsend	1933-1939
Sir Gerald Bernard Kaufman MP	1941-1949
Barry Cryer	1946-1953
Lord John Anthony Dyson PC	1951-1961
Ricky Wilson	1986-1996

About the Author

NEILL HARGREAVES WAS educated at Prince Henry's Grammar School, Otley, and later at Leeds University where he gained an Honours degree in English and History. In 1970, he was appointed as English teacher at Leeds Grammar School by the then Headmaster, Ernest Sabben-Clare, and served under John Scott who was an inspirational Head of Department. In 1985 the new Lawson Library was opened in the old Upper School at Moorland Road and Neill was appointed Lawson Librarian, in which capacity he remained until 2007. Alongside Mrs Stephanie Roberts, he saw the Library move to its new location at Alwoodley in 1997, a monumental task but one that provided a splendid facility. On retiring from full-time employment at the School, he continued to serve as SC RAF Section (CCF) and later as OC of the CCF as well as Editor of the *Leodiensian* until 2011 whereupon he then concentrated his efforts on the School Archive collection in a part-time capacity. Along with John Davies, a much-valued friend and colleague, he is in the process of cataloguing and organizing the huge assemblage of disparate material that makes up the archive collection. When not reading, he enjoys gardening, walking, travelling and attempting, wholly unsuccessfully, to comprehend the mystery of Anton Bruckner's symphonies. He lives in Shadwell with his wife, Pamela, and enjoys the company of his two sons, Richard and Stephen, and three granddaughters, Isla, Erin and Freya.